Antoine de Saint-Exupéry

Twayne's World Authors Series
French Literature

Maxwell A. Smith, Editor

University of Chattanooga

TWAS 705

**ANTOINE DE SAINT-EXUPÉRY
(1900–1944)**
*Photograph courtesy of
French Embassy Press
and Information Division*

Antoine de Saint-Exupéry

By Joy D. Marie Robinson

Twayne Publishers • *Boston*

Antoine de Saint-Exupéry

Joy D. Marie Robinson

Copyright © 1984 by G. K. Hall & Company
All Rights Reserved
Published by Twayne Publishers
A Division of G. K. Hall & Company
70 Lincoln Street
Boston, Massachusetts 02111

Book Production by Elizabeth Todesco

Book Design by Barbara Anderson

Printed on permanent/durable acid-free
paper and bound in the United States of
America.

**Library of Congress Cataloging in
Publication Data**

Robinson, Joy D. Marie.
  Antoine de Saint-Exupéry.

  (Twayne world authors series. French literature; TWAS 705)
  Bibliography: p. 170
  Includes index.
  1. Saint-Exupéry, Antoine de, 1900–1944.
2. Authors, French—20th century—Biography.
3. Air pilots—France—Biography.
4. Flight in literature.
I. Title   II. Series.
PQ2637.A274Z825   1984   848'.91209 [B]   84–10769
ISBN 0–8057–6552–2

For Pierre and Dorothy, my parents,
and Douglas, my husband

Contents

About the Author

Joy Marie Robinson, the daughter of a French father who taught English and an English mother who taught history, enjoys both her heritages and follows the family vocation of teaching. Born in Boulogne-sur-mer in northern France, she became a Parisienne when her father was appointed to a lycée in the capital. After studies at the Sorbonne, she started her teaching career at the American School in Paris. Later, she earned a special Teacher's Diploma from the University of London and then moved to the United States. She taught briefly in San Francisco and Philadelphia, then became a teaching assistant at Florida State University, where she earned her M.A. in French literature, under Dr. Maxwell Smith. She has since taught French at Georgia State University and at the Alliance française, both in Atlanta and in Washington, D.C.. While her husband was studying at Indiana University School of Music, she combined her love of music and language in teaching French for singers. Her B.A. Honors thesis on "La Provence dans *Les Lettres de mon moulin* d'Alphonse Daudet" and her M.A. thesis on "Le Dieu Pan dans la trilogie de Jean Giono" both reflect her strong belief in the essential values of life that led her to undertake this book on Antoine de Saint-Exupéry.

Since 1978 Mrs. Robinson has taught French at the Holton-Arms School in Washington, D.C., where she lives with her husband, tenor Douglas Robinson.

Preface

Antoine de Saint-Exupéry's ideas are so rich and intense that it seems impossible to imagine containing them or even holding their essence in one slim book. He himself did not write prolifically, and all his published works, including the 500-page posthumous work, are contained in some 1,000 pages. Yet each of his works, each of those pages, is so filled with ideas that every reading discovers more, so that the reader feels he can never really finish reading Saint-Exupéry.

Because of the richness of Saint-Exupéry's ideas he has been adopted and, indeed, used by many differing schools of thought. Religious writers have interpreted his works by theological symbolism, ignoring the fact that he was for several years an agnostic; political writers have variously made of him a Fascist or a Communist, ignoring his repeated, impassioned appeals against all totalitarianism; and philosophers have classified him as existentialist, despite his insistence on the importance of one's past and one's roots in realizing one's personality. He has been compared to Conrad, Lindbergh, and Stephen Crane, to theologian Teilhard de Chardin, and to aesthetist Elie Faure; and he has been called the spiritual heir of Rousseau, Nietzsche, Pascal, and even Plato. In fact, he may have something of all these, for he was a very cultured and sensitive man; but he was essentially himself, a unique figure in literature, and his writings reflect all the deep sincerity of his personal convictions, yearnings, and strivings.

Especially, Saint-Exupéry lived what he believed and what he wrote. He refused ever to write without "participating" in life fully. Only if he participated literally with his whole self, body and soul, did he feel that he had a right to speak to others. During World War II, he refused to accept a position of safety, to be "stored on a shelf like a pot of jam" until after the war. He demanded the right to share danger with his brother man, to stake his own life in order to save all that he believed in, that rich tapestry of culture and human relations that gives quality and meaning to life. He believed that only that for which it is worth dying makes life worth living. Saint-Exupéry did, indeed, die for that quality of life in which he believed and, just a month after his forty-fourth birthday, he disappeared in action, returning from a reconnaissance flight over occupied France.

The mention of Saint-Exupéry's name in America usually elicits the response, "Yes, the author of *The Little Prince*," with the implication that the book is a story for children only. Indeed, this book is usually filed on children's shelves in libraries, just as his *Pilote de guerre* is often categorized as "war literature" or "history of aviation." Saint-Exupéry is, of course, the author of the universally beloved little story, but he is much more than that, just as the story is much more than a child's story. He is the author of three novels, two of which won prizes; of a poignant autobiographical book, part meditation and part credo, which strongly influenced American thought during the war; and of a long, posthumous work, rich in parable, and biblical in style; and *The Little Prince* is a crystallization in allegory of most of the themes of Saint-Exupéry's philosophy.

These themes of Saint-Exupéry's philosophy begin to appear in his very first book, written at the age of twenty-eight, and reappear constantly throughout his work, weaving a continuously more intricate pattern throughout the tapestry which he creates. Even more than a tapestry, his work seems to resemble a musical composition, with themes introduced, repeated, developed, and finally majestically recapitulated in his *Citadelle,* where they return fully orchestrated. These themes of Saint-Exupéry's philosophy are many, each rich in itself yet all interrelated in this weaving or orchestrating of life at its fullest and most beautiful. They are themes such as "responsibility," which creates love and friendship through acceptance of commitment; such as "exchange," which transmutes personal life and effort into something greater than self; such as "solidarity," which is participation in a greater whole, which in turn enriches the individual with meaning. Throughout, Saint-Exupéry is concerned with the "founding of man," with the moulding of human clay into the finest that lies within it, and this through an acceptance of discipline and an exertion of self-discipline which will nurture the spirit within each individual. For this Saint-Exupéry has been accused of authoritarianism, yet his concern is for the recognition of the potential within each man, for its cultivation, that it be not stunted or withered by materialism or drudgery; and, in the beautiful, sleeping child of two worn-out migrant workers, he sees "Mozart assassinated" and laments that the uniqueness of each spirit is not cultivated as a special rose might be, for there are no gardeners for men.

The philosophy of Saint-Exupéry is expressed in an eloquent, distinctive style of his own, illumined with a personal vocabulary of vibrant key words, which grows throughout his work until it becomes almost another language. As the reader learns to respond to the full significance of this personal vocabulary, he comes to a closer understanding of Saint-Exupéry's thought. This is why it is wise for the new reader to begin with Saint-Exupéry's earlier works, before reading *Pilote de guerre* and, finally, *Citadelle.* He will then be rewarded with an awareness of a new richness both of language and of thought.

In preparing this study, I have relied most strongly on those biographies written either by those who knew Saint-Exupéry personally, such as Chevrier and Pélissier, or by those who had personal contact with his family and friends, such as Maxwell Smith. I have also referred extensively to the several volumes devoted to Saint-Exupéry by *Icare,* the French aviation magazine, to resolve conflicts of dates or names in other sources or to find new material. These are most reliable, as they often present photos of actual documents, some of which have only recently been brought to light. Since with many of Saint-Exupéry's works, for reasons of publication, the French edition is different from the English edition, I have worked directly from the definitive French texts, so most of the translations are my own. In these, I have tried to retain the distinctive flavor of Saint-Exupéry's style, often as surprising in French as its translation appears in English. I have also, of course, discussed textual differences between the different editions.

I wish to express my deep gratitude to Dr. Smith, who entrusted to me the privilege of presenting this beloved author and who has patiently awaited this manuscript; and to my husband, Douglas, who has patiently watched the growth of this book and encouraged me in this cherished undertaking.

Joy D. Marie Robinson

Acknowledgments

I am grateful to the following publishers and writers for their kind permission to quote from their books: to the Editions Gallimard, for permission to quote from all of Antoine de Saint-Exupéry's works, as well as to use poetic quotations from Louis de Vilmorin's *Fiançailles pour rire* and Pierre Chevrier's *Antoine de Saint-Exupéry;* to *Icare,* the French aviation magazine, for permission to quote from their several volumes on Saint-Exupéry, and especially for quotations from previously unpublished poems by Saint-Exupéry; to the Editions Robert Laffont, for permission to quote a poem by Louise de Vilmorin, from the biography by her brother, André de Vilmorin, *Poètes d'aujourd'hui, No. 91;* to Dr. Maxwell A. Smith, for permission to use the letter sent to him by Saint-Exupéry's American publisher, Eugène Reynal, which is quoted in his book *Knight of the Air.*

I am grateful, too, for the inspiration of the many excellent sources that I recognize in my bibliography, and for the encouragement of family and friends in writing this book on Antoine de Saint-Exupéry.

Chronology

1900 Antoine Jean-Baptiste Marie Roger de Saint-Exupéry born in Lyons, 29 June.

1902 Birth of brother, François.

1904 Death of father, Jean, and birth of sister, Gabrielle.

1904–1908 Childhood divided between two family homes, the Château de la Môle and the Château de Saint-Maurice de Rémens.

1908–1909 Schooling with the Frères des Ecoles chrétiennes, in Lyon.

1909 Family moves to Le Mans. Antoine enters the Collège Sainte-Croix.

1912 First experience of flight, his "baptême de l'air" near Ambérieu.

1915 Enters the Villa Saint Jean, a Marianist school in Fribourg, Switzerland.

1917 Successfully passes his Baccalauréat exam. Death of his young brother, François. Enters the Lycée Saint-Louis, in Paris, to prepare for entrance to the Ecole navale.

1919 After successful first part of exam, fails second part of entrance examination to the naval school.

1920 Audits classes at the Ecole des beaux-arts, in Paris.

1921 Mobilized for military service, sent to aviation regiment in Strasbourg. Starts flight training, which he continues throughout his military service. First contact with North Africa, a training period in Morocco. Obtains his military pilot's license.

1922 Transferred to Versailles and to Le Bourget. Engagement to Louise de Vilmorin.

1923 Accident at Le Bourget alarms the Vilmorin family. After demobilization, Antoine begins work in offices of the Boiron tile-works. Engagement broken by Louise.

1924 Begins work as traveling salesman for Saurer trucks.

1926 Short story, "L'Aviateur," appears in *Le Navire d'argent*, published by Jean Prévost. Enters the Latécoère aviation company, in Toulouse.

1927–1928 Flies for the Latécoère Company, on North African lines.

1928 Sent to Cap Juby, in charge of Latécoère's landing base there.

1929 Publication of *Courrier sud*. Navigation classes at Brest. Sent to Buenos Aires, as director of the new Aeroposta Argentina.

1930 Awarded la Légion d'honneur, for civilian aeronautics. Search for Guillaumet, lost in the Andes. Meets Consuelo Suncin de Sandoval.

1931 Return to Paris. Marriage to Consuelo Suncin. Publication of *Vol de nuit,* which receives the Prix fémina.

1932 The Latécoère line collapses, leaving Saint-Exupéry without a position. Pilots hydroplanes on the Marseille-Algiers line.

1933 Becomes test pilot in Toulouse. Accident at Saint-Raphael, in which he almost drowns.

1934 Joins Air France, for public relations, mission to Saigon. Applies for patent on landing device, first of many patents for inventions.

1935 Flies publicity tour of Mediterranean. Reporter for *Paris-Soir* in Moscow. Attempts speed-record flight to Saigon. Accident in North African desert. He walks five days until rescued.

1936 Reporter for *L'Intransigeant* on civil war in Spain.

1937 Reporter in Spain for *Paris-Soir*.

1938 Attempts speed-record flight from New York to the Terra del Fuego. Seriously injured in accident in Guatemala. Convalesces in New York. Made officer of la Légion d'honneur.

1939 Publication of *Terre des hommes,* which receives the Grand Prix du Roman de l'Académie française in France and the Book-of-the-Month award in America. Record flight to New York with Guillaumet. Mobilized at outbreak of war, as captain.

1940   Flies reconnaissance missions with the Groupe II/33 at Oronte. Awarded the Croix de Guerre. The Groupe is evacuated to Algiers after France is occupied. Saint-Exupéry is demobilized on 31 July, returns to France. In December he arrives in New York.

1941   Living in New York, visits Renoir in California. Article, "Books I Remember," published in *Harper's Bazaar*. Consuelo arrives in New York.

1942   Publication of *Flight to Arras* in America. Authorized for publication as *Pilote de guerre* in Vichy France, but banned soon thereafter. Clandestine editions would appear. Article, "An Open Letter to Frenchmen Everywhere," published in the *New York Times Magazine*.

1943   Publication of *Lettre à un otage* and of *Le Petit Prince*. Article, "Lettre à un Ami," published in *Amérique française*. Saint-Exupéry returns to Algiers, rejoins the Groupe II/33, although he is past the age limit to fly. Trains on new Lightnings. Promoted to Commandant. Grounded by American authorities after a bad landing. Moves into Dr. Pélissier's home, in Algiers, while trying to return to active duty.

1944   Obtains permission from General Eakers to fly five reconnaissance missions. Returns to Groupe, in Sardinia, in May. Disappears in action, 31 July, on tenth mission.

1948   Publication of Saint-Exupéry's posthumous *Citadelle*.

Chapter One

Childhood

Childhood, that great territory from which each person comes! . . . I belong to my childhood as I belong to a country.[1]

Antoine de Saint-Exupéry, almost forty years old and flying as a reconnaissance pilot over Arras in flames, draws on the roots of his being as he confronts an almost certain death. Throughout his adventurous life, his thoughts returned to this luminous world of childhood each time he faced death, for there he found the source and origin of the strands which linked him to life and to his fellow man. Pierre Chevrier, a biographer who knew him personally, wrote that "each time his pilot's profession brings him to the threshold of death . . . he will evoke the tender, protected world of his childhood . . . this park where a fountain of gentleness sings."[2] Indeed, all those who study Saint-Exupéry come to recognize the importance of his childhood in the growth of the sensitive and imaginative spirit that would always retain a youthfulness of wonderment, vision, and sincerity. Maxwell Smith says that "one of the charms of Saint-Exupéry is that in some ways he never grew up but always kept this feeling of wonder, of eager anticipation, in which the real world and the imaginary one blend."[3]

Saint-Exupéry's early childhood was spent in the freedom and seclusion of two large country estates, where his widowed mother took her five children alternately to her mother's or to her aunt's. They spent the summers mostly at her Aunt Tricaud's at Saint-Maurice de Rémens, near Ambérieu in the Savoie, and the summers at her old home of the Château de la Môle, near Saint Tropez in Provence. Both of these old houses became very special places to Saint-Exupéry, spiritual homes to which his mind would return in moments of meditation. Years later, during a lonely night in the desert, he thought of the Saint-Maurice house, saying "it was sufficient that it existed to fill my night with its presence. . . . I was the child of this house."[4]

1

Saint-Maurice de Rémens, not far from Lyons, belonged to Tante Tricaud, herself a widow, who adopted Antoine's mother when she also lost her husband. Later, Saint-Exupéry's mother inherited this house and it has now, most appropriately, become a "colonie de vacances," where groups of city children from nearby Lyons are brought for summer vacation. A commemorative plaque states: "In this house, Antoine de Saint-Exupéry spent all his vacations when he was a schoolboy and a student. It was in the park bordering on the earth of men that he learned to love plants, animals and life in its humble aspects."[5] The Château de la Môle, twenty miles from Saint Tropez, still belongs to the family.

His Family

Antoine de Saint-Exupéry came from an old, aristocratic family. A geneological tree shown in a commemorative issue of *Icare,* the French aviation magazine, traces his ancestry back to the eleventh century.[6] According to Chevrier, there are references to a Bishop Saint-Exupéry of Toulouse, in the fourth century, in the writings of Gregory of Tours; and in the history of the archbishopric of Bayeux, another Saint-Exupéry, bishop of Bayeux is mentioned.[7] Raymond de Saint-Exupéry, in the thirteenth century,was a knight, and the family historically had the knightly privilege of riding in the king's coach. Cate suggests a possibility that Guillaume de Saint-Exupéry was a crusader. In 1779 Antoine's great-great-grandfather, Lieutenant Georges Alexandre Césarée, serving under the Comte de Guichen, took part in the siege of Yorktown and was present at the surrender of Cornwallis.[8] His son, Jean-Baptiste, was an officer of the Military Household, under Louis XVIII in the Restoration; and his grandson, Fernand (Antoine's grandfather), was *sous-préfet* of four departments under Louis-Napoléon, during the Second Empire.[9] Antoine's mother also came of an aristocratic family, the Boyer de Fonscolombe, to whom Fragonard and others had dedicated their works. Yet with this distinguished ancestry, Antoine almost never used his title and he was, indeed, embarrassed when it was used. Saint-Exupéry's only concern for aristocracy was for nobility of soul or mind, and such aristocrats he constantly sought, finding them in all walks of life.

Antoine de Saint-Exupéry was born on 29 June 1900, in Lyons, yet he used to say "It was quite by chance that I was born in Lyons.

I am not a Lyonnais."[10] In fact, he was Limousin on his father's side, for the little medieval town whose name he bears is in the Corrèze department of the Limousin province; and he is Provençal on his mother's side, as the de Fonscolombe family had long been established in the south. His paternal grandfather, Fernand, had settled in Le Mans when his fortunes declined after the fall of the Second Empire, and he became an inspector for an insurance company there. Antoine's father, Jean, also an inspector for the same Compagnie du Soleil, was posted to Lyons, and it is there that he met Marie de Fonscolombe, whose aunt Gabrielle, Comtesse de Tricaud, had an elegant apartment in town, as well as the property of Saint-Maurice in the country.

Antoine Jean-Baptiste Marie Roger de Saint-Exupéry was the first son born to Jean and Marie de Saint-Exupéry after two daughters, Marie-Madeleine and Simone. Two years later, a second son, François, was born and then, in 1904, another daughter, Gabrielle. Just a few weeks before Gabrielle's birth, Antoine's father died, leaving Marie with five small children. Only once in all his published writings does Saint-Exupéry refer to his father, and this is in a letter to his mother in 1917, when he mentions having met a priest who had known him.[11] The death of his young brother, François, in 1917, is reflected much more in his writings, transposed as the death of Geneviève's child in *Courrier sud,* referred to directly in *Pilote de guerre* and echoed in the death of the chieftain's son in *Citadelle,* and in that of the Little Prince.

Childhood Games and Interests

Despite the early loss of his father, Antoine's childhood was an intensely happy one, as reflected in his own writings and in the recollections of his sister, Simone. The five children created a world of their own in the two homes which welcomed them, Tante Tricaud's at Saint-Maurice and their grandmother's at La Môle. Years later, Antoine would write to his mother that his family "forms a tribe,"[12] and it was in the security of this tribe that Antoine grew up.

In *Terre des hommes,* as Saint-Exupéry grows to understand the significance of the desert, he remembers his childhood at Saint-Maurice: "Before this transfigured desert, I remember the games of my childhood, the dark, golden park, which we had peopled with

gods, the limitless kingdom which we drew from this square kilome-
ter . . . ."[13] His sister Simone writes that the whole world was
contained in this park,[14] and in several articles she recalls their
childhood games and adventures together. All the brothers and
sisters were intensely interested in the animals and insects in the
gardens, and the oldest sister, Marie-Madeleine, nicknamed "Biche,"
wrote a book on animals called *Les Amis de Biche*. As an adult, Saint-
Exupéry kept his love of animals: Even when he was stranded in
the desert, almost certain to die of thirst, he still was fascinated by
the little desert fox who would later become so important in *Le Petit
Prince*. The boys were also interested in mechanical inventions, and
Simone de Saint-Exupéry tells how her brother attached wings to
his bicycle in an attempt to fly, declaring, "When I fly away on
my new machine, the whole crowd will shout, 'Long live Antoine
de Saint-Exupéry.' "[15] Another time, Antoine and François tried to
set up a garden irrigation system, powered by a steam engine. This
experiment ended in an explosion in which François almost lost an
eye. Antoine's distress was so great that Simone feels it gave him
the first intimations of that strong sense of responsibility that is
one of the keys to his philosophy[16] and that is reflected in another
reminiscence of Simone's. The five children had been hiking in the
mountains all day and were returning home when Simone realized
that she had lost her gold watch. Antoine immediately set off up
the mountain to try and find it. Late that night he was brought
home by a passing carriage, pale and exhausted, but concerned only
that he had not succeeded in finding his sister's watch.[17]

The adult Antoine remembered his childhood games in the strang-
est circumstances, and two of these reminiscences have become well-
known passages in his books. One night in Argentina, where he
was a mail-pilot, Saint-Exupéry was invited to stay with a family
in their old, dilapidated but cherished house, and he recognized the
permanence and love in this family home, as he had known it in
Saint-Maurice. At dinner, he met the two young daughters of the
house and he sensed that they were judging his quality, just as, in
a secret game, his sisters used to award new guests a score out of a
perfect twenty. Remembering how a mysterious "eleven" would
sound out during a silence in the dinner conversation, he wondered
how he was succeeding. Suddenly he heard a soft whistling sound
under the table and felt something brush against his legs, and the
younger girl explained quietly "It is the viper." Luckily, Saint-

Exupéry simply smiled contentedly, and so the girls condescended to explain about the vipers, and Saint-Exupéry knew that he had passed the test.

Saint-Exupéry recalled another game of his childhood as he was flying the reconnaissance flight over the flaming town of Arras, recounted in his *Pilote de guerre*. As he miraculously flew unscathed through the antiaircraft tracer bullets, he remembered how, with his sisters and brothers, he used to play a game of their own invention, "le Chevalier Aklin." They played it on stormy days, when a cloud was ready to burst. "We would start off from the very bottom of the park in the direction of the house, across the lawns, running breathlessly. The first drops of the storm-showers are heavy and scattered. The first person touched admitted defeat. Then the second. Then the third. The last survivor was thus revealed as protected by the gods, the invulnerable one. He had the right, until the next storm, to be called "the Knight Aklin."[18] And Saint-Exupéry, the war pilot, felt that he was still playing at being the Knight Aklin, running breathlessly through the deadly drops, although he knew that he was no longer invulnerable. Yet in this reminiscence, Chevrier recognizes the childhood awareness of the fragility of miracles and the desire to consecrate them.[19]

Young Antoine, usually called "Tonio," was also nicknamed "Le Roi-Soleil" ("the Sun-King"), because of his blond curls. This name must have suited the child, who not only was king in his small world, but who already had the radiance of mind and spirit that would characterize him for so many friends in his adult life. His curiosity and wonderment touched everything around him, from the world of nature, to mechanical inventions, to poetry and music. He was, indeed, regal in the demands he made of those around him, sometimes awaking his whole family to read them his poetry, as he would later require his friends to read his manuscripts. Yet he gave such sincerity of friendship and affection in return that such demands were always forgiven. Like the child, the adult Antoine showed an all-embracing curiosity into every creative area of the human spirit. Besides trying to write poetry, he also invented words, according to his older cousin, Yvonne de Lestrange, who remembers his stating that he did not like somebody because she was really "désagrante."[20] As an adult writer, too, he would create his own significant vocabulary, giving a new and rich vibrancy of meaning to ordinary words. Contrary to the opinion of some biographers, Simone de Saint-

Exupéry insists that her brother was quite musical.[21] Several books show a photo of the adolescent Saint-Exupéry playing the violin; and his friend, Jean Escot, claims that he still has the violin which Saint-Exupéry gave him when he left Paris to join the Latécoère company.[22] His radio navigator, Jacques Néri, remembers that Saint-Exupéry sang in tune, with a deep voice, and that he played the piano.[23] As a school boy, Antoine even wrote the libretto for an operetta, "The Umbrella," for which he hoped his old music teacher would compose the score.[24] Mechanical inventions also fascinated Antoine, who as an adult would later take out patents on many aeronautical instruments, and he was constantly designing motors and mechanical devices. His sister says that "Invention burst forth from him as from a bubbling spring";[25] and in the absence of a father to consult, Antoine often took his latest invention to the village priest for advice when he came for dinner.

During his early years, Antoine and his sisters and brother had governesses, first Paula and then "Moïsie." Both of these women live in his books, as symbols of his secure childhood world. In *Pilote de guerre,* flying doggedly through the antiaircraft fire, Saint-Exupéry thinks of Paula, the Tyrolean governess of his earliest childhood, whom he really only "remembers remembering," and calls out to her, "Paula, they are firing on me."[26] The later governess, Marguerite Chapuys, nicknamed "Moïsie," lives in pages of *Terre des hommes.* Saint-Exupéry, alone in the desert at night, feeling all the magnetic bonds which attached him to his world, remembered the house at Ambérieu and saw the old housekeeper tending the linen closets of the old house. This activity became symbolic to him, for she was protecting "the eternity of the house" as she repaired "these altar cloths . . . these sails of a three-master, serving I know not what that is greater than she, a God or a ship."[27]

This image of the family house as a ship is one that appears frequently in Saint-Exupéry's writing. Bernis, in *Courrier sud,* thinks of Geneviève's house: "Her house was a ship. It carried the generations from one shore to the other."[28] This image occurs again in *Pilote de guerre:* "The family house received him at his birth and carried him to death, then, like a good ship, from one shore to the other, it carried his son in his turn."[29] Remembering how, with his sisters and brother, he used to explore the attic of the old house, Saint-Exupéry says, "We alone knew that the house was launched like a ship."[30]

The clan formed by the five young Saint-Exupéry children was a brilliant one. Marie-Madeleine (Biche) published a book before her early death; Simone (Monet), who graduated from the Ecole des Chartes, published a volume of short stories in Saigon; Gabrielle (Didi) participated in the Resistance movement; and young François, when he died at the age of fourteen, already showed a dignity and wisdom which would strengthen Antoine when he, too, confronted death and which are immortalized in the death of the Little Prince.

Charles Sallès, a school friend who visited Saint-Exupéry's family, believes that Antoine "owes the essential of his genius to this family milieu and, first of all, to the admirable mother who raised him."[31] Devoted to the task of bringing up her five fatherless children, Marie de Saint-Exupéry created for them a home of warm affection, where each could develop his creativity within the security of family understanding and responsibility. Although she imposed no narrow religious ideas, she gave them a respect for the riches of their religious heritage which Saint-Exupéry would rediscover in his quest for a personal credo. She could understand and encourage her children in their artistic striving, for she was an artist herself: She played the guitar and she sang, she wrote poetry and she painted. When, in 1929, the year after *Courrier sud* was published, the town of Lyons bought three of her paintings, Antoine was immensely proud of his mother, writing "What a family we make!"[32] He remained devoted to his mother throughout his life, and his letters to her are perhaps the most expressive of his published correspondence, revealing his beliefs, his aspirations and, especially, that ascension of spirit which carried him in a continual quest until his death. To her he could write of the new, mature spirit which he felt growing within him. Strangely, perhaps symbolically, his last letter to her reached her just a year after his death in action.

His Education

During his earliest years, Antoine was educated at home, but in 1908–1909, he attended a Catholic school in Lyons run by the Frères des Ecoles chrétiennes. Then, in 1909, Madame de Saint-Exupéry decided to move her family to Le Mans in the north, where her family-in-law was living and where Antoine, and later François, could enter the Jesuit school that their father had attended, Notre Dame de Sainte Croix. It was here that Antoine became known as

"Tatane" and then acquired the nickname of "Pique-la-Lune" ("prick the moon") because of his upturned nose, a nickname which he thoroughly disliked. His two earliest letters to his mother were written from this school, where he was *demi-pensionnaire* ("weekly boarder"), while his mother was away at Ambérieu.

Antoine was a student at Sainte Croix from 1909 until 1914, and these cannot have been easy years. After the privileged years of early childhood, spent entirely within the warmth and security of a close-knit family, where discipline was never arbitrary but always the simple result of affection and mutual responsibility, the austere discipline of the Jesuits must have been hard to accept. At first, Antoine was often punished for day-dreaming, untidiness, and lack of concentration. Yet his family was still his security, and in one of his letters to his mother he recalled "When I was a child, I would come home . . . sobbing because I had been punished . . . (and) you made me forget it all . . . I felt safe in your house."[33] Gradually his school-work improved, although his inveterate untidiness remained incurable. According to Chevrier, Antoine's teachers recalled a child who was "restless, big-hearted, intelligent but too often absent-minded."[34]

As a young child, Antoine had eagerly written poetry and used sometimes to present a poem to his mother for her birthday. Now, at school, he continued to enjoy writing. His first composition to receive attention was entitled "The Burial of the Ant," and it was read aloud by his teacher. Still more successful was his "Autobiography of a Top-Hat," written when he was fourteen, and which is still kept at the Collège Sainte-Croix. It earned Saint-Exupéry his first literary award, the prize for the best French composition of the year. Antoine also decided to start a class magazine, "L'Echo de troisième," reserving for himself the poetry section, but this was a short-lived undertaking, as the very first issue was confiscated. He was also inspired to write poetry by his youthful admiration for Odette de Sinéty, the sister of some class-mates. Cate quotes one such romantic attempt, "L'Hallali," starting:

> Le son du cor s'élève et baisse lentement,
> Fait résonner les bois d'un long tressaillement.[35]

> [The sound of the horn rises and falls slowly
> And makes the woods resound with a long quivering.]

which seems strongly reminiscent of De Vigny's "Son du cor."

It was at this time, too, in 1912, that Antoine had his "baptism of the air," on the airfield of Ambérieu during a summer holiday at Saint-Maurice. Once again Antoine was moved to express himself in poetry, writing:

> Les ailes frémissaient sous le souffle du soir
> Le moteur, de son chant, berçait l'âme endormie
> Le soleil nous frôlait de sa couleur pâlie. . . . [36]
>
> [The wings shuddered under the breath of evening
> The engine, with its song, lulled the sleeping soul
> The sun brushed us with its pale color. . . .

Three years later, making new friends in a new school in Switzerland, Antoine would introduce himself to Charles Sallès by saying, "You know, I've been up in a plane. It's fantastic!"[37]

With the outbreak of war in 1914, the whole pattern of life changed. Antoine's mother, who held a state diploma in nursing, became head nurse at the station hospital in Ambérieu. Antoine and his brother, François, entered the Jesuit school of Notre Dame de Montgré at Villefranche, near Lyons, as boarders; but they were so unhappy there that their mother withdrew them after one term and sent them to finish the year at Le Mans, where they lived with their Aunt Marguerite. Finally, in November 1915, the two boys entered the Villa Saint-Jean at Fribourg in Switzerland, where they would stay for the next two years.

The Villa Saint-Jean was a school run by the Marianist fathers. Here Antoine found a very different atmosphere from that which he had known in the Jesuit school. The Marianist fathers taught that free acceptance of discipline and that sense of responsibility which would be so much a part of the adult Saint-Exupéry. The school motto, "De toute son âme," ("With all one's soul") was one which Saint-Exupéry could well make his own. Although it was here that the adolescent broke from the dogma of his church, it was here, too, that he began that "long inward ascension which will lead him toward light," in his quest of God.[38] Saint-Exupéry remembers these years with affection and, in *Courrier sud,* he imagined that he returned with Bernis to visit their teachers. The old teachers wanted to learn from their former students, grown to manhood, and they were proud to recognize in them the heroic ideas which they had taught: "These heroes whom they had always extolled, now they could touch them and, having at last known them, they could now die."[39]

Living in neutral Switzerland, the adolescent Antoine was inspired by patriotism for his war-torn country to write poetry again. In one poem, "Amertume," ("Bitterness"), he revolted against his own inactivity; in "Reims," he imagined the Kaiser ordering the bombing of the cathedral in revenge for his own losses; yet another, "Printemps de guerre," contrasted the cruelty of war with the beauty of spring; and in "Soleil d'or" the blood-red sunset symbolized a dying world. Strangely, the first lines of "Reims"

> Dans la profonde nuit, Reims agonise et brule!
> La Flamme vers les cieux scintille, monte, ondule. . . . [40]

> [In the deep night, Reims writhes, dying, and burns!
> The flame toward heaven, gleams, climbs, undulates. . . .

suggest that description of Arras in flames which he would write twenty-five years later in *Pilote de guerre:* "Arras is nothing except this red flame on the blue background of night. . . . The flame of Arras has grown."[41] Saint-Exupéry admitted being convinced at that age that he was a poet. Later, under the guidance of friends of his mother's, Madame Perrin (daughter of René Bazin) and Dr. Geniès, he realized the limitations of his poetry,[42] but his prose would always remain intensely poetic. Indeed, Cate actually quotes the first page of *Courrier sud* in poetic form to prove this quality.[43]

In 1917 Antoine successfully passed his "baccalauréat" examination, but his happiness in this achievement was obscured by the severe illness of his young brother who had developed rheumatic fever. Just a month later François died, and the dignity with which he faced and accepted his death so impressed Antoine's spirit that it seemed to condition his personal concept of death in which the body is extraneous to man, and the essence stands revealed. Twenty-five years later, remembering his brother's death, as he faces death himself, Saint-Exupéry declares: "One does not die. . . . There is no more death when one meets it. . . . When the body breaks apart, the essential is revealed. Man is only a knot of relationships . . . ."[44] With the death of his brother, Antoine felt a stronger responsibility toward his sisters. He tried especially to console the youngest, Gabrielle, who had been François's constant companion, promising to replace for her "all the brothers in the world."[45] Antoine and his three sisters spent the summer in Brittany with their aunt, Amicie Churchill, trying to recover from their tragic loss.

That autumn Antoine went to Paris to start the serious studies that would lead to a career. He had decided to enter the Ecole navale (naval school) in Brest, but he needed two years of training in higher mathematics before taking the entrance examinations. He therefore attended the special preparatory classes at the Lycée Saint Louis while living as a boarder at the Ecole Bossuet, under the Abbé Sudour who would later play such a vital role in guiding Saint-Exupéry's career. Now, for the first time, Antoine was really alone and living in a great city. The magical childhood years with his family, prolonged by school days with his brother in the provinces and by the gentle schooling of the Marianist brothers in the mountain villa, were now at an end, and Antoine confronted years of hard work and struggle to find his way in life.

Chapter Two
Student and Soldier Years

At the Lycée Saint-Louis

In 1917, armed with his freshly won *baccalauréat,* the young Saint-Exupéry arrived in Paris ready to face the challenge of the arduous preparation required to enter the Ecole navale, and eager from there to forge his career. His future seemed clear before him, and he had all the confidence of any adolescent preparing to enter the adult world. His frequent letters to his mother are full of excitement and confidence, despite occasional moments of homesickness, and he is proud of his ability to hold the pace in intensive mathematics courses. Soon he started planning what he would do when he was a naval officer, promising to rent a seaside house where he could invite his mother.

Amongst his school friends at the Ecole Bossuet and the Lycée Saint-Louis, he had now become "Saint-Exu," a nickname which he accepted. Although he was sometimes withdrawn, he often took part in student pranks, and he helped organize a type of class government, in which he was elected as *Préfet des moeurs* ("prefect for moral standards"). A lifelong friend whom he made at this time was Henri de Segogne, who looked back on this friendship as "the most precious treasure of his life.[1] It was Henri who helped him in an unsuccessful escapade when Saint-Exupéry tried to avoid evening study hours at the Lycée by escaping through the sewer-tunnels to a main branch under the rue Cujas. In the study hall, Antoine enjoyed the privilege of having an individual desk with a convenient storage under the lid. However, his chronic untidiness aroused the anger of the study supervisor who ordered Antoine to give up his precious desk and move to a work-table. Instead of moving, Antoine composed a poetic appeal on the blackboard, starting:

> J'étais dans le fond de l'étude
> Un petit bureau sans valeur
> Je faisais la béatitude

De mon illustre possesseur. . . .

[In the back of the study, I was
A little desk without value.
I made the happiness
of my illustrious owner.. . . .]

The final plea, "Préfet, laissez-moi mon petit bureau"[2] ("Prefect, leave me my little desk"), moved the supervisor to let him keep his treasured desk.

Despite such pranks, Antoine was in general a serious student. He respected his teachers, and he was encouraged by them as they recognized his special temperament. At Fribourg, Antoine had tended toward philosophical studies; now he was specializing in mathematics and sciences, and showing considerable gifts in these fields. Général Chassin, who met him at a navigational course several years later, believed that he could have become a great mathematician, and he had a physical sense of mathematical ideas.[3] Gifted with remarkable, quick intelligence, he could excel in any field to which he chose to set his mind, although he often refused to exert that intelligence in a study that did not appeal to him.

Meanwhile, although he was a boarder, Antoine was developing some social life in Paris. Sometimes it was as simple as an evening at the café with classmates and their sisters, or a visit to his old friends, the Sinétys. His Aunt Anaïs, lady-in-waiting to the Duchesse de Vendôme, introduced him into society, and he was exhilarated the day he had lunch with the Duchesse, sister of the king of Belgium. His distant cousin, Yvonne de Lestrange, was an especially good friend to him, often inviting him and introducing him to her friends. Later she would introduce him to Jean Prévost, who published his first work, and to André Gide, who wrote the preface to *Vol de nuit*. There were other cousins and friends of his mother's in Paris, too, including Aunt Rose whom he especially appreciated for her delicious *goûters* ("afternoon teas").

In 1918, under growing threat of bombardment and invasion in Paris, the Lycée Saint-Louis was evacuated to the Lycée Lakanal in Sceaux. One reason for this evacuation was the habit that the older students had developed of climbing onto the rooftops to watch the bombardments. Even in Sceaux they could hear the guns. Antoine was determined that if the *Boches* took Paris he would escape on foot, as he reassured his mother.[4]

After the Armistice in November 1918, which was celebrated boisterously by Antoine and his friends, he returned to the Ecole Bossuet for final studies, before the entrance examination to the Ecole navale. In June he took the examination and passed the written tests successfully, but he later failed in the oral tests. A persistent legend, perhaps encouraged by Saint-Exupéry himself, is that he failed the French examination, turning in a blank paper. The facts, as confirmed by Henri de Segogne, Pierre Chevrier, and others, are that he not only earned the highest grade in mathematics but also did, indeed, pass the French written exam, although he had not been inspired by the topic. In the oral exam he failed specifically on questions of history and geography; and the Little Prince's vague notions of geography maybe echo this disappointment. Simone de Saint-Exupéry remembers that her brother had come joyfully back to Saint-Maurice after his first success to spend the summer in his childhood home studying for the oral,[5] so his disappointment must have been intense.

The unexpected failure at the orals blocked Saint-Exupéry's entrance to the Ecole navale, toward which he had been working for two years, for he had passed the age limit for a second attempt. Henri de Segogne expresses his surprise at this failure, asserting that the Navy deprived itself of an exceptional cadet by refusing Saint-Exupéry.[6] Yet he wonders whether, indeed, Saint-Exupéry would have been content in a situation which would soon have appeared too narrow for him in its outlook. Indeed, we may wonder whether Saint-Exupéry would ever have become "Saint-Ex" if he had entered the navy with its structured, traditional world. Although he once said that if he had been a miner, beneath the earth, he would have written about the world of men just as he did as a pilot, above the earth, maybe he did, in fact, need the special circumstances of his life as a pioneer airman to discover the "favorable terrain" in which he could begin to mature as a man and a writer.

The Ecole des Beaux-Arts

After the failure in the naval examinations, Saint-Exupéry decided to try a completely different course. After a few months of indecision, he entered the Ecole des beaux-arts ("school of fine arts") in Paris as an auditor, in the department of architecture. Most biographers dismiss these fifteen months which Saint-Exupéry spent in the Beaux-

Arts as an interim period, when he was simply marking time while he tried to find his way in life, a period which had no creative influence on him. Even one of his fellow students, Bernard Lamotte (who later became a successful artist in America), states that Saint-Exupéry "was as much an architect as I was a dentist."[7] Yet one critic, in a lengthy dissertation on the esthetics of Saint-Exupéry's work and philosophy,[8] asserts on the contrary, that this period was of vital importance in developing his ideas. Specifically, Carlo François believes that Saint-Exupéry came under the influence of the art critic, Elie Faure, who lectured at the Popular University that year. Dr. François supports his theory by drawing interesting parallels between key passages in Saint-Exupéry's works and quotations from Faure's writing, going so far as to assert that the intensely personal vocabulary which Saint-Exupéry creates was, in fact, drawn from Faure's language. Convincing as these comparisons might appear, the whole argument is nevertheless weakened by the total lack of any reference to Elie Faure either by Saint-Exupéry himself or by any of the biographers who knew him personally. This is especially significant in the case of Léon Werth, Saint-Exupéry's special friend to whom he dedicated *The Little Prince,* who was both an art critic himself and a close friend of Elie Faure. In fact, Carlo François himself frankly quotes Léon Werth's assertion that Saint-Exupéry never met Faure and his opinion that all assumptions of such influence are based on coincidence. Strangely, the published letters of Saint-Exupéry to his mother, otherwise covering every period from childhood to a posthumous note, include no letter at all from this period at the Beaux-Arts.

All that we really know of this period at the Beaux-Arts consists of a few anecdotes, recurring in most of the biographies, which show Saint-Exupéry experiencing the life of most Parisian students of the time, living in a hotel room on the Rue de Seine, eating in simple restaurants and never able to make his allowance last to the end of the month. To earn a little money, he and Segogne signed up as extras at the Théâtre des Champs-Elysées, in Jean Nogès's opera, *Quo Vadis,* in which the "guard" Segogne attacked the "Christian" Saint-Exupéry with a wooden sword. Pierre Chevrier shows Saint-Exupéry refusing to accept dinner invitations unless he actually had the money to pay for a restaurant meal, a quixotic attitude reminiscent of Cyrano de Bergerac's refusal to accept more than a symbolic grape when he was penniless. Yet even the little that is

generally accepted as descriptive of the year at the Beaux-Arts seems
contradicted in part by fellow student Bernard Lamotte. In a recent
article in *Icare*,[9] Lamotte recalls visiting his friend in the "magnificent mansion" where Saint-Exupéry was staying with his cousin,
Yvonne de Lestrange, and then surprisingly states that Saint-Exupéry took him for a drive in his new Bugatti, thereby negating the
usual impression of poverty. It seems probable that both pictures
of these student days are exaggerated.

Military Service and Aviation

Whatever this mysterious Beaux-Arts period may really have been,
spiritually and materially, it came to an end when Saint-Exupéry
was mobilized in April 1921 to do his two years' military service.
At his own request he joined an air force regiment in Strasbourg.
Here Saint-Exupéry, who would later be content in the austere hut
at Cap Juby in Africa, or in the farmhouse room at Orconte during
the war, immediately rented an elegant room in town where, during
off-duty hours, he could withdraw from barrack life to read books,
drink tea, and entertain friends. In the same letter in which he
describes this room, he explains the indispensability of a motorbike
and in the next, he asks his mother for a monthly allowance of 500
francs. The next few years are well documented in letters, and these
are interesting in that they reveal both the rather immature, almost
spoiled young man who entered the air force in the ground crew,
and the birth of the passion for flying which would be the liberating
force for his spirit and would bring him to a new world of camaraderie and mature responsibility.

Saint-Exupéry had entered the air force regiment in the ground
personnel. However, before he even had his uniform, he was thinking of flying, writing to his mother: "Only let the moment of
piloting come, and I shall be perfectly happy."[10] Meanwhile, thanks
to the intervention of two friendly officers who recognized his su-
perior education, he was put in charge of teaching a course on
aerodynamics and the combustion engine, a promotion of which he
seemed rather naturally proud. Yet the desire to learn to fly seemed
to grow increasingly urgent in him. He immediately put in a request
to become a student pilot, and was ready to volunteer to go to
Morocco if he could not satisfy his longing to fly. Soon he had
arranged with friendly Capitaine de Billy to take private instruction

at the Strasbourg airfield and to earn a civilian license. This, however, cost a considerable amount of money, so Saint-Exupéry again called on his mother, trying to make her understand his urge to fly, and explaining that with a civilian license he could automatically take the military one. Almost in desperate ultimatum, he declared that he would sign up for three years in order to fly, rather than spend two years without flying. Stubbornly he made final arrangements with the Compagnie Transaérienne de l'Est, a civilian company which shared the Neudorf aerodrome with the military. Still trying to convince his mother, he insisted that his was indeed a mature decision and declared urgently that he had not a moment to lose.[11]

Finally, on 18 June, he took his first lesson in a Farman, with the instructor, Robert Aéby, who recounts these first lessons in volume sixty-nine of *Icare*. It is here that most of the major biographers situate the anecdote of the novice Saint-Exupéry climbing unauthorized into a plane to try solo flying before he had even learned maneuvers. The dramatic story then has the plane on fire before Saint-Exupéry finally lands safely, nonchalantly remarking that his uniform gaiters are burned. However, according to two aeronautically reliable sources, Robert Aéby, his instructor, and Marcel Migéo, a fellow pilot in Strasbourg, this story is ungrounded, forming part of the legend which has grown up around Saint-Exupéry. Robert Aéby explains how, after careful training in dual control, he deliberately decided to *lâcher* ("let go") Saint-Exupéry in solo flight on 9 July, telling him to land when he saw a signal flare.[12] Saint-Exupéry came in too high and too fast, so he circled off again, giving more gas to the motor, which caused it to overheat and smoke. Marcel Migéo gives the same technical explanation, but with more detail, explaining how the pilot of those early machines had to regulate the proportion of gas and air fed to the carburetor.[13] Although this simplified story is less dramatically heroic, it still shows that Saint-Exupéry already had good, instinctive reactions for a pilot, circling off and adjusting the fuel mixture the instant he realized he was wrongly placed for landing, and finally making his first solo landing correctly while he believed his plane was on fire. Both instructor Aéby and the commanding officer were satisfied, and Saint-Exupéry obtained his civilian license.

Another incident, however, which is just as colorful, did take place during Saint-Exupéry's training and it is authenticated by fellow pilots, Migéo and Escot, with slight variation of detail. Saint-Exupéry had just landed in his Sopwith and was waiting beside his plane to taxi into place when a large, four-seater Spad came rolling straight toward him, and Saint-Exupéry spotted it only just in time to leap aside before his light plane was crushed. Migéo comments with humor that Saint-Exupéry was lucky to have paid a comprehensive fee for his training, including "breakage"; while Escot reports Saint-Exupéry's wry comment that this accident meant that nobody would see his broken landing gear.

First Contact with Africa

Saint-Exupéry had volunteered for a transfer to Morocco where he could continue flight training and obtain his military license. Some biographers pass over this period in Morocco with a brief sentence, yet these months were surely important as they were his first introduction to Africa and especially to the desert, where he would find such inspiration. Already in anticipation, he wrote to his mother from Strasbourg, "The desert seen from a plane must be sublime."[14] His letters from Rabat and Casablanca were revealing in that they passed from initial nostalgia for France and her green countryside, to gradual understanding of the African landscape, which he would later come to love. Here too, in his letters, were the first suggestions of ideas that would reappear in his books. In one of these letters, he mentioned a navigation lesson with a sergeant who described the terrain intimately, just as in *Wind, Sand, and Stars,* the older pilot initiates the novice into the map of Spain, told in sheep and streams. For the first time, Saint-Exupéry, who would spend so much of his life traveling or in exile, was living out of his country; and nostalgia aroused in him his first awareness of love for France, which his later periods of exile would develop into an understanding of his country as an entity, inspiring his loyalty and devotion.

This was a pleasant interlude, too. In Casablanca, Saint-Exupéry met Sabran, an old school friend from Bossuet, and together they spent restful weekends of music and conversation in Rabat, Saint-Exupéry's "well-loved city," as guests of Capitaine Priou. In the captain's Moorish-style house, in a quietness punctuated only by the bell from the nearby mosque, Saint-Exupéry began to discover adult social life, after years of school and barrack life. During this period, too, Saint-Exupéry discovered the delight of making the rapid pencil sketches with which he thereafter illustrated many of his letters, and he wrote to his mother, "I have discovered what I was made for: the black charcoal pencil."[15] More exactly, he rediscovered this skill from which he had been discouraged as a child, as he tells us in *The Little Prince,* and which he would bring to its most sensitive refinement in illustrating that book. His letters began to show more maturity of spirit during this period, with some suggestion of philosophical reflection.

In December 1921 Saint-Exupéry obtained his long-sought military pilot's license and, in January, he was sent back to France to complete his training at the apprentice center at Istres, which Migéo describes as *le bagne des élèves morts* ("the penal colony of dead students")[16] because of its terrible conditions. Fortunately, Saint-Exupéry did not have to stay there long as, in Morocco, he had passed the entrance exam for the officer cadet school at Avord, near Bourges. However, his short stay at the sinister Istres, before entering the school at Avord, brought him his first meeting with Henri Guillaumet, whom he would meet again as a pilot of the Latécoère line, and who would become a beloved, lifelong friend.

In April 1922 Corporal Saint-Exupéry entered the school at Avord where he found Jean Escot, whom he had known in Strasbourg, and also met Marcel Reine, who would later be a fellow pilot in Africa and in South America. The training here was chiefly in theory, leading to an observer's diploma. To continue practical training in flying, the few qualified pilots had to put in early hours before the day's classes began. During a special training period that summer at Versailles, Saint-Exupéry and Escot again devotedly arose early to satisfy their passion for flying before class time, driving to Villacoublay aerodrome on a borrowed motorbike. Finally, in October, Saint-Exupéry completed officers' training well enough to be promoted to second lieutenant and to be able to choose his assignment. He chose the 34th aerial regiment at Le Bourget, the airfield near Paris, where he completed his two-year military service.

First Love

Life at Le Bourget was good, for it was near Paris, and Saint-Exupéry could renew contacts with old school friends and family friends. On free days he would visit Henri de Segogne, now working at the Cour des comptes, Bertrand de Saussine, whose sister, Renée, became a good friend, and the Vilmorin family, to whom he was very distantly related. This was a family much like his own, where four brothers and two sisters enjoyed a vital, close-knit life, with a charming, widowed mother. During school days in Paris, Saint-Exupéry, de Saussine, and many classmates had been attracted to the exhilaration of this household. Now, during that winter at Le Bourget, Saint-Exupéry fell in love with the younger sister, Louise (who would also become a writer). Her brother, André, writes that Louise felt a kind of passion for this young airman, who talked to her of poetry and wrote poetry for her. One poem that her brother remembers begins

> Hâtons-nous de rêver car voici que se dresse
> L'ombre qui dès midi campe au revers des monts[17]
>
> [Let us hasten to dream for already there arises
> The shadow which, as early as midday, is encamped beyond
> the mountains.]

Soon, the two young poets became engaged, despite the opposition of Louise's mother, who considered Saint-Exupéry unsuitable. However, the engagement was officially announced, and Saint-Exupéry gave Louise a family heirloom ring, sent by his mother.

Early in 1923 Saint-Exupéry suffered the first of the serious accidents that punctuated his career. He was flying over the Paris suburbs when his engine ran out of fuel. Rather than try to land there, amongst the crowded streets, Saint-Exupéry tried to bring his plane to Le Bourget, but he lost so much speed that he crashed. His skull was fractured and, when he awoke in the hospital, he curiously studied what he thought was the next world. As soon as he recovered, he valiantly returned to flying to prove his determination to continue. However, this accident had stiffened the Vilmorins' determination that Louise could not marry a pilot, so Saint-Exupéry was faced with the ultimatum: to choose Louise or flying. He still had several months to decide, however, until the end of his two years' military service.

When Saint-Exupéry was discharged, he could have entered the airforce as a career pilot, for he had the necessary license and had completed apprenticeship at Le Bourget, as well as theoretical training at Avord. Général Barès, a family friend, had indeed arranged a posting for him, but the Vilmorins were adamant that Saint-Exupéry leave aviation. Although Migéo considers that Saint-Exupéry left flying because he had not yet realized his own vocation for it, Chevrier and Cate recognize that he sacrificed his love of flight to his love for Louise. The Vilmorins had found him a stable, secure office job, as inspector with the Boiron tile works. So in June 1923 Saint-Exupéry left the airforce to return safely to civilian life for, as André de Vilmorin says, Saint-Exupéry thought only of Louise.[18] After two years of passionate struggle to fly at all costs, he tried to settle down to the life of the "anthill" *(la termitière)* if this would satisfy the Vilmorins and give him Louise.

Chapter Three

The Dark Years: "L'Aviateur"

La Termitière

The next three years were, in the words of Saint-Exupéry's friend Charles Sallès, his *années obscures* ("his dark years"),[1] or as Chevrier says, "the years during which he could find no trace of man."[2] These were the years when he struggled to fit himself into the "reasonable," secure life to which his family, friends and fiancée thought that he should adapt. He struggled financially, for he was not successful in the business world; and he suffered spiritually, for he felt stifled in this routine existence, the world of the *termitière*, which he would later condemn in *Wind, Sand, and Stars,* pitying those who are caught in it.

Yet at first, he must have entered this new period of his life optimistically and with happy hopes. He had an adult job in Paris and he was engaged to Louise, to whom he was completely devoted. He had many good friends in Paris, with whom he could enjoy a good social life, and several family members who would invite him and introduce him to artists and writers. There were his Aunt Anaïs, who lunched with him each week, his uncle, Jacques de Fonscolombe, and especially his older cousin, Yvonne de Lestrange, who became, as he said himself, his *meilleur copain* ("best pal"),[3] always encouraging and guiding him. Also he was not entirely deprived of flying, for he still sometimes contrived to fly at Orly.

Saint-Exupéry's engagement to Louise was at first idyllic. Once when she was sent to Switzerland to recover from a bad case of influenza, he determined to join her there and he sold his camera to pay the fare. There they wandered romantically hand-in-hand, picking gentians, and so obviously passionately in love that Louise's hosts feared lest they dramatically take a lovers' leap into the lake.[4] Yet the engagement did not last, perhaps because Louise was not ready for marriage. As she recalls, "Antoine thought only of flying, telling me about terrifying or sublime moments spent between sky and earth, and I, thinking only of furnishing our future house, interrupted him to ask him if he liked padded chair-seats."[5] (The Geneviève of *Southern Mail,* whom Bernis tries in vain to detach from her world of ordered things, is surely sister to Louise.) One day Louise broke the engagement by the simple means of disappearing, only letting Saint-Exupéry discover later that she had gone to Biarritz.

No published letter of Saint-Exupéry's mentions his engagement to Louise and its abrupt end, but it surely hurt him deeply. Marcelle Auclair, the wife of Jean Prévost, remembers seeing Saint-Exupéry arrive pale and shaken at Yvonne de Lestrange's house: he had just seen Louise, now married and expecting her first child, climbing into a car, her arms filled with flowers.[6] Louise herself must have recalled their engagement with emotion, as it is reflected in several of her poems, especially in "Il vole," where she plays on the two homonyms *voler,* meaning "to fly" and "to steal," in an image based on the fable of the Fox and the Crow:

> Mais où est mon amant?—Il vole
> C'est un voleur que j'ai pour amant,
> Le corbeau vole et mon amant vole,
> Voleur de coeur manque à sa parole
> Et voleur de fromage est absent
> Mais où est le bonheur?—Il vole

> [But where is my lover?—He is flying (stealing)
> It is a flyer (thief) whom I have for a lover.
> The crow steals (flies) and my lover flies (steals)
> Thief of hearts fails in his word
> And thief of cheese is absent.
> But where is happiness?—It flies]

ending with the line: "Je veux que mon voleur me vole" ("I want my flyer-thief to steal me away").[7]

Later, Saint-Exupéry and Louise renewed their friendship and corresponded when he was at Cap Juby. In one letter quoted by Louise's brother, Saint-Exupéry wrote to her in a moment of spiritual solitude, "There are so few people whom I can really reach. You, Loulou, how heavily you weigh"[8] already using his image of true friendship, whose value seems to have tangible weight. Years later when Saint-Exupéry had married Consuelo, and Louise had returned to France after an unsuccessful marriage in the United States, they would meet at gatherings in Yvonne de Lestrange's home. Comparing Saint-Exupéry's works and Louise de Vilmorin's writings arouses a wistful conjecture that they could, indeed, have created a happy marriage in maturer years.

When the engagement was suddenly broken, Saint-Exupéry was left with nothing but his unrewarding job as inspector in the tile manufacture, which he described to his mother as "such stupid work."[9] In this same letter, we can read between the lines an indirect reference to his heartbreak: "I know that I ought to confide in you and tell you my sorrows so that you could console me, as you used to do when I was a child. . . . You must not be angry with me for having been embittered, I have been through some bad days. Now I have overcome (my discouragement)."[10] That autumn, probably soon after his own disappointment, he had taken part in his sister Gabrielle's wedding; and these two experiences seem to have brought him some maturity, for his letters now contained a more adult expression of his affection for his mother and family, less demanding and more protective. Despite his financial difficulties, he became embarrassed to be an expense to his mother; instead, he wished that he could invite her and spoil her.

Dissatisfied with his present position, Saint-Exupéry was trying to find other openings; and all the facets of his future career seem to have come under consideration at that time. Journalism already seemed a possibility, through an acquaintance in *Le Matin,* but his office work left Saint-Exupéry no time to do the necessary preliminary reporting. Flying was always in his mind, and he was tempted by a possibility of going to China to direct an aviation school. Meanwhile, he still found opportunities to fly at Orly airfield, at the training center for civilian pilots of military age. Significantly, for the first time he mentioned writing, nonchalantly saying in a letter, "Half my novel is done. I think that it is new and concise."[11] Thereafter there were frequent brief references to "his novel."

By 1924 life began to look more hopeful, as two opportunities opened up. First, through the intermediary of Général Barès, Saint-Exupéry became a part-time pilot in the Compagnie Aérienne française, where he gave *baptêmes de l'air* ("first flight air baptisms") and also undertook contract flights, often photography reporting. He even considered founding a company for aerial photography, which apparently did not materialize. Then came what he believed was "an immense hope,"[12] a position as traveling sales representative for the Saurer truck company, which he felt would give him independence, both financially and in his daily activities. He entered into this new situation with enthusiastic high hopes, even accepting the two-month training period at the factory with comparative optimism.

During this period when he was confident in his new situation, Saint-Exupéry seems to have considered the idea of marriage again, but simply the abstract concept, linked with some paternal instinct: "I have a small, just a small desire to get married, but I don't know with whom. And then, I have so much paternal love in store. I would like to have some little Antoines . . . ."[13] The big Antoine would never have his paternal love fulfilled, although he was a wonderfully affectionate uncle to his sister's children, their much adored "Oncle Papou"; and not until he was thirty-one would Saint-Exupéry get married. He was discouraged by the empty young girls whom he met, who all seemed alike, nothing but "waiting rooms," until he should find the ideal girl whom he described to his sister as intelligent, restful, and faithful.[14] This abstract desire for marriage was intensified by the solitary life of a commercial traveler, but seemed later almost forgotten during his intense years flying in Africa.

Soon Saint-Exupéry completed his training period at the Saurer truck factory, and he was pleased with his assignment to the Montluçon area, feeling that he was established for life. At first this new work was exciting, and Saint-Exupéry enjoyed observing the life of the provincial towns which he visited, cheerfully describing them in letters to his mother and his friends. Soon, however, this nomadic life began to pall, despite the periodic visits of his friends, who sometimes joined him in his travels. Besides, Saint-Exupéry was not a successful salesman and, in eighteen months, he sold only one truck. But the enforced solitude of this unsettled life, alternating with long discussions with his friends, whenever he returned to Paris, must have encouraged meditation, and a new, significant maturity appeared in his letters.

Literary Interests

Already in 1923, a letter to Renée de Saussine showed philosophical meditation on the essence of writing: "One must not learn to write but to see. Writing is a consequence,"[15] he wrote, in discussing the writing of a friend. Again, in a letter to his mother in 1924, he suddenly mentioned a friend with whom he had discussed the philosophy of writing. Saint-Exupéry had taught his friend to reevaluate his empty, superficial style and to accept the need of personal growth in intelligence and vision before writing. Significantly, Saint-Exupéry adds that this disillusionment with self is a "healthy hygiene through which he has been himself."[16] Saint-Exupéry was glad at the success of his teachings, feeling for the first time that he had "moulded" someone, as he would later say.

Here we find the germ of some of the great "leitmotifs" of Saint-Exupéry's philosophy: the danger of language which can betray thought; the need to learn to think and to see, before trying to write; the contradiction between reason and understanding. He despised those who wrote only for effect "using words like a calculator"[17] to produce automatic thought. Saint-Exupéry was already quite uncompromising in his condemnation of any writer whom he suspected of simply playing with words; and he startled his friends in a café one day by a violent outburst against Pirandello, whose work he treated as *métaphysique de concierge*.[18] Writing to explain, if not to apologize for his outburst, he elaborated on the growing need within him for integrity of thought: "I cannot consider ideas as tennis balls, or coins for social conversation. . . . One cannot play at thinking."[19] Because his friends, Renée and Laure de Saussine, had compared Pirandello to Ibsen, he broke down this comparison: "Ibsen, whether he succeeded or not, tried to give us nourishment, not a new game of lotto,"[20] and then he entered into a long, detailed analysis of the weakness of Pirandello's work, which he characterized as "dramatic trickery" designed to make the spectator dizzy. This letter to Renée de Saussine is of major importance in understanding Saint-Exupéry's philosophy, his integrity, and uncompromising demands for himself and for others, and it is, indeed, the first appearance of the Saint-Exupéry whom the world would know through his writing. It contains a sentence written for Ibsen which could well epitomize Saint-Exupéry himself: "He tried to make you understand the things which he judged to be true. And in this case, the man goes beyond his work, whatever that may be."[21]

Another strikingly important letter in this period is one written to his mother from Montluçon in 1925, in which he tried to make her understand the new, mature Antoine who had grown behind the talkative, superficial man whom others saw in him: "I am so different from what I may have been. It is enough for me that you should know it and have some regard for me."[22] Now, the only important thing for him was the inner life of thought and spirit, and he set high standards by which he measured the fruitfulness of his days. Hard on himself if he did not meet his own high expectations, he admitted that he was hard on others who did not fulfill them, and he was hurt when he did not find in others what he sought there. Yet he felt a kind of modesty about revealing this inner self and he told his mother: "You must look for me as I really am, in what I write, which is the scrupulous, meditated result of what I think and see."[23]

Writing had become an increasingly serious activity for Saint-Exupéry. Although he had perhaps, as an adolescent, simply played with words, he had at some time disciplined himself to the "healthy hygiene" of re-evaluating his own work and ideas, just as he had made his friend do. Now when he wrote, he could "come face to face with himself and, avoiding all formulae or literary trickery, express himself with effort."[24] Then he felt himself completely honest and conscientious. The urge to write was growing stronger in him and he felt that if he could write every day, he would be happy, for then something would remain of each day's experience.

More and more frequently in his letters, Saint-Exupéry mentioned his "novel" which was growing, and most biographers presume that this was, in fact, the short story "L'Aviateur" which would be published in 1926. Yet there apparently was another, somewhat mysterious, earlier manuscript, entitled "Manon" or "Manon, danseuse" which elusively appears in various references. The magazine *Icare* lists "Manon, danseuse" as an unpublished manuscript in 1926.[25] Pierre Chevrier simply gives the title "Manon" to the article published in 1926, which was, in fact, "L'Aviateur,"[26] although there is no "Manon" in the published article. Cate believes that "Manon, danseuse" was a second short story, which Saint-Exupéry had written while at Montluçon, but that it was a "youthful and immature work" which he did not wish to see published.[27] In a footnote to the letter in which Saint-Exupéry says that his novel is "ripening page by page," his mother explains that this first manuscript was lost.[28] This could refer to the elusive "Manon" but it might also be a reference to a longer, original text from which "L'Aviateur" was supposedly drawn. Indeed, the editor's note to "L'Aviateur" says that he thinks Saint-Exupéry lost his original text, then rewrote it from memory as the short story.[29] The editor is obviously not sure of this fact, although the standard introduction in the Gallimard edition of *Un Sens à la vie* states the loss as a fact.

"L'Aviateur"

The editor of "L'Aviateur," when it appeared in *Le Navire d'argent* in 1926, was Jean Prévost, whom Saint-Exupéry had met at Yvonne de Lestrange's home. Prévost had for some time been working with Adrienne Monnier, whose book shop, "La Maison des amis des livres," on the rue de l'Odéon vied with Sylvia Beach's "Shakespeare and Company" as a literary center, and together Prévost and Monnier published *Le Navire d'argent,* a literary magazine. The magazine lasted only a year and would perhaps now be forgotten if its last issue had not included an article by an unknown young writer, Antoine de Saint-Exupéry. Prévost had been intrigued by Saint-Exupéry's gift for describing his impressions in conversation so, when he learned that Saint-Exupéry had been writing, he considered publishing his short story. Prévost read the text, admired its "straight-forward art and the gift of truth which seem surprising in a beginner's work"[30] and decided to publish it. He only had room in the issue for extracts, however, so the full "Evasion de Jacques Bernis" appeared as eight fragments entitled "L'Aviateur."[31]

Although the fragmentary "L'Aviateur" is usually passed over with a brief reference, as being simply Saint-Exupéry's first published article, it seems worth noting that these eight extracts already include many of the ideas that will recur, more fully developed, in Saint-Exupéry's better-known works. Indeed, Luc Estang considers "L'Aviateur" to be the "first version" of *Southern Mail,*[32] and one sentence is actually transplanted bodily into the later work. Briefly, these extracts are vignettes showing the essential facets of Bernis's experience as a pilot. In the description of takeoff, there is already a feeling of fulfillment in flight and, in the description of flight, a sense of fusion between the pilot and his plane. There is, too, a new perspective on the earth and a new realization of self discovered in flight that will be so essential in *Wind, Sand, and Stars.* The camaraderie born of a common craft is already recognized, and there is a sense of initiation into this select world of dedication. Finally, in the character of Bernis there is already an outlining of the chief who must hide his affection for his men under apparent hardness in order to mold them to greatness, just as Daurat in *Wind, Sand,*

and Stars or the Chieftain in *Wisdom of the Sands* will do. And the near-accident of a student pilot and Bernis's final fatal accident foreshadow the familiarity with death that Saint-Exupéry would experience all his life. Yet the intriguing question remains of the original title of the larger manuscript from which these extracts were taken, "The Escape of Jacques Bernis." In what sense was Bernis "escaping?"—from the treadmill of everyday life or from some hopeless love, as in *Southern Mail?*—and was death the ultimate price he had to pay for this escape?

Meanwhile, Saint-Exupéry continued to fly part-time for the Compagnie Aérienne Française, finding much satisfaction in this work, which kept alive his love of flying. Several years later, autographing a copy of *Wind, Sand, and Stars* for Général Barès, who had found him this opportunity, Saint-Exupéry writes significantly: "To General Barès, to whom I owe my first steps in commercial aviation, for without him I should not have entered the Compagnie Aérienne française. And thus I should not have realized this vocation, known the lines of the Aéropostale and written this book."[33]

Yet, despite publishing his article and flying more regularly, Saint-Exupéry was still unsettled, still seeking his way. He found no satisfaction in the lonely life of the traveling salesman, in which he could experience no warmth of companionship or sense of mission. Added to his latent dissatisfaction with his aimless life, came the tragedy of his sister, Marie-Madeleine's death, in 1926, after a long illness. Saint-Exupéry, who had enjoyed such closeness with his family during his childhood and who had felt himself drawn even closer by the early death of his brother, François, surely suffered deeply from this loss, both for himself and for the grief which it caused his beloved mother.

Turning-Point

During this period of distress and discouragement, Saint-Exupéry apparently confided in his old friend and teacher from the Ecole Bossuet, the Abbé Sudour, who had the perceptive wisdom to recognize what his young protégé needed to do. Sudour could have tried to find Saint-Exupéry some position in the academic world; instead, he introduced him to Beppo de Massimi, whom he had met during the war, and who was now director of the newly created Latécoère aviation company. This introduction would prove to be the vital turning-point for Saint-Exupéry, a moment from which his whole life and career would develop, as a pilot, as a writer, and as a man. Indeed, it is to be hoped that there exists somewhere a copy of *Wind, Sand, and Stars* autographed for the Abbé Sudour by Saint-Exupéry with much the same words as those used for Général Barès, for without Sudour's wisdom, Saint-Exupéry would not have realized his vocation and written that book.

When Massimi met Saint-Exupéry, he at first wanted to give the well-educated, distinguished young man an administrative position in the Madrid office, where he could be influential in diplomatic negotiations for the company, concerning the Rio de Oro on the Mauritanian border. However, already true to his lifelong principle of participation, Saint-Exupéry adamantly insisted that he must fly, proclaiming that he wanted to fly above anything else. His sincerity of purpose moved Massimi, who promised to recommend Saint-Exupéry to the director of the company operations office in Toulouse. Although Saint-Exupéry was eager to leave that same day, it was finally agreed that he would wait for the expected summons at his sister's home, at Agay in the south, conveniently close to Toulouse. At last, his ambitions of full-time flying seemed about to be realized. Yet at the moment of leaving Paris, where he had spent his "dark years," Saint-Exupéry sadly wrote to Renée de Saussine "I have had enough of this Paris, which makes one hope too much and never fulfills anything [any promise]," adding wistfully, "But then, it is really my fault."[34]

Saint-Exupéry had made his original application to Latécoère on September 1st, but it was not until October 11th that the long-awaited summons to the Toulouse office reached him at Agay. The very next day he reported to the Latécoère office at the Montaudran airport near Toulouse, armed with his references and air log. There he met the director of operations, Didier Daurat, the man who would prove to be such a great influence in Saint-Exupéry's life, by his stern dedication to purpose. As a man, Saint-Exupéry would feel himself strengthened by the strong demands placed upon him by Daurat, which "moulded" him into full realization of his potential; as a writer he would find in Daurat the model for the controversial Rivière in *Night Flight* and for the Caïd in *Wisdom of the Sands*. At this first meeting, however, he saw only a laconic man who questioned him briefly, then sent him to start the technical training in mechanics required of all pilots of the Latécoère Line.

Wearing workman's overalls and with his hands deep in axle grease, the dapper young second lieutenant began his initiation into the world where his spirit would grow and soar, a world of pride in work well done, and of companionship with his fellow flyers, striving toward the same purpose, a world of responsibility.

Chapter Four
La Ligne in Africa:
Courrier sud

The Latécoère Line, which Saint-Exupéry joined on 12 October 1926, was founded by Pierre Latécoère, an heroic pioneer in the domain of commercial aviation. As an airplane manufacturer during World War I, when early planes were first used in battles, Latécoère was inspired with the concept of the peaceful uses of this new device which could serve to bring people closer together. Even before the end of the war, he imagined an aviation line linking southern France, through Spain to Morocco, and then on across the Atlantic to South America. This was still the period of fabric-covered planes, flying at 130 kilometers per hour, with a flight radius of 500 kilometers, when pilots used carrier pigeons instead of radio. As Migéo says, Latécoère's concept seemed inspired by the imagination of Jules Verne,[1] yet it would soon become, in Kessel's words, "the chanson de geste of our times."[2] On Christmas Day, 1918, Latécoère and fellow pilot Cornemont made the first exploratory flight to Spain; and soon Latécoère founded his "Ligne" at the airport of Montaudran, near Toulouse. In his undertaking he was joined by many pilots in whom the armistice had left the nostalgia of flight. First among these men inspired by this passion for flight was former war pilot Didier Daurat who, in 1919, made the first airmail flight to Morocco and who then emerged as true leader of men in the Line. Supported administratively by Beppo de Massimi and encouraged by Lyautey, Latécoère officially founded his *Compagnie Générale d'Entreprises Aéronautiques* in 1921. Service was extended on the African lines, from Casablanca to Dakar to Oran. In 1925 the first reconnaissance flight to South America was made. When Saint-Exupéry joined the Line in 1926, his fellow pilots included Mermoz, Guillaumet, Reine, Lécrivain, Gourp, and others, destined to become famous for their own exploits or through his writings. In all of them there grew this "Spirit of the Line," nurtured by Daurat:

It is there that there begins that surprising ascension which would lead them to the most eminently human summits, so human that they have been called superhuman. It is true for Saint-Exupéry as for all the others . . . What one calls the spirit of the Line, that is to say the spirit of unconditional sacrifice or even the mystique of the mail . . . this condition of the soul which will soon be that of all these men who had come there to fly, it is Didier Daurat who created it.[3]

Daurat realized that Saint-Exupéry had found in the Line the fervor which he had sought in vain elsewhere.[4]

Saint-Exupéry had arrived in Toulouse expecting immediately to satisfy his passion for flying, but first he had to go through the practical, literally down-to-earth initiation of mechanical training. Before any pilot might start to fly for the company, he had to acquire thorough mechanical knowledge so that he could repair his plane whenever, as happened so often, he crash-landed on a Spanish plateau or in the North African desert. At first in his new world, Saint-Exupéry seemed to show a certain reticence, born of years of frustration and material failure. Yet as Daurat recognized, Saint-Exupéry saw before him a whole new world, sensing the expanse of it, and anxious to be worthy of it.[5]

Although Saint-Exupéry would soon find the comradeship of the Line very enriching, during the initial period in this new world, he missed the friends he had left behind in Paris. He wrote frequent letters to Renée de Saussine, hoping perhaps to find in her the ideal companion to fill the void left by Louise. Because she apparently responded only rarely, he lucidly admitted that he was writing to an image created by himself: "For I create you this evening at my will and if only you knew how kind you are! Indeed, these are the only conversations I have with you. Those invented within myself. What a revenge I am taking with my invented friend."[6] Indeed, his *Lettres de jeunesse* were first published as *Lettres à l'amie inventée.* These published letters continue until 1931, the year when Saint-Exupéry married Consuelo. At least one critic suggests that Renée, and not Consuelo, was indeed symbolized by the capricious Rose in *The Little Prince.*

For some time Saint-Exupéry continued his ground training, avidly listening to the laconic accounts of returning pilots. When Daurat considered that Saint-Exupéry had progressed sufficiently in mechanical training, he sent him out on his first flight for the Line.

His orders were summarized in the reminder "Beneath the clouds lies eternity."[7] It was then that Guillaumet gave Saint-Exupéry the famous geography lesson which recurs in *Southern Mail* and *Wind, Sand, and Stars,* and which had already been mentioned in his letters to his mother.

"Guillaumet did not teach me about Spain: he made of Spain a friend for me."[8] As Guillaumet told him about the orange trees, the farmers, the streams, and the sheep which he could spot from the air, "Spain became, beneath the lamp, a land of fairy-tale."[9] Thus initiated into the inner knowledge of the Line, Saint-Exupéry set out for an evening walk through the city crowds, feeling something of the detachment and commitment of a knight in his vigil before a first battle: "Amongst the unknowing passers-by, I walked with my young fervor. I was proud to brush against these unknown people with my secret in my heart. . . . I strode amongst them with a defender's steps but they knew nothing of my solicitude."[10] As he looked at the bright Christmas windows, displaying all the good things of the earth, he "proudly tasted the intoxication of renunciation"[11] and was exhilarated by his new responsibility.

During these first weeks with the Line, Saint-Exupéry soon acquired the nickname of "Saint-Ex," a name which he liked his friends to use, although he did not appreciate it from a stranger or a journalist. Pierre Chevrier, thinking that some foreigners might dislike this abbreviation, finding it perhaps presumptuous, points out that his friends used it simply, with respect and affection.[12]

At first Saint-Exupéry remained in Toulouse, making flights to Spain and on to Africa. Flying at last as a professional pilot, he was exhilarated by his new work, writing to Renée: "Do you know that aviation is a beautiful thing? And that here it is not a game, and this is how I love it. Neither is it a sport as at Le Bourget, but something else, inexplicable, a kind of war."[13] One day Saint-Exupéry almost had a fatal accident when the controls broke. As he faced death, he experienced that ultimate fear which he found to be "a new, undefinable intelligence."[14] Through this closeness to death, glimpsing "a world which one does not often return to describe," he felt an intense understanding of life, where everything has an order and a meaning, as he tried to explain to Renée de Saussine: "How can I say, 'I have understood the fields, the sunshine . . . ?' And yet it was true. I felt for a few seconds the brilliant plenitude of this day. A day strongly built like a house where I was at home. . . . And it was meaningful to put order in this house. I was back, I was protected, I really loved life."[15] In his life as a pioneer commercial pilot and later as a war pilot, Saint-Exupéry repeatedly came close to death, and each time it intensified his awareness of life, and his love for this world to which each landing brought him back.

Sometimes breakdowns were less dramatic, simply stranding him in some small town or village until he could repair his plane, much as he had visited the little provincial towns during his months as a traveling salesman. Even in Toulouse, where he lived with all the other Latécoère pilots, at the Hotel du Grand Balcon, he felt he was part of the quiet provincial life in which he recognized both the value of habits, which can give security, and the danger of them if they become a prison. "I trace my little provincial path . . . until I feel within myself . . . an immense need to escape and to be new."[16] This was the *termitière*, the "ant-hill" in which men turn blindly. Then it was that the rattling old bus which transported the pilots out to the Montaudran airfield became a means of liberation, or rather of transmutation; "it was simply a grey chrysalid from which man could come out transformed."[17]

This transformation which Saint-Exupéry felt within himself came from responsibility accepted, from the sense of the métier, that French word which combines, under Saint-Exupéry's pen, the meaning of "craft," "profession," and even of "vocation." "Thus the necessities imposed by the 'métier' transform and enrich the world. . . . [They] make the pilot of the line discover a new meaning to old sights. . . . Like a peasant who . . . forecasts by a thousand signs, the 'pilote de métier' also deciphers the signs of snow, signs of fog, signs of a peaceful night. The pilot defends his mail against three elementary divinities, the mountain, the sea, the storm."[18] For Saint-Exupéry, the plane became a tool through which man entered into contact with his world, as does a farmer with his plough: "The peasant, in his ploughing, wrests little by little some secrets from nature, and the truth which he discovers is universal. In the same way, the aeroplane involves man with all the old problems."[19] As Saint-Exupéry began to feel some security in his new position, one of the first impulses was to offer his mother a happy vacation in Spain just as, when he had hoped to become a naval officer, he had looked forward to renting a little house by the sea where she could relax. This impulse is too often ignored by biographers who like to stress Saint-Exupéry's embarrassingly frequent appeals to his mother for financial help during his difficult years. The simple terms in which he expresses his new material stability show his satisfaction in this reversal of his situation: "I am building a secure situation. . . . I will at last be able to invite you to lunch," and again, "I will at last be able to be a son such as I dream of being . . . ."[20] In this new material security and spiritual fulfillment, Saint-Exupéry was starting to write again, too, stating simply to his mother that he was going to send something to the *Nouvelle Revue française.*

By 1927 Saint-Exupéry was spending much of his time in Dakar and making his first contact with the desert and the people of the desert who would influence his life so significantly for the next few years, as well as with the adventurous life of the Line. In one letter he wrote of seeing the Moors for the first time, and he nonchalantly reported that his flight went well, "except for a plane crashed in the desert."[21] After this crash, he took refuge in an isolated little fort, where he met the sergeant who would reappear in *Wind, Sand, and Stars* as the man so homesick to see another of his own race after months of isolation. Saint-Exupéry's enthusiasm for the Line grew and he reassured his mother simply that he had a wonderful life, and that he was "as happy as a pope in that country."[22] He was becoming fascinated by the desert, "this gentle Sahara . . . a strange country. But captivating,"[23] and he was making personal contact with the Moors, hoping to be able to travel *en dissidence,* that is, into the unsubdued, unpacified areas. He already felt himself to be exerting the multiple profession of aviator, ambassador, and explorer.

Chief at Cap Juby

Saint-Exupéry showed such ability as an emissary that at the end of 1927 he was appointed *chef d'aéroplace* at Cap Juby, the isolated outpost between sea and desert where the Line was having difficulty both with the unsubdued Arabs and the Spanish who officially controlled the area. Cap Juby was one of the ten *escales* or "ports of call" for the company between Casablanca and Dakar, and it was located in the Spanish zone of the Rio de Oro. This was a particularly dangerous area over which to fly as, in case of a forced landing, the air crews were attacked by the hostile Arab tribes of the area, who often carried them off into slavery, held them for ransom, or even tortured and killed them. After an earlier visit to Cap Juby, Saint-Exupéry had described the dangerous isolation of the outpost: "If you venture further than 50 meters, you are sent off to join your ancestors or carried off into slavery."[24] There was a Spanish fort at Juby, as at Villa Cisneros, but these authorities did little to ensure the safety of the pilots. Furthermore, after several incidents confronting the French pilots and the Moors, the Spanish authorities had finally forbidden the Latécoère company to make flights over the Rio de Oro, thereby actually cutting the planned route from Spain through North Africa to South America.

It was in this crisis that Daurat decided to use Saint-Exupéry, sending him to Cap Juby to reconcile the Spanish and the Arabs, a mission which, by Daurat's own admission, was considered impossible.[25] The assignment was a vital one for the company, but it was also a vital one in Saint-Exupéry's growth, for it brought him both a deep sense of responsibility and the challenge of uniting men, of drawing them together. Talking to Saint-Exupéry just before he left for Cap Juby, Daurat had felt him to be already transfigured by the sense of his responsibility; and as Saint-Exupéry gradually won the confidence of both the Spaniards and of the Arabs, he began to perceive the full meaning of the human mission in which he was engaged, "of the possible miracle, which is to bring men together, to make them understand and love each other."[26]

The setting for this essential experience was in itself unique. Saint-Exupéry simply describes it by exclaiming "What a monk's life I am leading!"[27] He and his mechanics lived in a wooden hut built against the Spanish fort on the beach, between the sea and the desert. His room was like a monk's cell, with its pallet bed, jug of water, and wooden crates used as tables. At high tide the water came lapping near his wall on one side; but on the other side, there was the desert, with the mystery and threat of the unsubdued tribes. Airplanes of the Line came through once a week, and once a month the supply ship from the Canary Islands came sailing in. This monastic solitude, fully accepted, gave Saint-Exupéry the chance to seek and find himself, learning detachment from worldly goods and developing his untiring devotion to the search for the elevation of man.[28]

Saint-Exupéry quickly began to succeed in his mission of reconciliation. The Spanish commander, Colonel Peña, respected this aristocratic, cultured man, who played chess with him and admired his miniature "garden" potted in real earth; while the Arabs accepted the honest, unaffected man, who studied their language, played with their children, and took tea in their tents. The acceptance of the Line by the Spaniards was firmly established when Saint-Exupéry flew a rescue mission to save two stranded Spanish pilots, who were being threatened by an Arab *rezzou* ("raiding party"). As Saint-Exupéry gradually adapted to the rhythm and attitudes of desert life, the Moors began to consider him as a desert sage, or *marabout*, whom they would consult for advice on great questions of quarrels and maladies.[29]

As the *chef d'aéroplace* at Cap Juby, Saint-Exupéry shouldered the responsibilities of a chieftain, and as his planes flew off again after servicing, he was anxious until he heard from them, for "they are like my little chickens."[30] He was always ready to take off to search for the lost ones, and he did have to fly many rescue missions, some of which were dramatic. Indeed, Migéo declares that Saint-Exupéry's principal activity at Cap Juby was in the role of rescuer.[31]

Rescue Missions

The best known of these rescue adventures was the long struggle to free the pilot, Reine, and his radio mechanic, Serre, who had been captured by the Moors in July 1928, and enslaved while being held for ransom. Saint-Exupéry flew repeated missions with his other pilots to try to discover and rescue his lost men, then entered into long negotiations with the Moors for their liberation. On one of the first search flights over the vast, desert expanses, the three planes had a forced landing for various technical problems, and the pilots had to spend the night in the desert. It is this incident which Saint-Exupéry transforms into an almost mystical experience of human communion in *Wind, Sand, and Stars* and which gives its English title to the book. The three crews had improvised a camp with five or six packing crates from their planes, setting them up in a circle with a candle burning in the shelter of each. Only a few months earlier, their companions had been caught in a similar situation and had been attacked and massacred by marauding Arabs; and even now there was a raiding party on the move. In full awareness of this danger, Saint-Exupéry, Riguelle, and Bourgat, and their crews calmly began a vigil which might be their last, in their dimly lit circle of shelter:

Thus, deep in the desert, on the bare crust of the planet, in an isolation of the first years of the world, we built a village of men. . . .
We were waiting for the dawn which would save us, or for the Moors. And I don't know what gave to this night its taste of Christmas. We recounted our memories, we joked and we sang.
We savored this same light fervor as at the heart of a well-prepared feast. And yet we were infinitely poor. Wind, sand and stars. A hard style for trappist monks. But on this ill-lit cloth, five or six men who no longer possessed anything, other than their memories, were sharing invisible riches.
We had at last found each other. [32]

When Saint-Exupéry learned from the Arab interpreter who had been allowed to return to Juby exactly where Reine and Serre were imprisoned, he planned a daring attempt to carry them off by force. He found a friendly Moor, El Bark, and he set him down in the desert near the Arab encampment where the airmen were being held. With a supply of food and water and some smoke flares, El Bark was to try to contact the prisoners and, if possible, bring them back to this spot four days later when Saint-Exupéry would return. The rescue attempt failed because El Bark had mistakenly set off his signal flares too soon, when another mail plane passed over, and so had no means of signaling left when Saint-Exupéry returned. Magnanimously, in a report on this incident, Saint-Exupéry reassured his superiors, "I believe that it will be easy to disown me (my action) since I acted without any authorization. I did not ask for this authorization so that it would not be refused. [33]
Another heroic attempt to save Reine and Serre, never mentioned by Saint-Exupéry in his own writings, is reported by many biographers. During a search flight, the pilot Riguelle made a forced landing in the desert, about thirty-five kilometers from Cap Juby, en dissidence, in the unpacified region. Although he was rescued by a fellow pilot, his plane was considered lost. It was generally forbidden to try to salvage planes in these dangerous areas, where the risks were only justified to save men or the mail. Saint-Exupéry, however, decided on a daring, if unauthorized salvage attempt.
First, Saint-Exupéry managed to recruit six armed warriors and a number of workers willing to accompany him into dissidence. Saint-Exupéry then had a kind of wagon made, mounted on airplane wheels and drawn by camels, to carry the new engine. To complete his unlikely rescue caravan, he added two horses, two donkeys, and

a third camel to carry heavy tools and spare wheels. When he and his mechanic, Marchal, reached the disabled plane, Marchal started dismounting the old engine, while Saint-Exupéry organized the building of a take-off strip. The first night, the Arab guards were tense and, at a false alarm, they made Saint-Exupéry and Marchal mount the camels and set off in the dark. After some miles, Saint-Exupéry shamed the Arab warriors into returning to the plane. When on the second day Spanish planes dropped an order from Colonel Peña to return, Saint-Exupéry decided to comply, but in the repaired plane, so he continued his work. Hostile Arabs appeared on the horizon and there was an exchange of rifle fire. When the raiding party had been driven off, the repairs were completed, and Saint-Exupéry succeeded in getting the plane to take off from the improvised strip.

Although Saint-Exupéry never gives an account of this daring episode, his official report of it appears in both Migéo's and Chevrier's biographies. More recently it has been published in *Icare,* together with a more formal report on the adventure contained in a letter to Monsieur Tête, his immediate director.[34] While minimizing his own personal courage in the undertaking, the two reports reveal a humorous enjoyment of the situation, and stress the psychological effect which his venture had on the Arabs, who admire daring and courage. Saint-Exupéry concludes that he can give only a general estimate of the costs "since they have no accompanying bill." Forestalling criticism, he adds, "I cannot judge if the cost of this expedition is exaggerated, as it is without precedent.[35] The irony of these remarks, surprising in one who often declared that irony was for dunces,[36] always appeared in his relationship with any bureaucracy, as Chevrier points out.[37] His real feelings are better revealed in the letter to Monsieur Tête, to whom he explains that being borne off in the Arabs' panic retreat that night "seemed to lack serenity" and he can justify the whole expedition simply: "It was reasonable to start out. And if we stayed, it was out of simple elegance.[38]

Saint-Exupéry's letters to his family reflect no more than a quiet satisfaction in these acts of accepted responsibility, associating his companions in any suggestion of heroism. A brief note to his mother states simply, "A companion is a prisoner . . . we have done quite magnificent things."[39] Exposed to shooting for the first time, he discovered that in those moments "one stakes his life with a great generosity."[40] This revelation of courage for a cause in the face of death, which Saint-Exupéry would experience frequently in other situations, is explained more succinctly in a letter to his cousin, Yvonne de Lestrange: "But I understand also what had always surprised me: why Plato puts courage in the last place among virtues. It is not made up of very fine feelings: a little anger, a little vanity, lots of stubbornness and common sporting pleasure. . . . Never again will I admire a man who is only courageous."[41]

Saint-Exupéry's abortive attempt to rescue Reine and Serre by force had angered the Spanish authorities, who were officially in charge of the area. Yet soon after this attempt, Colonel Peña called on Saint-Exupéry for help in rescuing a Spanish pilot and his Arab interpreter, shot down by an Arab *rezzou*. The situation was critical, as three hostile groups were in the region, and the wounded Arab owed "blood debts" to all three. Taking a Spanish observer and another Arab interpreter, Saint-Exupéry flew to rescue the men, whom he found under the temporary protection of a small, friendly group. The accompanying Spanish plane also landed but broke down, so Saint-Exupéry flew the wounded men back to Cap Juby, then returned with a mechanic to repair the damaged plane. This successful rescue naturally won the respect of the Spanish authorities, who offered to refund the fuel expenses. Saint-Exupéry refused such material recompense for a humanitarian endeavor, explaining in his official report: "I thought that having made possible the rescue of two pilots, an observer and a plane, you would not be especially interested in a thousand liters of fuel."[42]

Desert Life

Saint-Exupéry's life at Cap Juby was not only one of rescue missions and danger. A true ambassador, he established good relations with the Arabs, playing with the children, visiting the chiefs, and learning Arabic. "Every day, the 'marabout' comes to give me a lesson of Arabic. I am learning to write. And already I can manage (to express myself) a little. I offer social teas to Moorish chieftains. And they invite me in turn to take tea in their tents, two kilometres into 'dissidence,' where no Spaniard has yet been. And I shall not be risking anything, because they are beginning to know me."[43]

Soon after arriving at Cap Juby, Saint-Exupéry wrote to his mother, "I have tamed a chameleon. It is my role here, to tame. It suits

me, it's a pretty word."[44] *Apprivoiser* in French, is, indeed, a good
word, for it has the sense of taming to win over, whereas in the
sense of "dominate" it is *dompter,* and *apprivoiser* was to become one
of the key words in Saint-Exupéry's highly personalized vocabulary.
In *Wind, Sand, and Stars,* talking about the unpacified Arabs who
occasionally emerged from the dissident zones to buy sugar or tea
at Cap Juby, Saint-Exupéry says "we try, when they pass by, to
tame some of them."[45] He realized that much of their hostility came
from disdain rather than from hatred, and that this was founded on
the illusion of their own strength and superiority. He decided to
show them the world beyond the Sahara, and flew some of them to
France: "Here are men who had never seen a tree or a fountain, or
a rose, who know only through the Koran about the existence of
gardens where streams flow, since this is how it names paradise.
This paradise . . . is earned by bitter death on the sand, . . . after
thirty years of wretchedness. But God deceives them, since he re-
quires of the French, to whom these treasures are granted, neither
the ransom of thirst nor that of death."[46] An even more striking
revelation to the Arabs was that of a great waterfall in the mountains
of the Savoy district. The Arabs tasted it and found that it was fresh
water, that mysterious life-giving divinity for which they must
constantly struggle in the desert: "They remained silent, they wit-
nessed, grave, silent, this unrolling of a solemn mystery. . . .
God, here, was manifesting himself."[47] Their guide wanted them
to leave, but they protested that they must await "the end." And
Saint-Exupéry understood that "they wanted to wait for the hour
when God would tire of his folly."[48] Before such a miracle, they
admitted that "the God of the French . . . is more generous than
the God of the Moors is to the Moors."[49] But even as Saint-Exupéry
pacified the Moors by winning them over in such ways, he could
understand the painful confusion in their spirits. He could empathize
with the aging chief who, in his apparent betrayal of his French
friends, was perhaps trying to redeem his betrayal of his God of
Islam, and to restore its meaning to the Sahara, "when each fold of
sand was rich with threatened dangers."[50]

   Saint-Exupéry experienced himself that strange revitalizing of the
desert through the hidden presence of danger. A sentry warned that
a raiding party was on the move, and the desert seemed magnetized:
"A *rezzou* on the march somewhere, which will never arrive any-
where, makes its divinity."[51] Watching an Arab tribe prepare to

march against the almost legendary Captain Bonnafous of the Méhari squadron, Saint-Exupéry realized that their enemy's presence fills the desert with meaning for the Arabs, so that each step toward the south becomes rich with glory.[52] Already in Bonnafous there was the *ennemi bien aimé,* who would reappear in *Citadelle,* and when he returned to France the Arabs lamented the loss of their well-loved enemy who had been a magnetic pole in their desert world. Saint-Exupéry believed that Bonnafous would come back to the desert where he possessed "the only true riches, this prestige of sand, the night, this silence, this homeland of wind and stars."[53] This *patrie* of wind, sand, and stars, which would give the English title to *Terre des hommes,* was revealed to Saint-Exupéry when he suddenly sensed instinctively the approach of a storm, through the quiet appearance of a dragonfly on a still evening: "What filled me with a pagan joy, was to have understood in half-spoken words, a secret language . . . it is to have read this anger in the wing strokes of a dragon-fly."[54] Like Bonnafous, he would always feel a yearning for the desert where he had found such spiritual riches amongst such material poverty. Although toward the end of his stay at Cap Juby he was growing impatient to return to France, he had indeed learned to love the intangible meaning within the apparently empty sand and had drawn from it the rich teachings of the desert, which had become a world magnetized with invisible forces.

This elusive meaning of the desert which Saint-Exupéry came to understand so well was perhaps the revelation to him of his recurring idea, that "the essential is invisible for the eyes," that secret given to the Little Prince by the Fox.[55]

The empire of man is interior. Thus the desert is not made up of sand, nor of Touareg nor of Moors. . . .

But today, we have experienced thirst. And that well which we know, we discover that it radiates over space. A well bears its influence far, like love. . . . The Sahara, it is within us that it reveals itself. To enter upon it is not to visit an oasis, but rather to make our religion of a fountain.[56]

The Sahara reveals itself within each man, but it also reveals man to himself. Huguet says of Saint-Exupéry that "Three years of desert fulfilled the man within him" and that "the desert gave to Saint-Exupéry, more than impressions and images, an art of living."[57] Indeed, Huguet entitles his study *The Teaching of the Desert* and devotes it to this spiritually rich period of Saint-Exupéry's life, specifically with reference to his posthumous work, *Citadelle* [*The Wisdom of the Sands*]. Although Saint-Exupéry probably did not realize it, as he waited to be relieved from his post at Cap Juby, there had been born within him a "vocation" for the desert: "It seems that twentieth-century man, in his desire to safeguard a certain inalienable part of himself, has a nostalgia for the desert."[58] Chevrier also recognized this creative influence of the desert on Saint-Exupéry: "The desert, the cradle of all our European religions, encourages his meditation and brings him face to face with God whom he will evoke in *Citadelle*."[59]

Yet, after the final release of Reine and Serre, Saint-Exupéry was eager to return to France and he was understandably frustrated when his successor, Vidal, also made a forced landing among the Moors. Again Saint-Exupéry had to wait, until Vidal could be ransomed and released. By October 1928, however, he was finally on his way home for a well-earned leave at Agay with his family. After this leave, he returned to North Africa for a few weeks to fly some regular flights until his transfer to the South America section of the Line. His first stop in North Africa was at Cap Juby, where he was enthusiastically welcomed by all the Spanish and Arab friends he had made during his mission there. As he finally left North Africa to prepare for his transfer to South America, he wrote to his friend, Charles Sallès, "my greatest melancholy is to have tasted a form of life, something like that of a 'gentleman of fortune,': one of austerity, destitution and adventure. I no longer know if I am capable of being happy. . . . I have tasted of the forbidden fruit."[60]

When Saint-Exupéry returned from Cap Juby, he brought with him the manuscript of a novel, written in those long months of solitude in the "monastic cell" of his desert hut. He had entitled this novel *Courrier sud (Southern mail)* from the name on one of the company files which he kept in that hut. In fact, it was the elaboration of his first short story, "L'Aviateur," and possibly included elements of the mysterious "Manon, danseuse" as Cate suggests,[61] episodes inspired perhaps by his broken engagement. Already in 1927 Saint-Exupéry had written to his mother from Dakar: "I am writing a large work for the N.R.F. *(Nouvelle Revue française)* but I am becoming a little entangled in my narrative."[62] Later he reported from Cap Juby that he was still tangled in the structure of the book, wanting "to bring into it many things and different points of view."[63]

Courrier sud

Southern Mail is essentially the story of Jacques Bernis, now a mail pilot for the Line, as it is told by the narrator, who is Saint-Exupéry himself at Cap Juby. The personal experience is framed and punctuated by the official radio reports reporting the departure and progress of his flight, and is itself divided between Bernis's life as a pilot and his private life. Furthermore, Bernis, who is presented as a close, childhood friend of Saint-Exupéry and now his companion-at-arms, is really a projection of Saint-Exupéry himself. Much of the pilot's experience is one openly shared by Saint-Exupéry the narrator, while Bernis's emotional adventure, recounted sympathetically by Saint-Exupéry the friend, is an autobiographical reflection of Saint-Exupéry's own private experience. These various levels of the narrative cause the complexity of structure with which Saint-Exupéry had struggled but, far from marring the work, they finally produce a faithful reflection of the strongly faceted life of a pilot of the Line, where the setting of his *métier* was so far removed, physically and emotionally, from that of his personal life.

After an official radio report, the first part opens with a short, sensitive description of the desert at Cap Juby, where Saint-Exupéry awaits the coming of Bernis's plane, en route from Toulouse to South America. Into this opening passage are woven many of the elements—the wind, the sand, the stars, and the night—which will recur so strongly in Saint-Exupéry's next two books, as well as the two key factors in *Southern Mail,* water and light. "A sky as pure as water bathed the stars and revealed them. Then it was night. Beneath our muffled steps, there was the luxury of thick sand. And we walked bare-headed, freed from the weight of the sun. This night, this dwelling place . . ."(7). We follow Bernis's preparation for his long flight, dressing in the cumbersome clothing so like a diver's suit, receiving final orders from the chief. Once in the air, Bernis experiences that growth and fulfillment with which Saint-Exupéry always describes the pilot's entry into the world of flight. As he settles into the peaceful solitude of his flight he begins to meditate first on his experience as a pilot and then, gradually, on his personal life, and this meditation moves subtly back and forth between Bernis and Saint-Exupéry himself. Bernis recalls his first mail flight and the evening preparation carefully studying his maps beneath the lamplight, under the guidance of a veteran. Saint-

Exupéry, the narrator, recalls with Bernis the visit to their old school, where they found their old teachers ready to admire the heroes they had helped create. These are surely Saint-Exupéry's old teachers in Switzerland, at Fribourg.

Bernis lands at Alicante in Spain, and he experiences the strange reentry into the proportions of the earthbound world which seems unreal after flight. He feels that this solid world is secure as a house. But, as Bernis takes off again, the plane jolts momentarily out of control, and he confronts the realization of the insecurity of his "house," from which the slightest incident can cast him for ever. As he flies into the night over the Mediterranean, Bernis feels that he is abandoning the towns and lights which only two months before he was rediscovering, as he returned to Paris.

The long central part of the book is the narration of these months when Bernis returned to Paris, and they echo Saint-Exupéry's own reactions and experience when he returned to his old setting. At first all the excited anticipation is suddenly numbed by the realization that his old friends are busy with their own activities and by the fear that he will lose his own new identity, his winged self, and become a prisoner of the set surroundings. "They were all prisoners of themselves, limited by this hidden shackle and not like him this fugitive, this child, this magician" (38), three symbolic words which throw light on Bernis's story and represent Saint-Exupéry himself so well. A long letter from Bernis to Saint-Exupéry reveals his unnamed yearning: "I was the water-diviner whose rod trembles and who moves it over the world to the treasure. . . . But tell me what I am seeking and why for the first time, I do not discover the spring of water and why I feel so far from the treasure. What is this hidden promise made to me and which a hidden god does not keep" (43). Then suddenly there is the declaration: "I have found the spring. Do you remember? It is Geneviève . . . ." Saint-Exupéry does remember the gentle, sensitive Geneviève, childhood companion to Bernis and himself, source of mystery and radiance in their young world.

Now Geneviève is married to an unimaginative, boorish businessman and she has a child, who is for her the essential link in the order of her world. For several weeks Bernis visits her, rediscovering through her the meaning of things. Then her child falls ill and dies, and in her distraction Geneviève begs Bernis to take her away with him. She hopes to be transformed and freed, as she moves into his life but, instead, she is discouraged by the mediocrity of every-day details. Soon Bernis realizes the impossibility of taking her from the world she knows, and in which familiar things give her the assurance of duration and order. Generously, Bernis sets her free from his own future.

Alone again, Bernis seeks for some meaning to his own life. To escape the aimless minutes outside, he enters Notre-Dame cathedral, hoping perhaps to find "a formula which expresses him, reunites him" (104). But listening to a sermon, he hears only another cry of despair. Later, he tries a nightclub and cheap adventure, but without finding contentment. As he detaches himself from this chance encounter, he detaches himself also from Paris, ready to return to his pilot's world.

The third part is a strange blend of factual account and symbolic imagery. As night falls, Saint-Exupéry follows the progress of Bernis's plane from Toulouse to Juby. At Casablanca a stubborn director wants to send Bernis on, despite threatening weather; just as stubbornly, Bernis takes up the challenge to continue. From Juby, Saint-Exupéry grows anxious waiting for news of his friend, lost in time and space.

Finally, Bernis arrives and, as the two narrative threads join, he tells Saint-Exupéry of his last visit to Geneviève in a little provincial town where he stopped between trains. From the first line, this account takes on a dreamlike quality, reminiscent of *Le Grand Meaulnes:* "It was not a little provincial station, but a hidden doorway" (149). The ticket collector, the stationmaster and the crewman are three guardians of a secret world, "this kingdom which since Merlin one knows one can penetrate beneath appearances" (150). As Bernis, like Orpheus, possesses three qualities required for such a journey, courage, youth and love, he is allowed to continue to seek for his lost love. At every step, he goes deeper into a world with a different sense of time, a timeless land of Sleeping Beauty. When he finally arrives at the mysterious domain, he finds Geneviève dying. She almost recognizes him but has already passed beyond his reach and turns away. As Bernis turns to leave, the whole radiant world of Geneviève seems to be growing dark, and the meaning which she gave to things is fading.

As Bernis leaves Juby again, Saint-Exupéry wonders where he will find the treasure now. Bernis flies on, moving through time rather than space, for his watch determines where he will find the next escale. He is in a fourth dimension, but if the watch hand misses its mark he will crash in the desert, cast into yet another, different scale of time. Briefly he stops at an isolated fort where an old sergeant greets his countryman ecstatically. Then Bernis disappears, and soon Saint-Exupéry sets out to look for him. Somewhere, Bernis is lying and "a lost child fills the desert" (180). At last Saint-Exupéry finds Bernis, arms outstretched in death on the dunes, facing up to the stars. "My companion. Here then was the treasure. . . . A dizziness caught you, and in the star straight above, the treasure shone, oh fugitive" (181–82). Like the Little Prince, Bernis has gone home to his planet, and Saint-Exupéry is left lamenting that his friendship was not strong enough to hold him, as he would later lament when that mysterious young Prince also left him. Abruptly breaking the mood, the official radio report states, "pilot killed, plane broken, mail intact" (182).

Autobiographical Elements

This book, so often dismissed as a young author's first attempt, holds a wealth of ideas, and it sensitively weaves delicate strands of autobiography, philosophy, and poetry into a hard canvas of astute factual observation to create an unusual tapestry. The autobiographical element is most easily recognized in Bernis's experience as a pilot, with incidents and ideas which recur in later works, especially in *Wind, Sand, and Stars* and in *Night Flight.* Two well-known incidents had already been announced in Saint-Exupéry's letters to his mother. In 1921 he told her how, preparing for a flight, he studied his map in the lamplight, coached by a veteran; and this becomes Bernis's symbolic *veillée d'armes* or "knightly vigil"; later Saint-Exupéry has his *leçon de géographie* from Guillaumet in *Wind, Sand, and Stars.* In 1927, telling his mother about a crash landing in the desert, he said that he spent the night in a little fort where "the sergeant in command had not seen a white man for months";[64] and this is the lonely sergeant who nostalgically sings with Bernis and later delights in sharing his wine with Saint-Exupéry in *Terre des hommes.* Bernis's *chef,* too, glimpsed as he harshly imposed a fine on a mechanic (12), is Saint-Exupéry's admired Daurat, who will grow into the dominant figure of Rivière in *Night Flight.* Another significant autobiographical aspect is Bernis's unsuccessful attempt to find meaning through established religion. At this time Saint-

Exupéry had lost formal religious faith, but his quest for God would grow as he matured, and it is reflected in later works such as *Pilote de guerre* and *Citadelle*.

Less obviously autobiographical is Bernis's love for Geneviève, as Saint-Exupéry never wrote openly of his loves, either as a young man or even later when he married. From biographers who knew Saint-Exupéry personally, however, we can suppose that Geneviève is essentially Louise de Vilmorin, his lost fiancée, although Chevrier suggests that characteristics of his beloved youngest sister may be blended into the portrayal,[65] and the present writer wonders whether perhaps Renée de Saussine, the elusive *amie inventée,* is not also a part of the composite portrait. Louise is obviously present in her attachment to her surroundings, for Geneviève needs around her "realities which last" (78). Yet in Geneviève this attachment to material objects has a spiritual essence, as perhaps Saint-Exupéry saw it in Louise. Walking beside her, Bernis discovers at last the inner aspect of the world for, through her, "each thing carried again within its center this secret which is its soul" (506). Here again is Saint-Exupéry's key theme of the invisible essential. Geneviève "reigned over books, flowers, friends. She maintained pacts with them" (56), and she creates an invisible, mysterious order. The birth of her child secures her in the ordered concert of things; but his death seems a great disorder, a breakdown of things. This child's death no doubt reflects that of Saint-Exupéry's young brother and also the death of Louise's little niece in 1924. Geneviève is also a source of radiance; Saint-Exupéry associates her with the rising moon and remembers her crowned with lamplight in the shadowy dining room. For her sick child she seeks bright things as "sun-traps" for his room, since "everything that held the light pleased her" (64). Later, as she herself lies dying, her room is filled with light but, as Bernis leaves her, light and the essence of things seem to be withdrawing with her soul. Geneviève always *is* her soul; and as she is dying, Bernis senses an immense presence, her soul, which seems to fill the room.

Geneviève is the only woman depicted in all of Saint-Exupéry's work (other than a brief sketch of Fabien's wife in *Vol de nuit*), and she is an elusive, beautiful creature, part Ondine, part Mélisande, part Yvonne de Galais. She dwells in a world that is filled with the shimmering of water and the moving of time, a world born of the pilot's unique perspective, where the land seems to be the bottom of the sea, on whose surface he travels, and where distance is measured in time not in space. Cate comments on the abundance of marine imagery in *Courrier sud,* going so far as to compare Geneviève to the Little Mermaid whom her prince tries to draw from her enchanted realm.[66] Interestingly enough, Saint-Exupéry states that the first book he ever truly loved was a collection of Andersen's stories;[67] and in "The Little Mermaid" the mermaid's concept of humans who "were able to fly over the ocean in ships"[68] echoes Saint-Exupéry's concept of the pilots sailing above the land so that the earth below seems to be a "sea-bed where all rests quietly" (39). Geneviève's soul inhabits her body, "like a sprite in the waters" (47), and the mysterious place where she lies ill was a "legendary kingdom beneath the waters" (151) where the darkness flows into her room like water when she dies. Most strongly, too, occurs the image of the house as a ship, an image which will become part of Saint-Exupéry's personal vocabulary of key words. Bernis is a traveler in the fourth dimension in which his watch miraculously transports him (162). And this awareness of time perhaps echoes Saint-Exupéry's interest in Proust's concept of time and Bergson's philosophical discussions.

The idea of "escape" in the original short story "L'Evasion de Jacques Bernis" recurs subtly throughout *Courrier sud.* As a boy, Bernis knew that travel was a metamorphosis and he would try to escape from "the old refrain of seasons, holidays, marriages and deaths. To escape, that is the important thing" (145–46). Later he will realize that "all his life had been spent thus trying to flee" (104). Breaking his ties with his old life, Bernis frees himself from his former self. Saint-Exupéry reminds him that he has escaped from that very framework of customs, conventions, and laws which Geneviève needs. Bernis, escaping from this framework, is, in the sudden, strange definition, "this fugitive, this poor child, this magician" (38), and these three unexpected words recur. Flying over the desert, Bernis can discover the hidden treasure since "it is for you, magician, only a veil of sand" (160). Lost in the desert, he becomes, in his simplicity, the "lost child who fills the desert with meaning" (179–80). When Saint-Exupéry finds Bernis's body, in a final call to his lost companion, he exclaims, "In the star overhead, the treasure shone, oh fugitive!" (182). The Little Prince, too, will be a child, a magician, and a fugitive.

This is the enigmatic, intriguing book which was published in 1929 by the *Nouvelle Revue française,* to whose editor, Gaston Gallimard, Saint-Exupéry had been introduced by Jean Prévost. Despite Saint-Exupéry's modest misgivings, the company was so pleased with this first novel that they gave him a contract for seven more novels, a contract which, unfortunately, he never fulfilled. In his preface to the work, André Beucler wrote: "When the hero lives in a man, that man always stands . . . at the highest point of aristocracy and silence. . . . He who is a soldier in his soul, that is, a hero, always has beautiful language, for there is nothing he need seek."[69]

Intuitively, Beucler had recognized the qualities of both the man and the writer in Saint-Exupéry, the aristocracy of soul, the eloquent silence, and the instinctive style born of his heroic soul, "the elegance of heroism."[70] By contrast, in an often-quoted review of the work, Edmond Jaloux, while admitting the charm of the book, summarized it in superficial terms: "What is there in this appealing little book? Almost nothing: a romantic adventure, like hundreds we have read, but placed in a setting so modern that one cannot see the romanticism and one cannot see the modernism."[71] Jaloux further criticized a lack of explicitness in the work, and he stated sweepingly, "All of this remains very literary and superficial. One cannot explain psychological impulses by poplar trees," referring to the trees lining the country roads on Bernis's and Geneviève's flight. Yet Saint-Exupéry has made of the trees, which they slowly pass in the night, the physical symbol of Geneviève's struggle to pull herself from her old life towards the fresh, new life with Bernis.

Although Saint-Exupéry took no exception to this review of Jaloux's, he did grow impatient with some critics. He was anxious to have the opinion of others but knew that everybody would not understand his book. As he says, "One must at least understand Giraudoux to understand it."[72] But the opinion which he really valued was his mother's, and he wrote "your letter on my little *bouquin* is the one which has touched me the most."[73]

Meanwhile, during the printing and publishing of *Courrier sud,* Saint-Exupéry had already started another *petit bouquin,* and was studying navigation at Brest in preparation for his next undertaking with "la Ligne."

Chapter Five
La Ligne in South America:
Vol de nuit

One spring day in 1929, Lieutenant Chassin, director of the advanced aerial navigation course at Brest, decided to meet his eleven new students at a café; young officers from the great military schools of Polytechnic and Saint Cyr, a civil engineer, and a pilot sent by the Latécoère Line. In this pilot, Chassin recognized Saint-Exupéry, the director of Cap Juby, whom he had met the year before when on duty at Agadir. During the weeks of the course, studying mathematics at the Ecole navale where he once had hoped to be a cadet, Saint-Exupéry soon distinguished himself both by his absentmindedness and his quick intelligence, as Chassin recalled. Although he might on occasion forget that he was in a hydroplane and manoeuvre for a take-off from land, Saint-Exupéry had apparently forgotten nothing of his mathematics studies, and he was "absolutely remarkable when there was a question of inventing something."[1] In this assessment Chassin was certainly right, since Saint-Exupéry would later take out many patents for various scientific devices, ranging from a mechanism for landing, to a route tracer, to a starter system.

During this time in Brest, Saint-Exupéry was also happily preoccupied with correcting proofs of *Courrier sud;* and when the final copy arrived, Chassin and all the class read the new work. Chassin recognized in it the début of a true writer and especially admired the beautiful, poetic description on the first page, which soon the whole class knew by heart. Despite this preoccupation, Saint-Exupéry successfully passed the final exams as did all the class; and yet he officially "failed" because the Ministry representative demanded at least two failures among the eleven candidates, in order to maintain the prestige of the course. Latécoère and Daurat paid no attention to this technicality, however. Soon Saint-Exupéry was on board ship, bound for Buenos Aires, to join the Compagnie

Générale Aéropostale, which was the development of the Latécoère
lines in South America.

Founding the Aéropostale

The Aéropostale had grown from the day in 1924 when Roig,
sent by Latécoère and Daurat to explore possibilities of a line in
South America, had been introduced to the president of Argentina
by Vincente Almandos de Almonacid, an old army friend. Encouraged by Almonacid's enthusiasm, by the president's promise of
support, and by a general expression of confidence in Brazil, Uru-
guay, and Argentina, Roig brought back an optimistic report. Latécoère and Daurat immediately sent out an aerial mission, headed
by Prince Charles Murat, to explore the terrain, find suitable air
fields, and establish the line. Difficulties arose when the Brazilian
government repeatedly refused to approve a tentative contract given
to the company. Murat finally persuaded Latécoère to go to Rio de
Janeiro himself. There Latécoère won the support of Bouilloux-
Lafont, a very successful French businessman in Brazil but, despite
his influence, the contract was again refused.

Early in 1927 Bouilloux-Lafont took Latécoère to Argentina, where
the loyal Almonacid had again arranged a meeting with the president. Finally in 1927 the Argentinian government granted the
French company a contract guaranteeing them the exclusive aerial
transport of as much as twenty-five percent of all mail to Europe.
Meanwhile, having tried unsuccessfully to obtain financial backing
from the French government, Latécoère sold the South American
section of his company to Bouilloux-Lafont. As the new head of the
company, Bouilloux-Lafont obtained a yearly authorization from the
Brazilian government to fly over their territory, while Almonacid
arranged a second contract to develop an internal postal service.
Thus the Compagnie Générale Aéropostale came into being, with
its subsidiary, Aeroposta Argentina. In March of the following year,
the first weekly flight was established from France to South America,
and on 14 July 1929, the first commercial flight from Buenos Aires,
via Mendoza to Santiago-de-Chile, was inaugurated.

It was this thriving young line that Saint-Exupéry was sent to
join, after a short period in Toulouse testing Latécoère planes. On
12 October 1929 he arrived in Buenos Aires, where he was welcomed
by his old friends, Mermoz and Guillaumet, who had already joined

the new line. Two weeks later, he learned that he had been appointed director of the Aeroposta Argentina, the subsidiary company of the Aéropostale, with a suitably large salary. Although he was pleased with his new position, the change also saddened him. In announcing this news in a letter, he wrote, "I liked my old way of life. It seems to me that this makes me older."[2] He later echoed this feeling in a nostalgic letter to Renée de Saussine, early in 1930: "I feel weighed down and aged by a role that I did not want . . . which draws from me . . . all that remained of youth and beloved liberty."[3]

Even his new financial security seemed a burden, for he adds, "I earn 25,000 francs a month, for which I have no use and which it exhausts me to spend." But at least this new wealth allowed him to start repaying his debts to his mother, and he also invited her to come to Argentina, offering to pay her fare. She finally accepted in December 1930, spending six weeks with him in Buenos Aires, then traveling back with him when he returned to France in February 1931. He did not like living in the big, modern city of Buenos Aires, in an apartment sandwiched between seven others above and seven below, with a huge town of reinforced concrete all around. "I would have the same feeling of lightness in the middle of the Great Pyramid."[4] He was nostalgic for the desert and even for his old student days in Paris, where the recurrent, penniless "month's end," gave a rhythm to life, and the horse-chestnut trees blooming in the spring shared their *joie de vivre* with him. "The world was magnificent, for I desired everything since I could have nothing."[5] His only consolation was flying, for he was constantly in the air, inspecting established airfields, setting up new ones, and developing new lines.

On one such inspection flight, Saint-Exupéry proved again his powers of diplomacy. Learning that an airport director had gambled away the company funds, Saint-Exupéry notified him that he would be coming for regular inspection the next day. The director hastily borrowed funds from all his acquaintances to replace the money in the box safe. When Saint-Exupéry arrived, he asked for the money box. After checking it, he approved the accounts; then he calmly tucked the box under his arm and climbed back in his plane to the consternation of the airport chief. By this device, he had protected the company interests without ruining a man's reputation.

Developing the Line

During this heroic period of the new Aéropostale, the chief concerns were developing the network of routes on the continent and
achieving complete air transport of mail from France to South America. As director of Aeroposta Argentina, Saint-Exupéry established
a string of new airfields toward the south, in small towns which
would become famous through his *Vol de nuit:* Bahia Blanca, Comodoro Rivadavia, Trelew, San Julian. He then flew all the way down
to Rio Gallegos in the Terra del Fuego, where he established the
southernmost airfield. He wanted to extend the Line to Punta Arenas, the southernmost town in the world, but the Chilean authorities
would not allow this extension. Saint-Exupéry did fly to Punta
Arenas himself and, even if he could not build an airfield there, he
did bring back rich material for his writing. After flying over bare
volcanic land, he was struck by the sudden miracle of life springing
from the layer of good earth covering the lava flows—green grass,
animals, then a town. In *Terre des hommes* he writes: "But, further
on, older volcanos are already covered by a golden turf . . . life
has taken possession of a new planet, where the good loam of the
earth has at last been deposited on the globe. . . . So close to the
black flows, how well one feels the miracle of man!"[6] For a few
hours, he stayed in Punta Arenas, watching the activity around the
fountain of the little town, and he became aware of the invisible
kingdom of each life, which the observer can never penetrate: "Old
women come there to draw water; of their life's drama, I will know
only this servant's movement. A child, . . . cries silently; there
will remain of him, in my memory, only a beautiful child, forever
inconsolable. I am a stranger. I know nothing. I do not enter into
their Empires."[7] As he flew over the surrounding countryside, he
observed a strange little lake, which pulsed inexplicably with the
movement of the tides, and he realized the fragility of the seemingly
secure setting in which man acts out his drama.

Eventually, after several months' work, the southern line was
completed, and, in April 1930, the weekly service from Patagonia
to Buenos Aires was inaugurated. Meanwhile, Didier Daurat was
working toward completing the air route from Toulouse to Buenos
Aires. At first the mail had been carried by ship from Dakar to
Natal, linking the air routes established in Africa and South Amer-

ica; but the four or five days of sea transport had to be eliminated
to compete with the rival German and American lines. For this
purpose, Daurat recalled Mermoz to have him make the first ocean
crossing to South America. The authorities were so skeptical about
the success of this undertaking that they sent their official flight
permit by the airmail carried in Mermoz's plane so that, if he crashed
in the sea, their authorization would disappear too.[8] But Mermoz
had already pioneered night flight to help the Aéropostale speed its
mails; now he was ready to attempt this venture. During his crossing
of the South Atlantic, Mermoz flew through the strange regions of
the *Pot-au-Noir* ("the pot of blackness") where great waterspouts are
whipped up by the tornadoes: "Water-spouts stood there clustered
and apparently immobile like the black pillars of a temple. . . .
And Mermoz continued his way through these uninhabited ruins
. . . skirting around these giant pillars . . . toward the door of
the temple."[9] Mermoz landed in Natal, and the mail was carried
on to Rio de Janeiro by Vanier; from there Reine flew it the next
lap to Buenos Aires. Finally Guillaumet flew the mailbags to Santiago, and on 15 May 1930, the first completely airborne mail from
France to the Pacific Ocean was accomplished. It had taken four
and a half days.

Adventures of Pioneering Days

In the chapter devoted to "Les Camarades" in *Terre des hommes,*
Saint-Exupéry first pays tribute to Mermoz, whose courage opened
up the different realms to flying; from the Sahara to the Andes,
through the night and over the ocean: "Thus Mermoz had cleared
the sand, the mountains, the night and the sea."[10] Mermoz may
well be the inspiration for Fabien in *Vol de nuit.*

One constant factor to be confronted in all these pioneering flights
was the wind, which blew so violently at times that it had actually
torn the wings off a plane, necessitating a reinforcement of the basic
design. Patagonia, the region where Saint-Exupéry developed his
Aeroposta Argentina, was called "the country where the stones fly."
Saint-Exupéry had to issue an order to his pilots not to try landing
at Comodoro Rivadavia when the wind velocity exceeded 135 miles
per hour; and once, landing in Rio Gallegos himself, he had to
enlist army help to hold down his plane and tow it into a hangar
against the wind. Flying from Trelew to Comodoro Rivadavia, Saint-

Exupéry was blown out to sea by a cyclone, and he describes his experience in a chapter added to the English edition of *Wind, Sand, and Stars,* under the heading "The Elements." Despite his masterful description of his battle with the storm, which critics have compared to Joseph Conrad's *Typhoon,* Saint-Exupéry felt that the experience of a physical drama cannot be communicated unless a spiritual significance has been found within it. (In fact, he himself pointed out that the strength of Conrad's description came from the social drama which he depicted, as the storm destroyed the passengers' world.) Saint-Exupéry can find only symbolic images to express his own experience, summing it up in the effort of will to keep his tired hands closed on the controls.

It was during Saint-Exupéry's constant flights to develop his Aeroposta Argentina, that he had the chance visit to an old house near Concordia (recounted in chapter one), a visit which becomes an enchanted step into another world in the chapter "Oasis" of *Terre des hommes.* The oasis is not in the desert, but is a spiritual one into which he was privileged to enter. After an emergency landing, Saint-Exupéry was welcomed into the home of Mr. Fuchs, an Alsation immigrant, who lived in an old, baroque mansion near the city. Saint-Exupéry "did not know that [he] was going to live in a fairy-story" but, as he came in sight of the house, Saint-Exupéry saw "a castle of legend which, as soon as the porch was passed, offered a shelter, as peaceful, as secure and as protected as a monastery." It is all beautifully dilapidated, yet cared for "like an old tree covered with moss," with a polished decrepitude which revealed only "extraordinary respect."[11] In this home, Saint-Exupéry is introduced to two young daughters, who gaze at him "like two judges placed on the threshhold of a forbidden kingdom," then disappear in the rambling house. Saint-Exupéry recognized in this home the quality of life he had known in the two beloved houses of his childhood. While he was seated in the lamplight at the table, Saint-Exupéry realized that he was being judged by the two girls. It is then that he passed the test of valor, smiling contentedly at the announcement of the vipers under the table.

Later, as Saint-Exupéry recalled the charm of this visit, he wondered what had become of his *princesses d'Argentine.* He imagined that, as they grew to womanhood, they might so much want to award a nearly perfect score that they would give it to an "imbecile" who would lead the princesses away enslaved. It almost seems that

Saint-Exupéry recognized in his "princesses" the same quality which he had given to the Geneviève of *Courrier sud,* for she, indeed, did give her "heart which is a wild garden to the one who likes only groomed parks,"[12] and Herlin led her away enslaved; so too had Saint-Exupéry's fiancée, Louise, let herself be "enslaved" and carried away by a rich American businessman.

Probably the most poignant memory of Saint-Exupéry's experiences in South America was the heroic adventure of his friend and fellow pilot, Guillaumet, which Saint-Exupéry recounts in the chapter "Les Camarades" of *Terre des hommes.* Guillaumet had taken off from Santiago on 13 June (the Chilean winter) to make his ninety-second crossing of the Andes mountains. Caught in a violent snowstorm over the mountain range, he struggled to get through, but when his fuel was exhausted he had to bring his plane down among the mountain summits. For five days Saint-Exupéry and Deley flew desperately over the range, trying to find their lost comrade. Finally the Chilean authorities advised them to give up the search, insisting that no man could survive the fatal cold of a winter night in those mountains. Even the hardened smugglers refused to venture into the mountains in a search party, proclaiming "The Andes never give up a man in winter."[13] Yet a week after Guillaumet's disappearance, Saint-Exupéry received the unbelievable news that his friend was safe. Leaping into his plane, he flew off to meet his brother pilot and bring him home. Recognizing by some telepathic impulse the car which was carrying Guillaumet, Saint-Exupéry landed beside the road to welcome his friend, who was the "author of his own miracle."[14] In telling his story, Guillaumet's first remark was "What I have done, I swear that no animal would have done,"[15] for it was the magnificent story of man's spirit dominating over his suffering, tortured body. After waiting out the tempest by his plane for forty-eight hours, he had walked through the frozen summits, for five days and four nights, sustained only by the sense of responsibility to his wife and friends: "My wife, if she believes I am alive, believes that I am walking. My comrades believe that I am walking. They all have confidence in me."[16] Resisting his body's desire to surrender, he walked on past exhaustion and despair, just as later Saint-Exupéry would do in the desert, and he finally reached a valley where a peasant couple succored him.

In Guillaumet's heroic adventure Saint-Exupéry recognized that essential quality of responsibility, which will become one of the key themes of his philosophy, and for the first time he developed this idea. Speaking of Guillaumet he said, "His greatness is to feel himself responsible. . . . To be a man, it is precisely to be responsible."[17] Throughout Guillaumet's adventure, as in Saint-Exupéry's own, it is his spirit which is the man, detached from the body which simply serves him. "The body, then, is no longer anything other than a good tool, it is only a servant. And Guillaumet, you knew how to express this pride in a good tool."[18] On the third day of his forced march without food, Guillaumet felt his heart fail and, just as he would have listened to his plane's engine, he listened to his heartbeat, hanging on to its sound and encouraging it (incorrectly translated in English as "hanging on the rock"). "But it was a good quality heart. . . . If you knew how proud I was of this heart."[19] As Guillaumet came near death he felt his life withdrawing from the "distant regions" of his body to take refuge around his heart: "Something gentle and precious nestled in the center of you,"[20] and this something is the spirit. This is why Guillaumet's remark that he has done what no animal would have done is for Saint-Exupéry such a significant one, for it "situates man, honors him, re-establishes hierarchies,[21] not only that of the animal kingdom, but specifically the hierarchy where the spirit stands above the body.

In Guillaumet, Saint-Exupéry found the brother whom he had lost, the true friend who never questioned and in whom he could rest his spirit. When Guillaumet married, his wife Noelle became a part of this friendship, and Saint-Exupéry watched over her like a brother when Guillaumet was flying a difficult mission.[22] Guillaumet was Oliver to Saint-Exupéry's Roland; they shared joys and sorrows, and rejoiced in each other's achievements. When, in 1939, Saint-Exupéry received the title of commander of the Légion d'honneur, just as Guillaumet also received a decoration, they proudly exchanged the Légion "rosette" and the medal at a joint celebration. When Guillaumet died in November 1940, and Saint-Exupéry learned the news in Lisbon, where he was about to embark for the United States, he turned a promised lecture at the Alliance française into a meditation on Guillaumet and on friendship. Now, at the Laguna Diamante high in the Andes, where Guillaumet's epic struggle began, a commemorative stone honors the memory of both Saint-Exupéry and Guillaumet, the brothers-in-arms who died in action, disappearing over the Mediterranean.[23]

Marriage

Another important event of Saint-Exupéry's eighteen months in Buenos Aires was his meeting with Consuelo Suncin, who would become his wife. For many years Saint-Exupéry's letters to his family and friends had reflected a growing desire to marry, and his hope of finding the ideal woman. Louise de Vilmorin had disappointed him deeply, and so perhaps had Renée de Saussine, who apparently refused to respond to his courtship by mail. Renée did write to say she was coming to Rio de Janeiro but she neglected to advise him in time of her date of arrival, and he missed her. It must have been soon after this disappointment that he met Consuelo, the attractive young widow of an Argentinian journalist who had lived and worked in France. There are many colorful legends about their meeting, ranging from revolutions to stormy flights, but in fact they met quite prosaically at a reception of the Alliance française, where they were introduced by Benjamin Crémieux of the *Nouvelle Revue française*. Although the petite brunette was the opposite of the type he usually preferred, Saint-Exupéry was soon fascinated by the vivacious, exuberant woman, with her quaintly accented French and her fanciful imagination. They met in September 1930 and, in April of the next year, after his return to France, they married, thereby fulfilling the fortune-teller's prophecy at his uncle's many years before, that he would marry a young widow; but instead of eight days, he had had to wait almost eight years.

Almost unanimously, Saint-Exupéry's biographers, especially those who knew him personally, have chosen to ignore his marriage to Consuelo or to dismiss it with a brief mention, as his mother does with a simple footnote. The only notable exceptions to this silence have been Migéo, who tries gallantly to explain the role of the enigmatic Consuelo in Saint-Exupéry's life and work, and Adèle Bréaux, who was puzzled by her when she met Consuelo in New York during the war. "I had never before met such a complex personality, unpredictable and, for me, incomprehensible," writes Bréaux.[24] Perplexity is a natural reaction in considering this temperamental woman who seemed incapable of giving Saint-Exupéry the generous understanding and peace of mind for which he had yearned in thinking of marriage, writing "What I ask of a woman is to quieten my unrest."[25] Consuelo showed little understanding of her husband's writing, and she had artistic aspirations of her own as a sculptress. In a book which she published years later about her experience in an artistic commune in Provence during the early war years, Consuelo declared "I love my husband, but I do not know how to make him happy."[26] It is generally recognized that theirs was a tempestuous marriage, yet Saint-Exupéry must genuinely have loved the young wife for whom he wrote "The Prayer which Consuelo must say every evening" which seems to explain their relationship: "Lord, make me always like the woman whom my husband can see in me. . . . Lord, save my husband, for he truly loves me and without him, I should be too much of an orphan . . . he is too distraught when he does not hear me making noise in his house, even if I must break something from time to time."[27] Although the couple often broke apart to live separately, Saint-Exupéry continued to feel an affectionate responsibility for the "grown-up, tempestuous spoiled child"[28] whom he had married. When during the early months of the war he was flying active duty, he felt this responsibility intensely and wrote to his mother: "Poor little Consuelo, all abandoned, arouses an infinite pity in me. If one day she takes refuge in the south, receive her as your daughter, out of love for me."[29]

New Manuscript

When Saint-Exupéry returned to France in early 1931, he brought Consuelo and a new manuscript first to Paris, then to his sister's in Provence. André Gide, a frequent dinner guest at the sister's home, wrote in his famous journal: "Great pleasure seeing Saint-Exupéry in Agay. . . . From Argentina, he has brought back a new book and a new fiancée. Read one, saw the other. Congratulated him warmly; but for the book in particular. I hope that the fiancée proves as satisfactory."[30] This book was *Vol de nuit* which, in December 1931, would win the Prix Fémina and which would be translated into fifteen languages and would also be made into a film (with Clark Gable and Helen Hayes and the two Barrymores in the lead roles).

The published work of *Vol de nuit* is very different from Saint-Exupéry's original concept of his second novel, which he described in a letter to his mother from Buenos Aires:

Now I am writing a book on night-flight. But in its intimate meaning, it is a book on night. . . .

Here is the beginning, it is the first recollection of night:
"We used to dream in the hallway, when night was falling. We watched
for the passing of the lamps: they were carried like a bunch of flowers,
and each one stirred shadows on the wall, shadows as beautiful as palm
fronds. . . .

"Then the day was finished for us and, in our cots, we were embarked
toward another day.

"Mother, you would lean over us . . . and so that this journey should
be peaceful . . . you would smooth from the sheet each wrinkle, each
shadow, each wave.

"For one smooths a bed as a divine finger stills the sea."
Then there are less protected crossings of the night, the aeroplane.[31]

In fact, the manuscript that Saint-Exupéry finally gave Gallimard
for publication, laboriously trimmed, refined, and tightened from
400 pages to 180, contained none of these Proustian elements so
evident in this suggested first draft, as they had been in *Courrier
sud*. While the "bouquets of the lamps" would reappear in the
"Oasis" chapter of *Terre des hommes,* the only sentence surviving in
Vol de nuit is that of the "divine finger calming the sea," given to
the pilot's wife watching her sleeping husband. Having been criticized for literary lyricism in his first work, Saint-Exupéry apparently
decided to impose a strict discipline on himself in this second book
and to write a suitably austere work, which became something of
a Cornelian drama, in which duty and will dominate personal emotion. Structurally, too, the book is simpler than *Courrier sud,* although there is an almost cinematic technique of flashing from one
field of action to another; Saint-Exupéry had started writing a film
script in Buenos Aires, entitled "Anne-Marie," and may well have
been influenced by the modern technique.

Vol de nuit

Vol de nuit is the story of three mail planes flying by night to
Buenos Aires from Paraguay, from Chile, and from Patagonia, and
of the plane which will leave for Europe as soon as they have arrived;
two of the incoming planes arrive safely, but the plane from Paraguay
is lost in a storm. Binding these simple events together is the
dominant figure of Rivière, the director, who must decide on all
the flights and who, by his decisions, creates not only the existence
and success of the Line, but the very spirit and courage of the men

who constitute it. The story constantly moves from following the pilot Fabien, on his ill-fated flight from Paraguay, to observing Rivière as he commands and as he meditates on his work. The crucial question which confronts him is whether to continue night flights in face of the danger proved by the loss of Fabien, or whether to stop them despite their essential role in the life of the Line.

Using this simple story line, Saint-Exupéry develops the ethical or philosophical question of creative action versus individual happiness, personified in Rivière and in Fabien's wife respectively, and eventually introduces the essential question of the significance of life which lies perhaps in that which surpasses it. There is throughout the theme of night, a constant, tangible presence, often felt as a surrounding sea.

The story opens with Fabien's flight, as night begins to fall. Resisting the temptation to stop at San Julian for the night when he refuels, Fabien continues his flight, feeling the tangible waves of night holding up his plane. He settles into the meditation of flight which Saint-Exupéry mentions so often: He is a watcher in the heart of night and he discovers that night reveals man.

While Fabien flies quietly on into the depths of night, Rivière in Buenos Aires is awaiting the return of his three pilots. Rivière, constantly responsible for each mail flight, feels momentarily discouraged, but renews his own faith in his work by talking to the old workman Leroux, quietly content in his craft. Soon Pellerin arrives with the mail plane from Chile and reports to Rivière, although he cannot tell him his experience over the mountains, feeling the first breath of the cyclone as an angry presence within the mountains around him.

Set in opposition to Rivière, is Inspector Robineau who invites Pellerin to dinner. Incapable of grasping the magnitude of Rivière's concept of the Line, Robineau is vicariously proud of the harsh strength of his director, although he himself has been reduced to the automatic application of rules and sanctions. Now uncertain of his role in the Line, Robineau invites Pellerin, hoping to make friends with a pilot. He proudly shows him some meteorites which he has brought from the Sahara, admitting that geology is his passion. At that point he is arbitrarily called back to the office by Rivière, who warns him against personal friendship with a pilot. Rivière makes Robineau impose a penalty on Pellerin for some imagined reason, to enforce his maxim "Love those whom you command, but without telling them so" (64).

Rivière, during his vigil, meditates on his life's work and the meaning behind it. In imposing his discipline on the men, he was creating not only the Line, but the men themselves. Now he reassesses his philosophy. For a moment he considers the possibility of pity, and is tempted to reprieve the old mechanic, Roblet, whom he had fired for a mistake, but the report of a mechanical failure proves that he must maintain his severity in order to control events. Although he cannot know if what he is doing is right, Rivière feels the need to create something lasting: "Life contradicts itself so much that one manages as best one can with life. . . . But to last, to create, to exchange one's perishable body . . ." (87). Here, for the first time is the idea of *exchange* which will become one of the strongest leitmotifs of Saint-Exupéry's work and philosophy.

Appearing as an interlude between alternating scenes of flight and control room, is the gentle chapter describing the awakening and preparation of the pilot who will fly the European mail. As the pilot's wife watches him sleep before she wakes him, there appears that one sentence surviving from Saint-Exupéry's announced initial draft; "she smoothed this bed as, with a divine finger, the sea is stilled" (88). She is proud of the responsibility which he bears so strongly but feels he is destined for a strange sacrifice. When he awakes, he is already a giant whose shoulders press against the sky; he is a knight who slowly dons his armor. Symbolically, his wife buckles on his belt as "she herself repaired the last defect in the suit of armor" (94). Then, as he leaves to conquer the skies, she remains alone amongst all the gentle things of life, flowers and books "which were for him only a sea-bed" (95), as they had been for Jacques Bernis. This chapter strongly demonstrates the theme running through *Vol de nuit,* the insoluble opposition between action and individual happiness, recognized by the pilot's wife herself: "she thought of all that must be given up in order to conquer" (93), just as Fabien, thinking of the quiet happiness in the towns beneath him, recognized that "he would have had to renounce action in order to conquer it" (21).

When the pilot arrives to take the European flight, Rivière reprimands him for having turned back during a previous flight, believing that in this way he "saves him from fear" (99). Half surprised, Rivière realizes the power of his own will to strengthen men, to control events and, specifically, to establish night flights, so essential to the growth of the Line. Meanwhile, Fabien is confronting the storm, lost in the night which seems like a dangerous river without banks, flowing nowhere, neither to a harbor nor to the dawn. Despite Fabien's danger, that seems to prove him wrong, Rivière must decide whether to continue night flights. To the surprise of his staff, Rivière prepares for the night flight to Europe.

Fabien's wife telephones for news, and once again, the opposing worlds of action and personal life confront each other. Rivière can pity the woman's quiet, sad voice but he senses an enemy, for "neither action nor individual happiness admits sharing: they are in conflict" (126). Hers is an absolute world, too, with its duties and its rights, the world of "lamplight on the table at night," and in the light of this humble lamp of home, Rivière discovers his own truth to be inexpressible and inhuman. Yet he believes in it, so he seeks to understand it. Remembering an engineer who had questioned whether the building of a bridge could ever be worth a wounded workman, Rivière had answered: "Even if human life is priceless, we act always as though something exceeded, in value, human life. . . . But what?" (128).

Rivière must now confront the question: in the name of what value may action break individual happiness? In the name of what principle has he drawn men from "the golden sanctuary of the evening lamp?" But these "golden sanctuaries" must disappear with time. So perhaps something more lasting exists to be saved, and it is to save that part of man that Rivière is working. Gradually Rivière comes to grips with his own truth, "a duty greater than that of loving," and a phrase recurs to him: "It is a question of making them eternal." Then an image comes to him, of an Inca temple, great stones painfully set up on the mountain; the Inca leader, in the name of some strange love, has forced his people to build their own eternity, so that the spirit of their race should live. In this image, Rivière finds his own truth.

Fabien and his radio operator are now isolated in the stormy night, desperately needing a light or a voice to prove that the earth still exists. As the storm increases, matter itself seems to be in revolt, and the plane seems to vibrate with anger. Fabien realizes that they have blown out to sea and, all hope gone, he is suddenly aware of the awful power within his hands on the controls: "He held in his hands his comrade's beating heart and his own" (135).

Just as Saint-Exupéry had done in the cyclone, he concentrates his will on keeping his hands closed on the controls. Discovering himself at last vulnerable to death, he gives in to the fatal temptation of a star, suddenly shining through a tear in the clouds, "a mortal bait in a net," and rises to the surface of his stormy sea of night: "This hunger for light was such that he climbed" (137) and he finds a cold, beautiful world of moonlight over the clouds, a lifeless world where he is ironically free to wander in the moments of life that are left to him and his companion. The tempest has spread everywhere and Fabien has only a half hour's fuel left. With all hope gone, Rivière has a vision of night as a great lake in which his men have drowned. Meanwhile, Fabien is wandering hopelessly in the beauty above the clouds, beneath which lies eternity, dramatically illustrating that warning given by Daurat to Saint-Exupéry on his first flight with the Line.

Now Fabien's wife comes to Rivière's office and, as they wait for the inevitable end, the two worlds, the two truths which they personify, are confronted: "She revealed to men the sacred world of happiness . . . what august substance one touches through action . . . what peace, without knowing, one can destroy" (154). As Rivière had felt before, she now senses that her world becomes inexpressible within the domain of the opposing truth.

Realizing how Fabien's death will make her life devoid of meaning, Rivière experiences a deep pity, which, strangely, brings him closer to understanding his own truth: "We do not ask to be eternal but we do ask not to see our acts and things suddenly lose their meaning" (156). With Fabien's imminent death, Rivière's life-work seems like a ship becalmed at sea, and he imagines a great sailing vessel, built by the people of a small medieval town: "so that men may see their hope unfurl its sails upon the sea" (158). Rivière then changes from his original focus on the goal alone: "The end perhaps justifies nothing, but action delivers from death."

Fabien's last message comes through, as the plane enters the clouds; and the passing seconds of silence destroy all hope. Robineau, convinced that now all night flight must be stopped, goes to stand by Rivière in his defeat; but Rivière emerges from his private meditation with renewed strength and determination. Daring Robineau to offer sympathy, Rivière simply issues orders for the departure of the flight to Europe. Night flight will continue.

The Patagonia mail plane arrives safely, vindicating Rivière's faith, and the European flight prepares to take off. The pilot for Europe, laughing at the idea that Rivière had thought he was afraid, challenges night as he climbs into his plane.

Rivière listens to the sound of the plane and knows that if he had held up a single departure, the cause of night flight would have been lost. His recent defeat can be a commitment which brings true victory closer. Rivière slowly walks back through his offices, bearing his heavy victory.

Criticism of *Vol de nuit*

This best-known of Saint-Exupéry's books has, in the French expression, "caused much ink to flow." Critics have written at length on the philosophy it expresses, some to praise and some to criticize, but most agree on the quality of its style. Anet calls it "a work which comes the closest possible to a poem extended to a book in prose. A work of perfectly balanced harmonic resonances, coherent and completed,"[32] and Cate reinforces this evaluation, labeling the book "a treatise on leadership written in the language of a poet."[33] Maxwell Smith points out the balance between the sense of reality and the poetry of space and of epic struggle that transfigures the realism. "This sense of fearful beauty which pervades the entire work is expressed, not with lyrical rhapsodies, but with sobriety and restraint."[34] Smith singles out as a supreme example of this transfiguring poetry the description of the "oasis of calm" into which Fabien climbs when he is lost: "He would never have believed that the clouds, at night, could dazzle. But the full moon and all the constellations changed them into luminous waves. . . . Fabien thought he had reached a strange limbo, for everywhere, was becoming luminous. . . . For the light did not come down from the stars but emanated, beneath him, around him, from these white reserves" (pp. 140–41). This poetry is also present in the extensive use of marine imagery to describe night and the constant reference to light as a magnetic force.

Critics are less agreed, however, on other aspects of the book, specifically on the philosophy of the work and the character of Rivière who personifies it. In his preface to the book, André Gide defines that philosophy as the paradoxical truth that "man's happiness does not lie in liberty but in the acceptance of a duty."[35] Here he has recognized the developing principle of Saint-Exupéry's philosophy of life, that of responsibility. In this interpretation, the philosophy of action is positive, "action which delivers from death" (158), action which allows man "to last, to create, to exchange his perishable body" (87) for that elusive something that surpasses human life in value. This is the conviction which had grown in Saint-Exupéry from his experience with the Line under Daurat: he had learned that his own happiness came from duty accepted and responsibility shouldered, while he had never found it in the undisciplined years before. Accepted responsibility and dedication to a chosen duty give the meaning to acts and to things essential to fulfillment in life. This is the truth which Rivière discovers to explain his world of action. It is the germ of a new theme that will grow through Saint-Exupéry's world, "to give a meaning to the life of men," recurring in many forms and finally giving the title to the collection of articles published after his death, *Un Sens à la vie,* "a Meaning to Life." (This is wrongly translated in the English title as "A Sense of Life.")

Interpreted in the less positive sense, the philosophy of action as expressed by Rivière becomes almost the Nietzschean concept of the "superman," and it is to this aspect that many critics have objected. Maxwell Smith, although he himself believes in Rivière, very fairly lists some of the early, adverse criticisms of the character: Bidou found Rivière "coarse, ferocious, unjust, blatant and brutal"; Quint considered his morality dangerous, for a man cannot decide whether a cause is worth the sacrifice of his life unless he is a free agent; and Fadiman condemned Rivière as a "transcendental martinet, driving and brutalizing his men like machines, sending them to their death for the sake of an idea he is unable to define himself."[36] Fadiman regretted the use of a fine, imaginative talent in defense of "spiritual Toryism" and felt that Saint-Exupéry's "deification of mere will and energy" led dangerously to the "megalomania of Mussolini." Yet another early critic quoted by Smith is Martin du Gard, who saw sadism in Rivière's insistence that Robineau invent a punishment for the pilot whom he had just befriended.

All of these criticisms can be discounted to a certain extent, as Smith points out, by a close examination of the text, which reveals Rivière's inner motives and feelings. For Rivière the important principle is to mold men into the full expression of themselves: "man was for him a virgin wax which must be kneaded. A soul must be given to this substance and a will created within it" (49).

In this way "the orders were like the ritual of a religion which seem absurd but which shape man" (48). It is to fulfill this duty that Rivière forced men to realize their own potential, expressing his love for them only by his severity. Perhaps the most positive argument in Rivière's defense is that it is through this character that Saint-Exupéry first introduces his great leitmotiv of "exchange". Yet, despite all such determined efforts to understand Rivière, he remains enigmatic and controversial, strangely at odds with the generous humanity of Saint-Exupéry's writing in general, finding an echo only in the Caïd of the posthumous work, *Citadelle.*

Autobiographical Elements

It is generally accepted by all critics that Rivière is, in fact, Didier Daurat, the director of the Line in Toulouse. Léon Werth, stating this as public knowledge, adds that although Saint-Exupéry never confirmed this relationship, he never denied it either. Daurat himself accepted Rivière as a reflection of himself, and Werth suggests that the character gradually contributed to Daurat's own concept of himself. Daurat cautioned, however, "If you identify me with Rivière, you detract from the conception and beauty of that character. There was a Rivière in each of us."[37] That "Rivière within each one" is, no doubt, the sense of responsibility and the self-discipline which Saint-Exupéry had come to recognize as essential qualities of life. As Daurat himself explained, "There are no miracles, only serious accomplishments animated by a sense of responsibility and a respect for hundreds of disciplines."[38] Rivière is sometimes compared to the Nietzschean figure of Zarathustra. Borgal points out that, like Zarathustra, Rivière is momentarily overcome by a certain type of revelation (that of another truth) but is then reborn, "a being who is literally transformed in the last line of the book in a veritable apotheosis: Rivière the Great."[39] This last line, with its overtones of Nietzschean "superman" philosophy, rings strangely in the context of Saint-Exupéry's works; and Cate terms it a "literary faux-pas."[40] At best Rivière remains an enigmatic figure and one whom even Saint-Exupéry's loyal friend, Léon Werth, found hard to accept, just as he found Daurat himself difficult to understand. Prolonging in his imagination an old discussion with Saint-Exupéry on the subject, Werth found many humanistic arguments to oppose Rivière-Daurat's arbitrary authority, and finally concluded that Rivière is the incarnation of a creative order.

One of the most criticized of Rivière's actions is his firing of the
old mechanic, Roblet, despite his years of devoted service to the
Line. Roblet is identified by Cate and others as a literary reincar-
nation of Toto, the mechanic whom Daurat had fired for drunkenness
but then rehired, moved by his fidelity to the Line. A startling
statement by Paul Descendit, in a recent article published in *Icare*,[41]
asserts not only that a Roblet actually existed by that name, but
that it was Saint-Exupéry himself who fired him. Descendit, a fellow
mechanic, explains that Roblet was about sixty years old and physically weak, so unsuited to the work which required health and
strength. Although this explanation exonerates Saint-Exupéry, the
fact suggests a new interpretation of Rivière and, indeed, of the
philosophy of the book. When Saint-Exupéry was writing *Vol de
nuit,* he had just been appointed director of the Aeroposta Argentina
and was, for the first and only time in his life, in absolute control
of a group of men. He now had the position that Daurat had in
Toulouse, where he had to decide which flights to maintain and
which pilots to send, when to cancel a flight or to reprimand a
pilot. He wrote, both to his mother and to Renée de Saussine, that
this authority made him feel old, just as Rivière seems to feel.
Although he flew as much as he could, this was not the simple
responsibility of full participation that he had discovered in Africa
and would rediscover as a war-pilot; this was often the arbitrary
authority of rank, which must sometimes have divorced him from
contact with his fellow pilots.

In accepting the isolating responsibility of authority Saint-Exupéry must have recognized the experience of Daurat and perhaps
sought to emulate him. *Vol de nuit,* this starkest of Saint-Exupéry's
books (the only one in which there is no reference to his childhood),
was perhaps a rationale for the role he had been required to assume.
In this work he seeks to justify the role of the arbitrary chief, as he
had seen him personified in Daurat, showing the dominant, creative
principle behind the strict discipline, and the concealed love for
those whom the chief must discipline. In identifying Rivière simply
as Daurat, it has always been ignored that Daurat was not director
in South America but in Toulouse and on the African line, and
especially, that it was not Daurat who championed night flight,
but Mermoz in South America.

An interesting conjecture occurs: it must have been Saint-Exupéry
himself as director of Aeroposta Argentina, who authorized the flight

during which Guillaumet crashed. This traumatic event must have led Saint-Exupéry to question the absolute authority of the director and may have brought him to seek such a rationale as he attempts in *Vol de nuit*. This enigma of the stern chief who disciplines as an expression of his love in order to mold man's clay into strength, obviously continued to intrigue Saint-Exupéry, for his posthumous *Citadelle*, written as notes over many years, produced the character of the Caïd, the ultimate benevolent despot. Yet, in considering this interpretation, it must be noted that, as director, Saint-Exupéry always sought to participate in action. As Werth points out, Daurat commanded from his office, while Saint-Exupéry commanded from his pilot's seat. In his new position of authority, however, Saint-Exupéry found reassurance in the stylized figure of the admired Daurat, as Werth senses: "Saint-Exupéry, idealizing Monsieur Daurat and transforming him into Rivière, was obeying his moral code of order, of giving and of sacrifice. But also, contemplative and troubled, he sometimes received simplifications from Rivière or a setting at peace from Monsieur Daurat, and a solution to his anxiety."[42]

In *Vol de nuit* we also find the one example of personal animosity shown by Saint-Exupéry. The strange, pathetic figure of Robineau is actually Saint-Exupéry's revenge on an unscrupulous inspector of the Line in Africa who borrowed Saint-Exupéry's collection of aeroliths and never returned them. As Saint-Exupéry recounts in *Terre des hommes*, when he crash-landed on an otherwise inaccessible plateau of the desert, he discovered strange stones which could only have fallen from another planet; and he had been moved by the sudden awareness of this slow shower of meteorites, like apples falling from some celestial tree. These were the stones, vibrant with symbolic significance for Saint-Exupéry, which the amateur minerologist had borrowed, supposedly to write a study on them. The study never appeared, and Saint-Exupéry never saw his stones again. This inspector becomes Robineau who, in the emptiness of his life, finds consolation in his little collection of stones, which he shows to Pellerin. Remembering his lost collection, Saint-Exupéry comments that these little, blackish pebbles "opened a door onto mystery," but remembering the inspector, he scathingly says of Robineau, "in life, only stones had been gentle to him" (59–60). As Pélissier points out, in all of Saint-Exupéry's work there are only two examples of personal bitterness or hatred: one is Saint-Exupéry's hatred of

Hitler; and the other is the portrait of Robineau, satirizing the dishonest inspector.

Yet, for all its controversial complexities of philosophy and personal involvements, *Vol de nuit* is also very much a book on night. Writing later on books that had influenced his childhood, Saint-Exupéry remembers *Les Indes noires* by Jules Verne: "The action takes place in a subterranean passage . . . where light never penetrates. It is quite possible that the fantastic atmosphere of this book, persisting in my memory, was the genesis of my own *Vol de nuit,* which is itself an exploration of the dark."[43] *Les Indes noires* is set in an abandoned coal mine, made fearful by a seemingly mysterious presence, and indeed, there is one passage of *Vol de nuit* which is strongly reminiscent of this atmosphere: "This man must go down into the intimate heart of night, into its thickness, and without even that little miner's lamp which lights only the hands or the wing, but which thrusts aside the unknown by a shoulder's breadth" (101). Taking this clue, Cate tries too hard to read extensive symbolism and imagery from Verne's book into *Vol de nuit;* more pertinently, he points out that the moral of Verne's novel is that "resolution and courage and hard practical sense can, in the end, get the better of crippling mysteries and a supernatural belief in irrational phenomena."[44] This is, indeed, the moral of Saint-Exupéry's book, expressed through Rivière, who wants to free his men from fear by teaching them their own courage, declaring, "It is of mystery alone that one is afraid" (101).

Imagery

In Saint-Exupéry's own statement, *Vol de nuit* is "an exploration of the night" and almost exclusively, with the notable exception just discussed, Saint-Exupéry describes night in terms of marine imagery. Throughout the book Fabien discovers the realm of night, its moods and beauty, as though he were exploring an unknown sea. As he flies on into night, he feels he is entering the quiet waters of a harbor; the lights below are lighthouses signaling human presence, and he feels the waters of night holding up his plane. When he is lost, the night seems a vast river without banks, and he yearns to swim toward the beach of the dawn where he would be safe. Finally, as he climbs desperately above the clouds, like a fish rising to the surface, he was entering protected waters, a part of the sky which is like the bay of the islands of the blessed. Rivière, too, seems to sense the night as a sea, feeling that as each plane arrives, tossed up like a treasure from the sea, he is pulling the pilot to the safety of the shore. When Rivière knows that Fabien's plane is lost, he thinks of the men as drowned by the night, lying now on a peaceful seabed; only when the tide of night withdraws will they be found: "Rivière thinks of the treasures buried in the depths of night as in seas of fable" (148).

Vol de nuit is an exploration of the night, a confrontation of the themes of action and of individual happiness, the epic of the Line; it is a eulogy for Daurat and a rationale of the role of the chief; it can even be analyzed as the story of victorious defeat, as Pélissier chose to do. All of these it may be, but in the final analysis it is a search of that elusive value to which man seeks to dedicate his life and for which he will be willing to die. Rivière sets the question: "If human life has no price, we always act as though something exceeded human life in value. . . . But what?" (128). This is the question which Saint-Exupéry had asked of his friend, Henri Delaunay, "By virtue of what feeling did we keep risking our lives so easily, sometimes, to carry letters?"[45] Delaunay, writing thirty years later, still could not find the answer. Saint-Exupéry, in *Vol de nuit,* had not found the full answer either, but he discovered two leitmotifs, a "meaning to life" and "exchange," that would grow throughout his later books.

Chapter Six

The Collapse of la Ligne and Return to Europe: *Terre des hommes*

A few days after Saint-Exupéry's return to France on leave, in March 1931, and only a month before his marriage to Consuelo, the first signs of the downfall of the Line appeared and, within a few months, the Aéropostale was being liquidated in the midst of a scandal on the scale of the Dreyfus Affair; Saint-Exupéry's position as director of the Aeroposta Argentina had disappeared. The complex affair started when Bouilloux-Lafont refused a government proposal to reduce his personal holdings and so lost the government subsidies. Because the air minister called on Daurat to keep the air service going, during an investigation of the company finances, Bouilloux-Lafont accused Daurat of disloyalty, and engineer Serre, jealous of Daurat, brought ludicrous accusations against him. Mysteriously some documents appeared, apparently proving that government officials had been bribed by the Germans to force Latécoère and Massimi into selling Aéropostale holdings to Lufthansa. In good faith, Bouilloux-Lafont's son André sent these documents to the government, but when they proved to be forgeries, he was arrested. Thus within a few months, Daurat was fired, Massimi had resigned in protest, and Bouilloux-Lafont's son was put on trial and convicted. The Aéropostale was to be liquidated and most of the shares went to Air-Orient; eventually, both companies were merged with others into Air France.

The epic era of pioneer flying, which had aroused the loyalty and enthusiasm of Saint-Exupéry and his comrades, had ended in the bitterness of scandal and resulted in the formation of a simply commercial company. Not only did Saint-Exupéry lose his new position, but more painfully, he saw destroyed the work which he had helped to create and his revered chief maligned and rejected.

74

Saint-Exupéry, Guillaumet, and Mermoz stood loyally by Daurat, flying to Toulouse to urge Dautry, head of the "liquidation committee," to rehire him. Later, during the long months of the liquidation, Saint-Exupéry courageously wrote to Dautry, defending his old chief at the risk of his own position with the company.

Meanwhile, *Vol de nuit* was meeting with great success and, in December 1931, it was awarded the Prix Fémina. Ironically, however, this very success added to the bitter disillusionment that Saint-Exupéry was experiencing with the Line, for many pilots strangely resented the success of this book written in their praise, and they turned against their old comrade, whom they now considered a dilettante. Jules Roy says that "it seemed as if the success of a book which sang the praises of his comrades, of the nobility and beauty of their craft, had been considered by them as a betrayal."[1] In Cate's opinion, the book became "a literary millstone around his neck,"[2] and his disillusionment explains why it was several years before Saint-Exupéry ventured to publish another book. To his faithful comrade, Guillaumet, Saint-Exupéry wrote in his distress: "Because I had written that wretched book, I have been condemned . . . to the enmity of my comrades. Mermoz will tell you what a reputation those who no longer see me and whom I loved so well have given me. . . . Perhaps you also thought I had changed. And I could not bring myself to justify myself before perhaps the only man whom I consider as a brother."[3] Fortunately, Guillaumet always remained Saint-Exupéry's loyal friend, as did Mermoz and Daurat.

Added to the heartbreak of this difficult period was the insecurity of Saint-Exupéry's position. The Aéropostale was being liquidated, and his chances with the new company were endangered by his continued support of Daurat, as well as by the misunderstanding of the intentions of his book. Until December 1931 he went back to simple piloting on the African line, from Casablanca to Port-Etienne. After the award of the Prix Fémina, he took a leave of absence, hoping perhaps to live from the award money. However, he and Consuelo were chronically incapable of saving money so, by February, he requested another posting and was sent to Marseille, where he obtained the Certificate of Public Hydroplane Transport, and piloted hydroplanes on the Marseille-Algiers line. After another leave of absence, to help his mother, Saint-Exupéry was sent back to Africa as pilot on the Casablanca-Dakar mail line.

Return to Flying

Flying once more on an African line, piloting over the desert, Saint-Exupéry found that the spirit had gone from the line as he had known it in its pioneer days. He writes nostalgically of this in *Terre des hommes*: "We were nourished by the magic of the sands, others perhaps sink their oil wells and grow rich . . . but they will have come too late. For the forbidden palm groves . . . offered only one hour of fervor, and it was we who lived it."[4]

Taking yet another leave of absence in his disillusionment, Saint-Exupéry tried to enter Air-Orient, which had absorbed most of Aéropostale's shares. He was rebuffed on the pretext that the merger into Air France was under way, but probably because of one engineer's enmity to Daurat, whom Saint-Exupéry had praised in his book and defended in his letter. Eventually Daurat was rehired by the newly formed Air France, but it took longer for Saint-Exupéry to be recognized. Meanwhile Duarat arranged a position for him as a test pilot for the old Latécoère firm in Toulouse. After selling over ninety percent of his Aéropostale to Bouilloux-Lafont, Latécoère had started the production of two- and three-engined planes, some mounted on floats as "flying-boats"; and these were the planes that Saint-Exupéry was now to test.

A serious incident during this period was Saint-Exupéry's near-fatal accident when he was caught in a submerged seaplane and only survived because a large bubble of air was trapped in the cockpit. Biographers give conflicting accounts of this accident, ranging from the highly dramatic one in Albérès's first book, quoted by Smith,[5] in which the plane crashed in two pieces, to the very prosaic report given by Cate[6] of an uneventful flight marred only by the bad touchdown on the surface. The latter, less dramatic version is verified by Vergès in *Icare*.[7] In any event, Saint-Exupéry's danger was very real and it was his second close brush with death, after his accident at Le Bourget in 1923. As Guillaumet had experienced in the snow of the Andes, as he himself would experience in the sands of Libya, Saint-Exupéry felt the invading peace of death, with its physical temptation to give up the struggle, and he only made the supreme effort to survive through the returning sense of responsibility. Chevrier says, "he must still give an account of himself, protect, continue the fight."[8] Yet, in his own writings, Saint-Exupéry's reference to this incident is the simple statement: "Nothing is intolerable. I thought one day that I was going to drown, imprisoned in a cabin, and I didn't suffer very much."[9]

There was a dramatic result to this accident, however, for Saint-Exupéry lost his job as test pilot. He returned to Paris and tried again to obtain a position with Air France. Finally, in April 1934, Air France offered him a post, but not as a pilot; he was to be a representative of the company on publicity flights in France and abroad. Despite his earlier insistence on a post as pilot, Saint-Exupéry accepted this offer.

One of the first trips which Saint-Exupéry made for Air France was a "study-mission" to Indochina, where he was met by Pierre Gaudillière, an old friend from his days at Brest. They visited the ruins of Angkor, recently made famous by a scandal involving André Malraux in thefts of Khmer art there. When the seaplane broke down, they had to spend the night on the waters of the Mekong, while awaiting rescue. Saint-Exupéry found this a strangely enriching adventure; and in an article in *Icare,* Gaudillière recalls Saint-Exupéry's pensive, philosophic mood that night.

Films and Inventions

With the comparative security assured by his position at Air France, there now began a new period for Saint-Exupéry, still filled with his old activities of flying and writing, but developing new interests of cinematography and journalism. For Air France, Saint-Exupéry flew around the Mediterranean, giving lectures in most of the cities on its shores. For the new Air France magazine, he wrote several articles, at least one of which would later reappear in *Terre des hommes.* Soon he received reporting assignments from well-known newspapers, and many of these articles would later be included in *Un Sens à la vie.* As a recognized author and pilot, he was frequently asked to write prefaces for books on aviation, including one by Anne Morrow Lindbergh. Although he was not consulted for the American film of *Vol de nuit* in 1933, he did participate actively in the filming of *Courrier sud* in 1934 by a French company. When Air France decided to produce a publicity film, *Atlantique Sud,* on the history of the line, director Félix Forestier consulted Saint-Exupéry, who became, as he says, the "spiritual father" of his film.[10] Long intrigued by the new techniques of cinema, Saint-Exupéry had started writing a film scenario, *Anne-Marie,* during his stay in Argentina.

When, in 1935, he met film director Raymond Bernard (the son of the playwright, Tristan Bernard), the director was intrigued by the possibilities of this scenario, and soon Saint-Exupéry was involved in filming his story.

Anne-Marie is the story of five pilots of the line, inseparable Musketeers, who adopt a beautiful girl pilot into their group. All half in love with her themselves, they stand together to resist any outsider who falls in love with Anne-Marie. To console Anne-Marie when they have persuaded her suitor, the Inventor, to give up his love, the five Inseparables start writing joint love-letters to her, to be drafted by the Thinker; but soon the Thinker is cheating, adding pages of his own. When the Thinker is killed in a test flight, Anne-Marie discovers the identity of the letter writer and weeps both for him and the Inventor. (Surely Saint-Exupéry was thinking of Rostand's Cyrano de Bergerac here.) Anne-Marie takes off on a record-breaking flight but soon is lost in a storm. The Inventor saves her by flashing a signal to her through all the city lights; whereupon the four remaining Inseparables give her to the Inventor. Curtis Cate, who was fortunate enough to borrow this script from Raymond Bernard, believes it should be included in anthologies of Saint-Exupéry's work, as it is "unmistakably 'exupérien,' full of those quaint flashes of whimsy which were already brightening his letters twenty years before he wrote *Le Petit Prince.*"[11] Despite these experiences, Saint-Exupéry was never satisfied with films of his works, telling Pierre Chevrier, "I do not consider a film as my work. It is, indeed, always a collective work, the result of compromises which never satisfy any author."[12]

Yet another aspect of Saint-Exupéry's genius was developing at this time. Since childhood Saint-Exupéry had been intrigued by mechanical inventions and, in 1935, he took out the first of a series of patents on inventions which he continued to devise for several years. This first patent was for a landing device; later would come some ten more inventions, including a "goniograph," a propulsion system, a takeoff device, a route tracer, and finally a method of location by electromagnetic waves. The text of all these patents can be found in *Icare III;*[13] in an accompanying article, Gerard Trocmé states that, although Saint-Exupéry never obtained any practical application of his inventions, all the concepts developed by him are now to be found in American planes. Saint-Exupéry's old chief, Daurat, writes of the importance of these inventions and considers that his death "deprived French aeronautics of a researcher gifted with a rare imagination."[14]

Newspaper Reporting

In 1935 Saint-Exupéry undertook his first newspaper assignment, traveling to Moscow for *Paris-Soir*. His articles, which are now an important section of *Un Sens à la vie*, were very different from usual journalistic reporting, for Saint-Exupéry constantly sought and discovered the essential human values which transcend the passing event. Watching the disciplined crowds assembling for the massive May Day parade in Moscow, he suddenly recognized the "human miracle" as, in a moment of relaxation, the marchers became individuals, laughing, singing, and dancing. On the long train journey to Moscow, he saw the sleeping crowd of Polish miners returning to their country and felt the quiet drama of their repeated uprooting, leaving behind "all that they had succeeded in taming in a stay of four or five years in France."[15] Especially he was moved by the coarsening effect of drudgery on the fine clay of humankind. This was for him an essential human problem on which he meditated in his *Carnets* and which he again developed in *Terre des hommes*. As he watched a sleeping couple, now heavy and numbed by hopeless work, he imagined how they must have met, alive and quickened by emotion: "The mystery is that he should have become this lump of loam. . . . Why is this fine human clay spoiled?"[16] Then, in the well-known passage of "Mozart assassinated," he contemplates the beautiful, delicate child sleeping between his work-worn parents: "There had been born from that couple a kind of golden fruit. . . . I said to myself: 'Here is the face of a musician, here is the child Mozart, here is a beautiful promise of life.' . . . Protected, surrounded with care, cultivated, what might he not become? When, by mutation, a new rose is born in the gardens, all the gardeners are moved. But there is no gardener for men. . . . Mozart is condemned."[17] This passage is so essential to Saint-Exupéry's concern for men that it recurs, almost word for word, in *Terre des hommes*. This concern can find no answer in any political system, for such systems do not solve the basic problem of the wounding of humankind: "It is something like the human species and not the individual which is hurt here, which is deprived. . . . What distresses me . . . is the gardener's point of view. . . . It is a little, in each of these men, Mozart assassinated."[18] For within each of these work-deadened men lies the lost potential. The wakened travelers might contentedly eat their breakfasts and watch the passing countryside, but Saint-Exupéry can no longer be reassured. "The magic of the night has shown me, beneath the matrix, the child Mozart who was sleeping."[19]

In Moscow, trying to understand the revolutionary society, Saint-Exupéry confronted the dichotomy between man as species and man as individual, between Man and man. He suspected that in the arbitrary justice of the system there was "a great lack of respect for the individual, but a great respect for man, for the one who is perpetuated throughout the individuals."[20] The problem posed by this dichotomy was to remain in Saint-Exupéry's thought, for, throughout his later writings, there is an ambivalence in the focus of his constant concern for his fellow men.

In other articles Saint-Exupéry reported on the crash of the giant Soviet plane, the Maxim Gorki, in which he had just flown the day before. He was intrigued by the travelers camping for years in a station, awaiting the travel permit which will satisfy their nomadic yearnings. But it was a group of little, old French governesses which awakened his most human response, as he reported their patient life of memories and humble hopes. In an article of gentle sensitivity, Saint-Exupéry recounted his visit to these old ladies, who welcome him as a prince charming.

Crash in the Desert

During 1935 Saint-Exupéry in some way acquired a "Simoun" plane, but biographers disagree as to whether he won it in a competition or somehow found the means to buy it. In any case, he was very proud of the plane, which he used for his lecture tour around the Mediterranean. He hoped to be able to win prizes with it, too, for this was the era of the record-making "raids," when pilots competed in speed flights. When Saint-Exupéry returned from his Mediterranean tour in late November, he heard that the Air Ministry was offering a prize of 150,000 francs to break the record set by André Japy of 98 hours 52 minutes from Paris to Saigon; but the record had to be broken before December 31st. Saint-Exupéry persuaded René Delange of the newspaper L'Intransigeant to give financial backing in exchange for a promised article on the "raid." He also discussed the project with Daurat, who reluctantly agreed to have his mechanics rush through the necessary changes in the plane. With only a few days to make all the preparations the atmosphere was soon feverish in the headquarters which Saint-Exupéry set up at the Hôtel du Port-Royal. Departure was delayed for several days because of bad weather, but Saint-Exupéry finally decided to leave before dawn on 29 December. Driving to the airport, he stopped to buy two thermos flasks and he had them filled with coffee and wine which soon were to save his life. At this point, Saint-Exupéry had not slept for two nights, but, as Chevrier says, he discounted fatigue at the prospect of the joy of flight. In the article which he eventually wrote for *L'Intransigeant,* Saint-Exupéry expresses his feelings: "I walk around my plane and, with the back of my hand, I caress the wings, no doubt it is almost with love. . . . And I can already savor these treasures which I feel lined up before me, this yellow, green and brown expanse of the maps, this rosary of singing names which I shall count off, these hours which I shall climb toward the East, this progress to meet the day. . . ."[21]

Flying over the Mediterranean, Saint-Exupéry and his mechanic, Prévot, noticed a severe fuel leak and had to return to the Marignane airfield for repairs. Once more they set off across the sea and landed in Tunis to refuel. Then they flew off through the night toward Benghazi, and on again toward the valley of the Nile which, with a favorable tailwind, they expected to reach in three and a half hours. These would be hours of darkness and silence, for there were no airfield lights to guide them and they had no radio. "We are crossing the great, black Valley of Ordeal. Here, there is no help. Here, there is no pardon for errors. We are handed over to the discretion of God."[22] Then they made the error which could not be pardoned. Lost in a sea of cumulus clouds, unaware of a headwind, they thought after four hours that they had over-flown the Nile valley. They came down beneath the clouds seeking the valley lights, heading north to the sea. Lured, like Fabien, by a light, they flew toward a phantom lighthouse, apparently three hundred yards beneath them. Suddenly they crashed on the desert. Here began what Maxwell Smith calls "one of the great epics of modern times,"[23] the story of their long struggle to survive and to escape the desert, which constitutes one of the best-known chapters of *Terre des hommes,* entitled "The Center of the Desert."[24]

Miraculously, Saint-Exupéry and Prévot both escaped the crash unharmed, but the precious water canisters had been smashed open. Their only supply of liquid was the coffee and wine in the two thermos flasks. After an initial moment of despair, they rallied and, for five long days, would struggle valiantly to rejoin the world of men. The story of their agonizing physical struggle is illuminated by the discoveries of spiritual riches and joys within them. Just as Guillaumet, in the Andes, had realized that he must resist the temptation of death and struggle to live out of responsibility to his wife, so did Saint-Exupéry and Prévot struggle to live for the sake of those who believed in their courage to continue. They discovered the paradoxical truth that it is not they who are stranded or "shipwrecked": "The shipwrecked, it is those who wait. Those whom our silence threatens. . . . One cannot do other than run towards them" (187–88). Guillaumet had told Saint-Exupéry this, for it is a universal truth; so they will struggle and survive through their sense of responsibility.

Hoping for a rescue plane, they returned to their plane for the first two nights, after exploring the harsh, stony desert around them. Then on the third day, realizing that no plane could find them and that they must save themselves, they decided to set out walking in one direction until they dropped dead in their tracks. Although Saint-Exupéry believed that they were already east of the Nile, he chose instinctively to walk eastwards, against all logic and hope, simply because this was the direction in which Guillaumet had walked; and later they would discover that this was the only direction that could have saved them. Without food or water they covered incredible distances each day. Desert lore taught that one could live only nineteen hours without water; yet they walked on.

Finally on the fifth day, when they were at the point of death from exhaustion and thirst, and past all hope and sorrow, they sensed the desert come alive, for in the sand were human footsteps. Miraculously, they had crossed the path of a Bedouin caravan. The first Arab passed without seeing them, and their throats were too parched to call out. Finally one Arab slowly turned toward them and, like a god, restored life to them: "At the very second when he will face us, all will be accomplished . . . he will have erased in us thirst, death and mirages . . . by the casting of his glance alone, he creates life and he seems like a god" (206). The Arab gives them water and Saint-Exupéry realizes the divine qualities of this precious element: "You are not necessary to life: you are life. . . . With you, there enters into us all the powers which we had renounced. By your grace, all the dried-up springs of our hearts are opened" (207).

If the account of this harsh ordeal has become one of the most frequently quoted passages of *Terre des hommes,* it is not because of the heroism of the two men, which Saint-Exupéry understates. It is rather because of the sensitivity and intensity with which he continued to discover life as he faced death. "It is not danger that I love. I know what I love. It is life" (199). In all the small incidents of those days of struggle, Saint-Exupéry discovered manifestations of life. Finding traces of a little desert fox, he imagined it licking the dew off the stones and sparingly eating the little snails off the desert brush. Forgetting his thirst for a moment, Saint-Exupéry enjoyed these signs of life. This is, indeed, no ordinary fox, but a desert "fenech" who will become the Little Prince's teacher in the desert.

When the two stranded men discovered a miraculous orange in the wreck and shared it, Saint-Exupéry experienced one of the greatest joys of his life. For a moment he was infinitely happy and suddenly he understood the condemned man drinking his last glass of rum: "he has changed perspective and has made a human life out of this last hour" (186). One night, to escape the cruel cold of the desert wind, he buried himself in the sand. Then, forgetting his body, he withdrew into his thoughts and meditated on the life he had chosen: through the airplane, as a farmer through his plow, he has discovered "a peasant truth": "One does a man's work and knows a man's concerns. One is in contact with the wind, with the stars, with the night, with the sand, with the sea. One fends with natural forces. One awaits the dawn as a gardener awaits the spring. One awaits the landing-place like the Promised Land, and one seeks one's truth in the stars" (198).

While the English title of *Wind, Sand, and Stars* appears in this passage, the French title is suggested repeatedly throughout this account of the desert ordeal. When Prévot and Saint-Exupéry lit a signal fire near their plane, it was a call to mankind: "only men have fire, let them reply to us" (168). Returning to Prévot at the wreck, after desperately pursuing a mirage, Saint-Exupéry stopped to call out to mankind: "ohé, les hommes!" (185)—for this planet is inhabited. As he lay buried in the sand, he saw his plight simply:

"I tried to rejoin my kind, as I had forgotten where they lived on earth" (198). Thus his cruel ordeal became simply a search for the world of men. Most poignantly, the Arab who saved them became Man: "You are Man and you appear to me with the face of all men at the same time" (208).

Reporting in Spain

When in January 1936 Saint-Exupéry returned to the "world of men," he had to confront again the material difficulties of that world. After writing the article about his "raid," promised to *L'Intransigeant,* he had to find a means of livelihood: journalism and the cinema were again two resources. First, the producer Pierre Billon offered a contract to film *Courrier sud* from Saint-Exupéry's own scenario. Saint-Exupéry went with Billon to help in the filming and actually flew Bernis's takeoffs, but he was not happy with the film. But soon, in July 1936, there was the outbreak of the civil war in Spain, and Saint-Exupéry was commissioned by Delange to write a series of articles for *L'Intransigeant* on the tragic events there. These articles, together with those written for *Paris-Soir* in 1937 to 1938, now constitute an important part of the collection, *Un Sens à la vie.* Sent to report on the horrors of a civil war, Saint-Exupéry once again discovered the richness of man's spirit, as he had in the emptiness of the desert or the regimentation of Moscow. Recognizing no difference between the two sides in the bitter struggle, he saw only the common striving toward an ideal, toward a fulfillment of one's reality, toward a *meaning to life.*

At first Saint-Exupéry was simply saddened by the meaningless destruction of the struggle which seemed more like a sickness than a war. Here there was no respect for man, for the miraculous kingdom within each individual which is thoughtlessly blotted out by the firing squad. Yet soon, after the initial shock of witnessing trench warfare and a bombardment, Saint-Exupéry began to sense the poignant revelations of the tragedy around him. Seeing the bewildered despair of the man whose fiancée was killed in front of him, Saint-Exupéry recognized that invisible essence which the bereaved lover sought in vain in the dead body: "the angel without weight who clothed it."[25] Watching the bombardment of Madrid, he recognized the power of the human spirit which grows strong by resistance. "Men are thus: ordeals strengthen their virtues . . .

the blow resounds on the anvil: a giant blacksmith is forging Madrid."[26]

Best known, perhaps, of the passages in these Spanish articles is the story of the old sergeant who knows he must take part in a hopeless and senseless attack at dawn, yet sleeps peacefully until the fateful awakening. This story appears both in *Un Sens à la vie* and in *Terre des hommes,* and is obviously essential to Saint-Exupéry's ideas on man's need to discover and know himself. As Saint-Exupéry watched the sergeant roused from his heavy sleep, he pondered the reasons that could make such a man risk his life. Like the wild ducks migrating, like tame gazelles suddenly struggling to break free, the sergeant responded to a yearning nostalgia for something he did not even understand. "And so you felt yourself borne away in this inner migration of which nobody had ever told you."[27] Now, in this ordeal of renunciation as he faces death, the sergeant has discovered a new person within himself, whom he did not know, and he is, in a sense, fulfilled. "He who is no longer tied to material things, who accepts to die for all men, who enters into something indefinably universal, that man within you has opened his wings. A great breath passes over him. Then he is delivered from the matrix, the sleeping lord whom you sheltered: Man."[28] Once again, Saint-Exupéry returned to the discovery of Man.

In the original newspaper report, as it is reprinted in *Un Sens à la vie,* the attack was actually called off just before the sergeant awakes. Later, as Saint-Exupéry tightened the fabric of his work for *Terre des hommes,* he interestingly eliminated this fact, so that the sergeant actually does face death when he awakes. The English translation, *Wind, Sand, and Stars,* which strangely appeared before the French text, still contains the original version. In the definitive French text of *Terre des hommes,* the single story of the old sergeant appears in the final chapter, entitled simply "Les Hommes," whereas in the intermediate English version, the final chapter, entitled "Barcelona and Spain" contains most of the Spanish reports. As Saint-Exupéry refined his material he discarded most of these reports to retain only this essential story, setting it in the context of this final important chapter in which he discussed those paradoxical truths which liberate and fulfill man; these truths are the "favorable terrain" in which man may thrive: "If this religion, if this culture, if this scale of values, if this form of activity and not certain others favor this plenitude in man and deliver in him a great lord of which he

was unaware, it is because this scale of values, this culture, this
form of activity are the truth of man."[29] For lack of "favorable
terrain," man can hibernate without ever knowing the greatness
dormant within him; the old sergeant found within the tragic circumstances of civil war the "favorable terrain" which freed him from
his matrix. And in the final form of *Terre des hommes,* Saint-Exupéry
simplified his long declamation to the essential: "It is here that man
appears."[30]

In 1937 Saint-Exupéry was sent by Air France to reconnoiter a
new route on the north-east coast of Africa. Meanwhile, that summer, he returned to Spain as a reporter, this time for *Paris-Soir,*
and this is when he wrote the long article entitled "Madrid," which
appears in both *Un Sens à la vie* and in *Wind, Sand, and Stars.* All
his life Saint-Exupéry would refuse political affiliation, caring nothing for any regime, but only for the kind of man founded by that
regime. Now, after seeing communism at close range, he decided
to visit Germany to see fascism. He soon learned firsthand about
the restrictions in Nazi Germany, for he was almost arrested as a
spy, when he mistakenly landed at a military airport near Wiesbaden.

In this patch-work year of 1937, it is surprising to find the only
reference of Saint-Exupéry's going to England. According to his
friend, Henri Jeanson, Saint-Exupéry and he were both invited to
London by the film producer Alexander Korda, to discuss making
a film on the history of aviation, a project which apparently came
to nothing.[31]

Crash in Guatemala

The short reconnaissance flight for Air France in Africa, as well
as a flight to Rumania for the Air Ministry, had reawakened Saint-
Exupéry's nostalgia for flying and, by September 1937, he was eager
to attempt another "raid," despite his nearly tragic failure over the
desert in 1935. Besides this nostalgia, there was perhaps also the
desire to escape for awhile from the complications of his private
life, at which various biographers discreetly hint, while Cate forth-
rightly mentions problems with Consuelo, debts to *Paris-Soir* for
articles which he had failed to complete, and the burden of taking
advances from Gallimard for a book which he somehow could not
write. Saint-Exupéry suggested to the Air Ministry the idea of a
"raid" from New York south to Punta Arenas at Cape Horn, over

the land route, the region where he had pioneered the routes in his days with the Aeroposta Argentina. In January 1938, accompanied by his mechanic, Prévot, he sailed for New York with his "Simoun" plane crated in the hold; and so he arrived in the United States which would be his land of exile during the war.

After several days of necessary formalities and a short trip to Montreal and Quebec, takeoff was planned for February 1st, but blizzards caused several delays. Saint-Exupéry and Prévot finally took off on 15 February, on the first stage of the "raid" that was supposed to take them all the way to Punta Arenas. Yet the next day, on takeoff, after refueling at Guatemala City airstrip, Saint-Exupéry and Prévot were again struck down by a violent accident. This time they could not walk away from it, for Prévot was unconscious, with a broken leg; and Saint-Exupéry was seriously injured, with a lacerated face, a broken wrist, a cracked shoulder, skull fractures and concussion. Biographers generally suppose that the fliers had inadvertently taken on too much fuel, making the plane too heavy to lift off at that altitude. Whatever the cause, the projected, glorious "raid" of 14,000 kilometers was ended after only 5,500 kilometers, and it would take Saint-Exupéry months to recover.

For several weeks Saint-Exupéry remained in the Guatemalan hospital. Gradually he regained consciousness, and then began his battle with the doctors who wanted to amputate his arm. Three weeks after the accident Consuelo came to help him; and after more than a month in hospital, he flew to New York, where good friends, including Guillaumet, settled him into the Ritz Carlton hotel and surrounded him with care. Slowly his terrible wounds healed, although he would never again be able to raise his left arm fully; but the shock of the accident had shaken him emotionally. An American friend, General Donavan, invited him to convalesce in his apartment on Beekman Place. Here, in his room overlooking East River, Saint-Exupéry began at last to put together the notes and some articles which he had been collecting for seven years and which would become his third "novel," *Terre des hommes.*

Genesis of His New Book

While Saint-Exupéry was still working on his new manuscript, his friend Jean Prévost (publisher of his first story, "L'Aviateur") introduced him to the American publishers Hitchcock and Reynal,

who were immediately interested in the work. They chose a translator, Lewis Galantière, and when Saint-Exupéry returned to France
in April, he left a batch of manuscripts with Galantière. Thus arose
the strange situation of Galantière's working on the translation of
a book which Saint-Exupéry was still writing and reshaping; and
this accounts for the very marked differences between the French
and English versions, which will be discussed later. Although Galantière felt he had an established manucript to translate, Saint-
Exupéry was still refining his text, as was his habit, gradually freeing
it from the matrix.

During the whole summer of 1938, Chevrier tells us, Saint-
Exupéry wandered in search of tranquillity, with his manuscript
under his arm. After resting in the Var he went to Switzerland,
where he spent days on the lake steamers, vaguely hoping for Byronic
inspiration. He then undertook a nostalgic sort of pilgrimage to his
childhood, first to his school at Fribourg, then back to his childhood
home of Saint-Maurice de Remens, which had become a children's
summer camp. Finally he visited the old family housekeeper Marguerite, the "Moïsie" of *Terre des hommes*. Somehow he found time
to write the preface for Anne Morrow Lindbergh's *Listen, the Wind*
and, according to Chevrier, to return to New York in July to deliver
more manuscript to Galantière. In September, however, during a
"cure" at the Vichy spa, he was still reworking his manuscript.

In October 1938, after the Munich crisis, *Paris-Soir* commissioned
three articles from Saint-Exupéry, and these would later be included
in the anthology, *Un Sens à la vie*. In confronting the ethical problem
of the political choice made at Munich, Saint-Exupéry returned again
to the contradictory truths discovered in his reporting of the Spanish
civil war: he again recounted the fraternal conversation across the
trenches, both sides fighting for the same ideals, and again developed
the theme of man's instinctive drive to fulfill himself, even at the
risk of death. The concluding article is devoted to the need to give
meaning to life, to help man break free from the "ant-hill." (Here
is the source of the title, *Un Sens à la vie*.) In these articles, as in
the earlier Spanish ones, many themes are introduced which are
developed in *Terre des hommes* and which will swell through *Pilote
de guerre* to their recapitulation in the posthumous *Citadelle:* a meaning to life, the ascension of man, the freeing of man from the
"matrix," the need for a common language, for understanding. In
another recollection of the Spanish front, Saint-Exupéry described

the impromptu botany lesson given by a corporal to some rough, uneducated soldiers who seem to be struggling to catch up with humanity: "Thus, I had watched that ascension of the consciousness, like the rising of the sap and which, born of the clay in the prehistoric night, had little by little risen to Descartes, Bach or Pascal, those high summits."[32] In November 1938 *Paris-Soir* published another series of articles by Saint-Exupéry, strangely ignored or forgotten by most biographies and bibliographies, but brought to light by *Icare* in its third volume on Saint-Exupéry. These articles, entitled "Aventures et Escales," seem to constitute a preliminary sketch of *Terre des hommes,* recounting episodes which have become essential sections of that book: Saint-Exupéry's *veillée d'armes* before his first flight for "la Ligne"; the night he and Néri were lost over the sea and expected to die; another night when three stranded crews created a joyous camp in the desert; Saint-Exupéry's forced landing on the mysterious plateau where no human had set foot; a discussion of the haunting magic of the desert; and, finally, a discussion of his contact with the nomadic Arab tribes.

Understandably, these constant reworkings of the themes, the very substance of which *Terre des hommes* is created, made it difficult for Saint-Exupéry ever to be fully satisfied with any final version of that book, which was now in the hands both of his translator in America and of the publishers in France. He had made so many refinements in his original manuscript, cutting away a third of the text, that Galantière protested that Saint-Exupéry could write but not read, for he was throwing away beautiful passages. Saint-Exupéry finally agreed to let Galantière send his version to the American publishers while he sent the reduced French version to Gallimard in August. Yet even after this compromise agreement, Saint-Exupéry kept anxiously sending changes both to Galantière and to Gallimard, prompted by his own striving or by his friends' suggestions. When his friend, Dr. Pélissier, suggested his cutting out the long description of his flight across the Mediterranean before the desert crash, Saint-Exupéry protested that he had never described a normal flight, but he accepted Pélissier's opinion for his French edition, although the passage was reinstated in the American edition. Ironically, when early in 1939, Saint-Exupéry impulsively went to New York, apparently just to "apologize" to Galantière for his many deletions, he was immediately reminded that he had promised extra chapters for the English edition. Saint-Exupéry was some-

how forced to produce a new chapter within a few days, and the
long passage "The Elements" resulted. This time Saint-Exupéry was
so pleased with the chapter produced under pressure that he tele-
graphed Gallimard to include it in the French edition, but it was
too late. Disappointed, he later published it in *Marianne* (August
1939) under the title "Le Pilote et les puissances naturelles," and
it became well known in the anthology, *Un Sens à la vie*, as well as
appearing in the *Confluences* anthology.

Even the title of his laboriously evolved book produced more soul
searching for Saint-Exupéry. The original title, *Etoiles par grand vent*,
closely related to the English title, was too dramatic for his taste.
With the help of his cousin, André de Fonscolombe, Saint-Exupéry
thought of some thirty alternative titles, which he showed to Yvonne
de Lestrange; and, in a moment of inspiration, from a suggested
"Terre des humains," Saint-Exupéry discovered "Terre des hommes."
As a photo published by *Icare* shows, on proofs dated December
1938, the original title is crossed through and the new one, *Terre
des hommes*, is written in Saint-Exupéry's hand.[33] This French title
is so rich in connotations that it is difficult to translate fully; as
Smith says, it has the meaning "the planet where men live."[34] It
is the world of men, the earth of mankind; and the whole book is
a quest for the discovery of the essence, the soul of Man.

Terre des hommes

Although *Terre des hommes* received the Grand Prize for the Novel,
offered by the Académie française, it is, in fact, essentially autobiographical and historical, as well as being an instrument for the
expression of Saint-Exupéry's philosophy. To summarize the book
would be to repeat the adventure of Saint-Exupéry's life as we have
already followed it, with the story of the Line, of his comrades, and
of his travels as a journalist. Yet a short, though important, introduction sets the theme which will tie these reminiscences together
into a philosophical whole. Looking down from his plane, the pilot
sees the earth which "teaches us more than all the books" (7), because
it resists us, and man discovers himself when he is measured against
an obstacle. To do this, he needs a tool, and the plane can be this
tool. Scattered below are lights, showing where men are on the
earth. We must reach out to communicate with those men, on the
earth of men.

The first chapter, entitled simply "La Ligne," recounts Saint-Exupéry's introduction to his craft, with the geography lesson given by the veteran and the old airport bus, a grey chrysalis from which the new pilot will emerge transformed. In the second chapter, "Les Camarades," Saint-Exupéry tells of Mermoz, pioneer of night, desert, and mountains: he describes the night when he is encamped on the desert while trying to rescue his friends, Gourp and Erable; and he recounts the valiant story of Guillaumet, struggling through the frozen summits of the Andes.[35] Remembering those days, Saint-Exupéry realizes that "The greatness of a craft is, perhaps, above all, to unite men" (42). The short third chapter, "L'Avion," is a poem to the airplane, in which Saint-Exupéry sees a tool, like a plough, to enter into contact with life: "Beyond the tool and through it, it is (old) nature which we rediscover, that of the gardener, of the navigator, of the poet" (65). In the fourth chapter, "L'Avion et la Planète," the airplane becomes an instrument to analyze the world and to understand it. Here are Saint-Exupéry's discoveries of the "earth of men," where Man's presence is so miraculous. Reaching Punta Arenas, the southern-most town in the world, poised between volcanic lava and polar ice, Saint-Exupéry feels the "miracle of man," on an earth where lakes pulsate to the rhythm of the tides. Landing on an isolated plateau in North Africa, he marvels at the aeroliths fallen from the sky over the centuries; even more marvellous is man's mind which can conceive of this long shower of aeroliths. Lying on the desert sand at night, he feels himself bound to the earth by gravity and feels the earth beneath him, bearing him up like a ship.

Then comes "Oasis," the chapter of enchantment, where the airplane "plunges you into the heart of mystery" (85). This is his visit to the old house in Argentina where he found the two "princesses" who put him to the test of the vipers, then admitted him for a short moment into the beautiful realm of their home.[36]

After this oasis, in the next long chapter, Saint-Exupéry returns to his beloved desert. This is the seemingly empty expanse that becomes vibrant with significance as one enters into its life: "We accepted the rules of the game, the game formed us in its image. The Sahara reveals itself within us. To enter into it is not to visit the oasis but to make one's religion of a fountain" (98). He tells of the phantom *rezzou* (raiding party), whose presence magnetizes the folds of the dunes. Here are the desert Arabs whom he took to see the Alpine waterfall, amazed at the generosity of the Frenchmen's

god; and here is Captain Bonnafous, the "beloved enemy" of the
Arabs, who fills the desert with his "legendary presence" and who
is himself caught in the rules of the game. One of the best-known
episodes is the story of the old slave, Bark, who refuses to "abdicate"
his own personality, despite long years of servitude. When Bark is
finally freed, ransomed by Saint-Exupéry, he passionately tries to
find his true weight among men. "Nobody had shown that he had
need of him. He was free but infinitely so, until he could not feel
himself bear upon the earth. He lacked the weight of human relations" (138). And so Bark spends his gift money to buy golden
slippers for the street urchins who cluster around him, until the
weight of their hopes holds him.

The significance of the desert was in the "rules of the game,"
within which Saint-Exupéry had learned to live in his years at Cap
Juby. It was in the vibrant web of relationships woven between the
men of the desert, within these rules. Now, as the "dissidence" is
subdued, the desert has changed, its "hour of fervor" gone. As with
the childhood world which seems so infinite within the garden walls,
one would have to reenter the game, not the park or the desert, to
find again that closed civilization of which one had been a part.

Once Saint-Exupéry had reentered the heart of the desert when
he had crashed there. In the chapter, "The Center of the Desert,"
he tells the long, poignant adventure of his ordeal. This often-
quoted story (presented earlier in this chapter) again reaches through
the anguish of the moment to the discovery of man, whom Saint-
Exupéry recognizes in the Arab who saves them: "You are Man and
you appear to me with the face of all men at once. . . . You are
the beloved brother. And, in my turn, I shall recognize you in all
men. . . . All my friends, all my enemies in you walk toward me,
and I no longer have a single enemy in the world" (208).

In the extreme adventure, reaching almost to death, Saint-Exupéry had again found the strange truth that such moments of re-
nouncement bring plenitude, and a discovery of oneself. In the final
chapter, "Men," Saint-Exupéry tries to follow the extreme "vocation," to find the "favorable terrains," which enable man thus to
discover and fulfill himself. Here is the often-told story of the old
sergeant whom he had met in the Spanish civil war, ready to die
to satisfy an instinctive drive awakened within him.[37] The sergeant
found fulfillment risking his life in the companionship of battle, as
Saint-Exupéry found it risking his in the companionship of flight.

It is the web of human relations and the meaning to action which bring this fulfillment. "Truth for man is what makes of him a man" (228). The essential is to give meaning to men's actions and this is the urgent problem of the modern world. War may dangerously seem to offer such meaning but "we do not need war to find the warmth of neighborly shoulders in a race toward the same goal" (252). Rather should we seek a goal which unites us all.

Saint-Exupéry then recalls witnessing the death of an old peasant woman, with her sons gathered around her. Here life flowed richly from generation to generation, bearing the patrimony of language, traditions, and myths, through the metamorphoses, in continuing growth, ascending like a tree: "It was life, but it was also consciousness. What a mysterious ascension. From a lava in fusion, from the clay of a star, from a living cell germinated by a miracle, we have issued forth, little by little, we have raised ourselves to writing cantatas and weighing milky ways" (237). And again, Saint-Exupéry remembers the train filled with Polish immigrant workers, and the beautiful sleeping child between the work-worn parents.[38] But unless a meaning can be given to life, this potential Mozart will never know the true music within him. This is what troubles Saint-Exupéry as he ponders on the "earth of men." He concludes his long, rich book with the almost biblical thought: "Only the spirit, if it breathes on the clay, can create Man."

In January, just before the publication of *Terre des hommes,* Saint-Exupéry was made an officer of the Légion d'honneur. Then, in February 1939, almost simultaneously with its American edition, *Terre des hommes* was published in France. Within a few weeks it had received the Grand Prix du roman of the Académie française; and in June it was named Book-of-the-Month in America. And so 1939 began well for Saint-Exupéry, that year which would involve him in the intense emotional growth of his war experience, the final stage in the spiritual ascension which had begun with la Ligne.

Before the war broke out, however, Saint-Exupéry had the joy of flying with Guillaumet once more. Together, on Guillaumet's birthday in May, they celebrated Saint-Exupéry's Légion d'honneur. Then, as Guillaumet was attempting a record flight over the North Atlantic, Saint-Exupéry joined him and they arrived in New York to see *Wind, Sand, and Stars,* just published, in all the bookstores. On Bastille Day, 14 July, they flew back to France in a record-breaking twenty-four hours and twenty-four minutes. Within two weeks,

however, Saint-Exupéry was called back to New York to receive all
the honors bestowed on his latest book: Book-of-the-Month, American Booksellers Association Award, and National Book Award. It
was during this visit that he met Charles Lindbergh and his wife
Anne, for whom he had just written a preface to her book, *Listen,
the Wind*. In her diary Anne writes at length about his visit to them:
"When one finds a person who has the same thoughts as yours you
cry out for joy, you go and shake him by the hand."[39] Very soon,
troubled by the rumors of war, Saint-Exupéry returned to his country, arriving at Le Havre on August 26th; and on September 4th
he was mobilized as an aviation instructor. The final chapter of the
epic was opened.

Chapter Seven

War and Exile:
Pilote de guerre

Captain Saint-Exupéry was mobilized and ordered to report for duty to the Toulouse airfield on 4 September 1939. There he was to be a flight instructor, as he was considered too old to be an active combatant, especially as he had a stiffened shoulder after his Guatemala accident. Far from welcoming such relative security in time of war, Saint-Exupéry desperately sought to get into active duty, becoming miserably restless as long as he was kept from it.

In a letter quoted by Chevrier, he explained his urgent need to participate, if he was to continue to grow as a man and as a writer. Responding to those friends who wanted to protect him because of his value as a writer, he declared: "It is by participating that one plays an effective role. Those who have a value, if they are the salt of the earth must mix themselves with the earth . . . Everything that I love is threatened. . . . I cannot *not* participate. . . ."[1]

The Group II/33

Soon, by insistence and perseverance, Saint-Exupéry obtained the active posting which he sought and was sent to join the Reconnaissance Group II/33 at Orconte. There, in the barren simplicity of village billets, he rediscovered the close-knit fraternity and the monastic austerity that he had known at Cap Juby. In that setting, Saint-Exupéry seemed once again in the "favorable terrain" where he could grow and continue his ascension of spirit.

At first he was not in physical danger, for it was the period of the *drôle de guerre,* the "stalemate" of those first months of the war. After all his years of flying, Saint-Exupéry quietly accepted the new training required to fly war planes, the Potez 63. Then, in January and February 1940, he was sent to the Toulouse base again to retrain on the new Bloch 274 with which the Group was to be equipped. He returned to Orconte in March, happy to find his simple village

quarters again. Soon he began making reconnaissance flights over
Germany. In all, he would fly seven missions in 1940.

Meanwhile, Saint-Exupéry's friends kept plotting various means
to remove him from danger. As Saint-Exupéry wrote to Dr. Pélissier,
"I have thwarted three successive transfers which sought to save my
precious person. . . ."[2] Early in the war, Giraudoux had offered
him a post in the Ministry of Information which Saint-Exupéry had
refused. Then, in January 1940, the National Center for Scientific
Research requested his transfer there, to work on questions of applied
aeronautics. Such was Saint-Exupéry's distress at this order that he
persuaded Commandant Alias to go with him to the Air Ministry
to explain the absolute necessity of his staying in active service. As
the war intensified, Giraudoux, from the Ministry of Information,
tried to have Saint-Exupéry sent on a lecture tour to the United
States. When he replied that his absence from his squadron would
be morally impossible, the Ministry appealed to the Group commander to help Saint-Exupéry "reconcile" his duty as an officer and
his responsibilities as a writer which "make of him at present the
obvious spokesman to let the voice of France be heard in the United
States."[3] Saint-Exupéry, summoned by Paul Reynaud to be offered
this assignment, again refused to abandon his comrades-in-arms. In
Pilote de guerre he expresses his indignant reaction to the apparently
reasonable arguments of his well-meaning friends: "Intellectuals are
kept in reserve, like pots of jam, on the shelves of Propaganda, to
be eaten after the war. . . ."[4]

In one of its several issues devoted to Saint-Exupéry, the French
aviation review, *Icare*, published recollections by many of his comrades in the Group: Gavoille, Alias, Dutertre, Israel, names familiar
to the readers of *Pilote de guerre*.[5] They all echo the same warm
affection for their simple, unaffected comrade who, despite his experience and his fame, desired nothing more than to be accepted as
one of them and to serve his country. For his comrades, Saint-
Exupéry is the storyteller, the conjurer, the debater, delighting
them with tales and card tricks, and joining in their songs. Sometimes he would mystify them with demonstrations of graphology
or would challenge them to a high-level game of chess. In all of
these, they sensed the power of his spirit, which could somehow
reach out to comprehend another mind. Gavoille recalls Saint-Exupéry as a complete man (in the sense of the Renaissance man),
open to science as to literature, a universal genius; but especially

he recognizes in Saint-Exupéry a kind of spiritual radiance and magnetism which attracted others to him.

Saint-Exupéry was, too, an imaginative scientist, and he found a solution for the problem of the controls freezing in high-altitude flying. As he recounts in *Pilote de guerre,* this was a major problem, for a reconnaissance plane's only defence was in quick maneuvering, which became impossible when the controls froze. As this was caused by a water vapor given off by the combustion of the gas, Saint-Exupéry suggested the use of methyl-glycol as a lubricant, since it tends to absorb moisture. He also invented a system of "luminous camouflage" consisting of hiding an airfield or other objective behind intersecting beams of light. Later, much in advance of his time, he imagined an electromagnetic system for measuring distances. American scientists would soon develop a similar system, and Saint-Exupéry's friend, Jean Israel, wondered whether Saint-Exupéry actually gave them the germ of his idea during his war exile in America. In his article on the subject in *Icare 78,* Israel concluded that Saint-Exupéry's scientific spirit, as Leonardo de Vinci's, was equal to his other gifts.[6] When Commandant Alias accompanied Saint-Exupéry to see Professor Holweck at the Sorbonne, to test his ideas, the eminent professor expressed his admiration for Saint-Exupéry who, by his instinct for science, could act as a "revealer" to more formally trained scientists.

During this comparatively quiet period of the early months of the war, Saint-Exupéry positively enjoyed his simple "home" with the Group. In writing of it in *Pilote de guerre,* he speaks with proud possessiveness of "his" village where he will walk at night, if he returns from mission, of "his" farmer, whom he will try to amaze with accounts of his instrument panel and, especially, of "his" room in the farm, which has become a whole kingdom to him. In his frigid room on winter mornings, as he summoned up the courage to leave his warm bed and run across the icy expanse of floor to light the fire, he discovered three "provinces," three "civilizations" of sleep, of fire, and of desert.[7] Saint-Exupéry became completely devoted to the Group, collectively and individually: "I love the Group II/33 because I am part of it, because it nourishes me and I contribute to nourishing it,"[8] or again, "My love of the Group does not need to be spoken, it is composed only of bonds. It is my very substance. I am of the Group. And that is all."[9] Individuals stand out to exemplify the spirit of the Group: Alias, the commander, a brother to Daurat; Hochédé, the personification of disciplined devotion; Gavoille, who quite simply "is"; and heroic Israel, who was famous, like Cyrano, for his nose, which alone could betray his well-mastered fear as he went bravely to battle.

The Battle Breaks Out

In early May 1940 the war broke from stalemate into savage violence, as Hitler's forces overran Belgium and marched into northern France. Fully aware of the menace threatening his country, Saint-Exupéry took up the challenge with his comrades and participated fully. The Group had to evacuate from Orconte in the north, and moved to Orly near Paris.

On 23 May Saint-Exupéry carried out the famous mission over Arras which became the source of his book, *Pilote de guerre,* known in English as *Flight to Arras.* This was a reconnaissance mission from the Orly airbase, over the wide strip of land already occupied by the Germans, to still-unoccupied Arras, north of that strip. Pilots on these flights were, as Saint-Exupéry writes in *Pilote de guerre,* almost certainly condemned to be sacrificed and, even if they successfully returned with reconnaissance photos, these would by then be useless, such was the chaos of the constantly changing battle patterns. Yet Saint-Exupéry, like all his comrades in turn, accepted his mission simply because one must play the game to the end. In all the incoherence of the invasion and of inconceivable defeat, the commander who gave the orders and the men who continued to accept them were maintaining the semblance of orderly battle and of possible victory.

Although Saint-Exupéry and his fellow crew members had hardly expected to return from this mission, they did successfully complete it, after being struck by flak. They brought back the required photos and, more important, Saint-Exupéry brought back the intense perception of the war pilot's meditation, from which he would create the rich soliloquy of *Pilote de guerre.*

Meanwhile, Saint-Exupéry was decorated with the Croix de guerre for his mission. The citation reads: "Officer uniting the finest intellectual and moral qualities, constantly offering himself for the most dangerous missions. Brilliantly succeeded in two photographic reconnaissance missions. Is a model of duty and the spirit of sacrifice for the personnel of the unit."[10] It was after this flight that Saint-

Exupéry was summoned to Paris by Paul Reynaud, who wanted to send him on a mission to the United States. Refusing the assignment which would place him in safety, he returned to his unit more determined than ever to stay with his comrades-in-arms to whom he declared: "I understand absolutely nothing of what they are doing, nor what they want to do. There is only one thing I know, and it is that my place is here, with you, beside you."[11] Together with his Group, Saint-Exupéry faced the utter chaos of the exodus. (In French, *L'Exode* refers to the flood of refugees fleeing the Nazi invasion on the French roads, in the spring of 1940.) Repeatedly the Group was moved to other bases, with Commandant Alias trying desperately to hold them together as a working unit. Saint-Exupéry obtained a brief leave to help Consuelo close their house, and to send her south toward safety. Then, in June, the Group was ordered to Algeria. Commandant Alias sent men ahead to the Bordeaux airfield to have their Bloch planes serviced and to take any planes or spare parts they could save. Saint-Exupéry chose a large four-engined Farman, which he flew across to Algeria, picking up many stranded Polish officers when he stopped to refuel in Perpignan. In Algiers Saint-Exupéry immediately contacted his old friend, Dr. Pélissier, to whom he recounted his immense despair at the exodus.

Commandant Alias and his Group had hoped to find a means of continuing the struggle from North Africa, perhaps carrying the fight back into Italy. Cate suggests that Saint-Exupéry was actually sent on a confidential mission to Morocco to determine the readiness, spiritual and material, for such continued resistance. In all events, it soon appeared that such hopes were vain. The planes could only carry out a few more missions without repairs, and there were neither spare parts nor factories to supply them. The Armistice had been signed in France on 22 June, and already the armistice commissions were being set up to do their demoralizing work in North Africa, and the armed forces were being demobilized.

On 31 July Saint-Exupéry was demobilized and he prepared to return to France. At his farewell party, Commandant Alias said, "With Saint-Exupéry, the Group II/33 loses its soul."[12] Saint-Exupéry arrived back in France, at Marseille, on 5 August. He went first to Agay, to visit his family, while he tried to decide what he must do in the disaster which had befallen his country.

How does a man who had struggled so hard to fight for his country accept defeat? Like millions of Frenchmen, Saint-Exupéry was completely bewildered by the unbelievable situation of the Armistice and of the provisional government at Vichy, so inconceivable after his passionate personal battle to defend his country.

At first Saint-Exupéry stayed quietly at Agay with his sister, trying to work on the manuscript which would become *Citadelle.* Then he began to move about the so-called "free zone" in the south, visiting friends or going to Vichy, capital of the Pétain government, in an attempt to understand the situation. In Vichy he obtained a permit to travel to Paris in the officially occupied zone; but just a few days in the city controlled by Germans convinced him that he could not live in occupied territory. His New York editors had written to urge him to go to America where his *Wind, Sand, and Stars* had received such acclaim, but he was hesitant to leave his country. Meanwhile, the Vichy government tried to associate Saint-Exupéry with them by announcing his appointment to the National Council, an appointment which Saint-Exupéry vehemently rejected. Some friends of Saint-Exupéry even tried to persuade him to accept a Vichy post and then act as a double agent but, as Galantière says, Saint-Exupéry had no gift at all for intrigue or dissimulation.[13] Progressively, Saint-Exupéry came to the decision that he must go to America to get a perspective on the situation.

The question naturally arises of why Saint-Exupéry did not go to London to join de Gaulle and the Free French there, and there is considerable controversy on the subject. Smith quotes Léon Werth, Saint-Exupéry's close friend, as saying that Saint-Exupéry wanted to go to London and could perhaps have been encouraged to do so by him. According to Cate, Saint-Exupéry told Dr. Henri Comte, a Casablanca friend, "I do not know if I shall have the courage *not* to join the R.A.F."[14] Galantière, Saint-Exupéry's friend and translator, felt that Saint-Exupéry was hesitant to join any one group of Frenchmen who might be called to fight another, even to free the country. Since then, most biographers have let their own political prejudices color their analysis of this question, culminating in Cate's vicious (and undocumented) attacks on de Gaulle. To this writer, it is deeply sad that these two great Frenchmen, who both loved their country so intensely, should never have met and understood each other's passionate patriotism. That Saint-Exupéry was indeed of the same heart as de Gaulle was recognized even by the puppet government at Vichy, whose collaborators condemned Saint-Exupéry's *Pilote de guerre* as a "Gaullist manifesto" which expounded "total and unconditional adherence to Gaullism."[15]

Into Exile

Having finally decided to go to America, Saint-Exupéry obtained his visa from the Vichy government, then went to say good-bye to his mother whom, indeed, he would never see again. He planned to sail from Lisbon, but had to travel there via Algiers, as the Spanish government refused him passage across the country because of his reporting during the civil war. Général Chambe recalls meeting Saint-Exupéry in Algiers at that time, and Saint-Exupéry declared that he would return to Africa: "When the Americans land, I swear that I will be with them."[16]

In Lisbon, waiting to sail, Saint-Exupéry encountered for the first time the flow of rich, facile refugees who would later swarm into New York and disillusion him, those who "leave their country, going far from their people to put their money in safety."[17] It was in Lisbon, too, that Saint-Exupéry learned of the death of his friend, Guillaumet, who had been shot down over the Mediterranean. His grief was profound, and he wrote to Pierre Chevrier: "Guillaumet is dead. It seems to me that I no longer have any friends. . . . It will take me so long to learn his death, and I already feel heavy with that terrible task. It will last months and months, and I shall so often have need of him."[18] Saint-Exupéry had agreed to speak at the *Ecole française* in Lisbon, and he dedicated his speech to the memory of his lost comrade, drawing extensively on *Terre des hommes* and the story of Guillaumet's heroic struggle, to give the students a message of the meaning of life.

Finally in December he sailed for America. On the Portuguese steamer, he found himself among the crowd of refugees who had so distressed him in Lisbon. They were like extras on a stage, like plants without roots, for they no longer had a function or any responsibility. Like the old slave, Bark, in *Terre des hommes,* Saint-Exupéry refused to abdicate his identity, saying "I am willing to be a traveller, but I do not want to be an emigrant. I have learned so many things at home, which will be useless elsewhere."[19] On the last day of 1940, Saint-Exupéry landed in New York, where he began two and a half years of exile which would be, as Smith says, at once the saddest and most productive years of his life.[20]

New York

When Saint-Exupéry arrived in New York, his publishers, Reynal and Hitchcock, soon settled him into an apartment on Central Park South, trying to provide for his physical comfort, even if his spiritual anguish could not be relieved. These first months must have been extremely hard for Saint-Exupéry. He was suddenly cut off from everything that was his spiritual sustenance: his country, his comrades, his family, and his craft. He had been forced by circumstances into the position he abhorred, that of the spectator.

Furthermore, in the French circles in New York, Saint-Exupéry found himself caught in the partisan struggles between supporters of the Vichy government and followers of de Gaulle and his Free French in London. Galantière suggests that Saint-Exupéry could not join de Gaulle because he feared he might engage in a fratricidal war: and because he did not declare for the Free French, he was accused of being for Vichy. Each group wanted to claim such an illustrious man for their side, and, when they could not, each group accused him of working for the other.

During these first months, by Galantière's account, Saint-Exupéry was constantly tormented by what was happening to his country: "Desperate as he was at not participating, he was not the type of those who shut themselves in an ivory tower. . . . Whatever the conversation might be, he always returned to his major preoccupation, France. He was 'of France' and could not disassociate himself from his people. . . ."[21] After allowing him a few weeks to settle into his new home and recover from the traumatic experiences of the past months, Reynal and Hitchcock began to urge Saint-Exupéry to write again, insisting that he must take up the defence of France after her fall. Saint-Exupéry at first resisted the idea, unwilling to write to command and indignant at the suggestion that his country needed any justification. Soon, however, he began to recognize that some strong voice must speak for France, amidst the welter of slander and vilification which was being spoken and written about his country. He must speak too, to convince America to enter the struggle, in order to counteract the strong isolationist movement which was growing. He therefore began to work on what would become *Pilote de guerre*. Bernard Lamotte, his old friend from student days in Paris and now established in New York, would illustrate the book, and Lewis Galantière would again be his translator.

At this time Saint-Exupéry was increasingly unwell, troubled still by the injuries from his Guatemala crash. In July, while visiting Jean Renoir in Hollywood, Saint-Exupéry actually fainted and, much concerned, his friends sent him to a specialist, who discovered that an operation was necessary to correct persistent dislocations. While convalescing from this operation in Pierre de Lazareff's Hollywood home, Saint-Exupéry had the leisure to read through all the voluminous notes of his "posthumous work," the future *Citadelle*. This perhaps helped him to crystallize his ideas, for when he returned to New York he began to work on the new book in earnest.

In November Consuelo arrived in New York. Since Saint-Exupéry had sent her south during the exodus of early 1940, she had been living with a community of artists in a village in the Alps. She did, in fact, publish a book about this experience, entitled *Oppède* or *Kingdom of the Rocks*. In it one can find references to Saint-Exupéry or echoes of his ideas, and she describes herself as "waiting for a flying knight."[22] In New York Saint-Exupéry set her up in her own apartment near his for, although he still felt responsibility for her, he had long ago renounced trying to share life with her.

In 1941 Saint-Exupéry published only an article for *Harper's Bazaar,* in which he described the "Books I Remember." Amongst these were Anderson's *Fairy Tales* and Jules Verne's *Indes noires* which, as we have seen, may have had direct influence on his earlier works.[23] Certain books he always carried with him: the philosophers, Pascal and Descartes, and the poets Baudelaire and Rilke. Significantly, the contemporary playwright whom Saint-Exupéry most admired was Jean Giraudoux, who is probably the modern French writer who uses the language to its richest and fullest potential. Saint-Exupéry was so devoted to the purity of the language that he apparently refused to learn English while he was in the United States lest the study of a second language should weaken his awareness of the language in which he was writing. Meanwhile, Saint-Exupéry was working on the manuscript of the book requested by his publishers, while continuously adding to the notes for the eventual *Citadelle*.

The year 1942 was marked by the publication of *Flight to Arras* in January, by his "Letter to Young Americans," published in the *Senior Scholastic* in May, and then by "An Open Letter to Frenchmen Everywhere," in the *New York Times Magazine* in November. Also in May, Saint-Exupéry finally accepted an invitation to give lectures in Montréal. This lecture tour, which was supposed to last two days, caused him the aggravation of being forced to wait for a visa to reenter the United States which the organizers had naively thought unnecessary. Saint-Exupéry appealed to his editor, Curtice Hitchcock, to intervene and soon he was back in New York.

Pilote de guerre

Flight to Arras, which was published in its English edition in early 1942, is a unique work—intense, passionate, and almost impossible to define. Saint-Exupéry's editors had told him that he could make Americans understand what had happened to France and uphold their belief in her. As Fleury says, Saint-Exupéry wanted "to purify the idea which Americans imagined of France" and for him this work had the value of bearing witness.[24] In his driving hope of making the world understand his country, of holding up her essence for everyone to see, Saint-Exupéry starts wisely and simply with the account of how he discovered that essential himself, through serving his country, seeing her suffer, and then pledging himself to her spirit. From the deceptively quiet opening passages of the briefing for the flight over Arras, the book gradually develops in swelling crescendo, through the agonizing awareness of the exodus and of the physical defeat of France, to a hymn not only to Saint-Exupéry's country but to all mankind, and finally to his own personal credo, as he discovers it.

Pilote de guerre (the French title) is as difficult to summarize as it is to define, moving subtly from factual account to philosophical meditation. Interwoven into the skeleton of events are the thoughts and meditations of the pilot, as he accepts the almost certain threat of death in his "sacrificed mission" and then gradually comes to know both himself and his country through this liberating acceptance. At first everything has the quiet, orderly security of a classroom, as Saint-Exupéry sits talking to his companions. Soon he and his navigator, Dutertre, are called before Commandant Alias, who must send them on a hopeless mission to preserve the pattern of war, while everything is disintegrating about them. Saint-Exupéry seeks the images to describe the otherwise inexpressible chaos of that time, and he sees it symbolized in the clocks that have all stopped and the water running to waste from the village fountains.

Saint-Exupéry expects to die, as so many of his comrades already have, but he wants to understand for what he must die. He promises himself, if he survives the mission, a quiet walk in "his village to meditate and discover the answer." It is this pensive walk that evening, after his almost miraculous survival of the mission over Arras, which carries his long meditation exultantly to the discovery of himself and of his country, and to his affirmation of belief in mankind and in the civilization of which he and his country are born. Yet, within the vaulting arch of this meditation, from its first promise to its fulfillment after the accomplished mission, there are many stages, and many interruptions for material considerations of the flight.

Descriptions of the war pilot's mission start with the actual preparations for the flight, the briefing, then the dressing in all the special equipment. Yet immediately, the spiritual significance takes over from the factual, and this strapping on of the equipment becomes the ceremonial donning of sacramental garments for the sacrifice to which Saint-Exupéry feels himself destined. As Saint-Exupéry climbs into his plane the trained habits of his craft take over, and he rediscovers his identity in his familiar responsibilities.

For awhile the flight is strangely peaceful as they fly north over the chaos below, the burning villages and roads glutted with refugees. In this deceptive peace of this flight, Saint-Exupéry has time to meditate upon this war, comparing its "false adventure" to the "true adventure" of his room in Orconte,[25] for adventure "depends on the richness of the bonds which it establishes" (76).

As Saint-Exupéry meditates upon this war, which is an illness, he becomes aware of his country in a death agony beneath him. Everything is breaking apart and losing its meaning. Saint-Exupéry, already rebutting the criticisms which will later be made of France, proclaims his country's intense good will in continuing to "play the game" against all reason: "I will hear foreigners reproaching France for the . . . villages which have not burned, for the men who have not died. But it is . . . exactly the contrary which strikes me so hard. It is our immense good will in covering our eyes and our ears. . . . It is to play the game that our men are dying" (93). The terrible exodus is draining the lifeblood from the very body of France, drawing her people away from the towns and villages where their life had meaning. The hopeless thousands struggling down the congested roads become the embodiment of defeat; and Saint-Exupéry has a sudden vision of a France that is losing its inner substance.

As Saint-Exupéry flies on toward Arras, he tries to analyze victory, which binds together, and defeat, which divides. The very face of France seems to have disintegrated in the division of defeat. Yet Saint-Exupéry again refuses the judgment of the outside world. "One must not judge France on the effects of being crushed . . . (but) on her consent to sacrifice" (137). France could not refuse to fight, even to avoid defeat, so she accepted the role of the vanguard which must die. Yet, paradoxically, defeat can become a pathway to resurrection: "I know that to create a tree, one condemns a seed to perish. The first act of resistance is always a losing one. . . . A tree will perhaps come from it, as from a seed (138).

As the plane draws close to Arras, Saint-Exupéry realizes the full acceptance of death, which constitutes war, and he once again rejects the judgment of those who would condemn France. For his beloved Group, which is melting away "like wax in the fire," he declares, "We are fighting in the name of a cause which we believe to be a common cause" (143). Affirming that there is a truth higher than the concepts of intelligence, he declares: "Something passes through us and governs us, which I experience without grasping it yet . . . I do not die to oppose invasion, for there is no shelter. I do not die to save an honor which I refuse to consider at stake. . . . Nor do I die out of despair. . . . And I shall accept" (145).

The plane approaches Arras, and Saint-Exupéry can now see the great tree of flames going up from the burning city. As he realizes what little chance he has of surviving, he thinks of the security of his childhood and, as he seems to move unscathed among the anti-aircraft fire, he recollects the childhood game when, with his brother and sisters, he used to try to run between the raindrops.[26] For awhile he is tempted into a kind of desperate hope, and he can even admire the strange beauty of the pattern traced by the shells rising slowly from the guns. Dazzled by the visual splendor, he feels strangely immune.

Suddenly the plane is struck. The beauty is still there, but all reasonable hope has gone. It is in this ultimate moment of confrontation with death that Saint-Exupéry's long meditation breaks through to a full realization of his beliefs and values. First he asserts that the body does not count for man; rather, man is what he does: "You reside in your act. Your action is you. . . . Your body is of you, it no longer is you" (169). Then Saint-Exupéry expresses one of his key ideas: the *exchange*. As a father gives his body to the flames to save his son from the fire, so each person will exchange himself for that which he holds most precious, and at this point his significance becomes dazzling. Saint-Exupéry declares that, projected forth from his body by loss of all hope, he lacks for nothing. Though he had confronted death several times before, he realized that he first learned this truth from his young brother who died courageously at the age of fourteen. Again comes one of Saint-Exupéry's key ideas: "When the body breaks apart, the essential is revealed. Man is only a knot of relationships" (172).

Miraculously, the plane continues to fly and, after this moment of supreme renunciation, Saint-Exupéry feels a resurrection. With each moment that he continues to be alive, he is filled with the joy of life. The passion of life fills him like a spring and he proclaims that the enemy fire is forging him and his comrades, as the bombardment of Madrid had forged that city.[27]

From this point of approach to death and then resurrection, the book reaches a new level of philosophical thought, where we can find many of the ideas which Saint-Exupéry had been slowly evolving for years in his notes for *Citadelle*. As he thinks of all his comrades in the Group or in the Line, he considers the "density" of their being and the "bonds" which create the "substance" of each man. Once again, Saint-Exupéry protests his need to participate: "Who am I if I do not participate. In order to be, I need to participate. I am nourished by the quality of my comrades . . ." (185). Again he rejects the possibility of any post of safety, for "it is only the liberty not to *be*. Each obligation makes one *become*" (186). Because Saint-Exupéry had staked his own flesh in the mission over Arras, he now feels that he has become even more intensely a part of the Group and has acquired the simple right just to *be*, "to participate. To be linked. To receive and to give. To be more than myself. To attain that fullness which swells so strongly in me" (188).

Flying slowly back towards his base, Saint-Exupéry thinks of those comrades who form the Group, as others had formed the Line. As Daurat had forced his men to discover the best in themselves, so does Commandant Alias force the pilots to "become" what they must be. Each man is strongly formed by the ties with his world which weave through him. And, in his strong, personal idiom, Saint-Exupéry declares his substance and his loyalty: "I am of the Group II/33. I am of my country. And all those of the group are of that country. . . ." (191). ("To be *of,*" in the sense of "to come from," "to be made of," "to be one with. . . .")

The writing has now moved to an intensely philosophical, almost mystical level, shot through with the highly personal idiom of key words which Saint-Exupéry had evolved and which will become so dominant in *Citadelle.* There are several richly complex key passages, alternating still with the simple conversation between crew mates, with Commandant Alias, or with the farmer. As Saint-Exupéry accepts responsibility for the people of Arras he becomes bonded to them: "I am only linked with those to whom I give. I only understand the one I espouse" (194).

Saint-Exupéry issues forth from the acceptance of death as from a sacrament, filled with solemn, lasting jubilation. He and his crew mates have matured as though after years of meditation in a monastery. Now they hasten towards the warmth of their comrades' welcome and the communing in the evening bread. This warmth is symbolized in two images: the spiritual warmth of Christmas night, and the mysterious, invisible warmth of a fire for a blind man; and these are images which Saint-Exupéry will often use. The reward to which they hasten is that of essential love: "a network of bonds which brings us to fulfillment" (200).

At last Saint-Exupéry is home in his farm billets, having supper with the farmer's family. As the farmer cuts the rich, country bread, knowing that the next day may bring invasion or death, the gesture takes on a ceremonial significance. As in *Terre des hommes* Saint-Exupéry sang a hymn to water, so now he sings one to man's daily bread:

> Wheat is something other than a bodily food. . . . Bread plays so many roles. We have learned to recognize in bread, an instrument of the community of men, because of bread broken together . . . an image of the grandeur of work, because of bread gained by the sweat of the brow . . . the essential instrument of pity, because of the bread which one gives . . . the savor of shared bread has no equal. . . . It is for bread as it is for the oil in lamps. It is changed into light. (203)

It is for this that Saint-Exupéry has fought, "to preserve the quality of a light, . . . for the special radiance into which bread is transfigured in the homes of my land" (203).

Aware suddenly of the precious heritage of the village, personified in the farmer's family, Saint-Exupéry feels responsible for this invisible treasure. He walks out for the "conversation with his village" which he had promised himself, and it becomes a deep, philosophical meditation, prefiguring and echoing all of the wealth of ideas in *Citadelle*. He builds up image upon image to establish his humanist faith in Man, which is the foundation of his belief in his country: with time, the buried seed will triumph; with vision, the tumbled stones will form a cathedral; through errors, the sculptor will mould his creation. Here resides the very principle of victory for "whoever bears in his heart a cathedral to build is already victor. Victory is the fruit of love" (207). Here, Saint-Exupéry proclaims the substance of Man, too long neglected in favor of Intelligence: it is his essential Being. Eventually, each one moves where the weight of his being carries him, another exuperian theme. But what must he, Saint-Exupéry, be and weigh, to save his country? "Tomorrow, we shall enter into night. . . . I want my country to be—in her spirit and her flesh—when the day returns. To act for the good of my country, I shall have to bring my weight to bear each instant in that direction, with all my love" (209). Thus Saint-Exupéry sets rules for himself, in the dark night of loss, vowing never to deny his people or to disassociate himself from his country in her defeat. He accepts this responsibility for his country as essential, in order to be. "Each one is alone responsible for all. I understand for the first time one of the mysteries of the religion from which came the civilization which I claim as mine: 'to bear the sins of men.' And each one bears the sins of all men" (213).

As Saint-Exupéry meditates in his village, he realizes that, although he has kept the image of his civilization, he has lost sight of the "rules of the game" which create it and so he has lost its fervor. So he seeks the keystone of his civilization and finds it at last in Man. Remembering the moment of revelation over Arras, Saint-Exupéry understands: "Man appeared. He settled in my place. . . . He looked at the scattered crowd and saw a people. His people. Man, the common measure between that people and myself" (219).

This new awareness of Man, or humankind, within him gives a feeling of a "miraculous kinship" with all peoples and all races. (It is important to notice the frequent change between "Man" and "man" in this meditation.) Man is not simply a sum of individuals but rather the expression of the civilization of which he is the essence, as a cathedral is the expression of stones. "It is he (Man) the essence of my culture. He is the key of my community. He is the principle of my victory" (222).

The philosophical meditation now intensifies and grows more complex as Saint-Exupéry reaches the questions of free will and of God. His civilization delivers man by "teaching him thirst and tracing a road to a well" (223). As a stone is freed by gravity, so is man freed by the "invisible slopes of love" which move him. Contemplating God through man, his civilization has made of each man "the Ambassador of the same prince" (224). In God and through God, men are equal: "Expressing God, they were equal in their rights. Serving God, they were equal in their duties" (225).

Moving from one revelation to another, Saint-Exupéry proclaims the principles of his civilization in progressive steps: "My civilization, inheriting from God, made men equal in Man . . . founded the respect for man through the individuals . . . made men brothers in Man. My civilization, heir of God, preached also self-respect that is the respect for Man through oneself, . . . made each one responsible for all men, and all men responsible for each one" (225–28). And so Saint-Exupéry perceives the significance of Liberty: "It is the liberty of a growth of a tree in the lines of force of its seed. It is the climate for the ascension of Man" (229).

Yet the rich heritage of this civilization has been squandered by a false conception of humanism which has forgotten the essentials. Language has become a barrier to essential acts, and by talking about the "collectivity" and the "individual" we have lost sight of the essential "beings" or entities, such as country, craft, civilization, and religion, which can only be "founded" within us by commitment: "A Being is not of the empire of language but that of acts. Our humanism has neglected acts. . . . The essential act here has received a name. It is sacrifice . . . (which is) a gift of oneself to the Being of which one claims to be a part" (233).

By losing sight of both God and of Man, our civilization has falsified even the essential concepts of equality, liberty, charity, and fraternity. Equality must be within something; liberty is not vague license; charity must honor God through man; and fraternity is more than mutual tolerance. Emptied of their real substance, these words have led us to contradictions, to anarchy, and to totalitarianism. Deprived of these entities, these "beings" in which they can find their meaning, as do stones within a cathedral, men have remained scattered and meaningless. Thus the war is reduced to these terms:

"I am no longer surprised that a pile of stones, which is heavy, should overpower loose stones" (240).

It is in this moment of defeat, however, that Saint-Exupéry rediscovers his strength and that of his country: "I am the strongest, if I find myself again. If our Humanism re-establishes Man. If we know how to found our Community, and if, to found it, we use the only instrument which is effective: sacrifice. . . . I am the strongest, because the tree is stronger than the materials in the earth. . . . The cathedral is more radiant than the pile of stones" (241). Declaring that he is "of" a civilization which has chosen Man as its keystone, Saint-Exupéry then proclaims his personal credo, by which he will live, fight, and die: "I believe that the prime importance of Man founds the only Equality and the only Liberty which have any significance . . . and I believe that Liberty is that of the ascension of Man. . . . I believe that my civilization names Charity the sacrifice given for Man, to establish his reign. Charity is a gift to Man. . . . I will fight for Man. Against his enemies. But also against myself" (242–44). After his long meditation, Saint-Exupéry returns to his comrades. Once again, the Group must move. Tomorrow it will seem that they are defeated, but they will only await the moment of rebirth. "The vanquished must remain silent. Like seed" (248).

Response in America and France

Flight to Arras was published in New York early in 1942, dedicated to Commandant Alias and to Saint-Exupéry's friends of the Group. The immediate response in America was generally very positive, and critics noted the radiant poetry and poignant sincerity of the work. Katherine Wood, of the *New York Herald Tribune,* recognized Saint-Exupéry's stance of solidarity with his country: "In a patriotism as profound and passionate as its expression is restrained, Saint-Exupéry finds himself one with his country in its glory and in its humiliation, its weakness and error and its immortal hope."[28] In the February review, *Time* declared that *Flight to Arras* was "The most important book yet written about this war . . . a magic text, at times almost Biblical, of why men fight and how they feel in the presence of death."[29] The reviewer also saw in the book "a personal proof of the profoundest of Christian texts: Except a corn of wheat fall into the ground and die, it abideth alone, but if it

die, it bringeth forth much fruit." Strangely, Galantière, the translator, was among the few to question the book's influence on American readers, feeling that the response to their questions about France
was too abstract.[30] Yet the *Atlantic Monthly* suggested that, together
with Churchill's speeches, the book was the best answer which the
democracies had discovered to Hitler's *Mein Kampf.*[31]

Surprisingly, *Pilote de guerre* was authorized by the Nazis for
publication in Vichy France, in December 1942. The censors pre-
sumably did not understand the true message of the book, asking
only that a direct reference to Hitler be suppressed. At first the
Vichy press was enthusiastic, reading into the book a philosophy
of resignation, but soon they recognized the true message of fervent
patriotism and courageous hope, and the book was banned, as a
"Gaullist manifesto."[32] Soon clandestine editions appeared in the
country, published first in Lyon, by Gaston Rigby, who was caught
by the Gestapo, and then in Lille, by Paul Angelo. After the Liberation, when *Pilote de guerre* could finally appear openly, the bare
covers of those clandestine editions, published for beliefs and not
for money, prompted one newspaper to write: "It is not merchandise,
it is a masterpiece, and masterpieces are always naked . . . it has
reached us a little like the *Chansons de Geste* (epic poems) of the
Middle Ages."[33]

It is moving to note another book by an aviator, published on
the same date and by the same publishers as *Flight to Arras,* Richard
Hillary's *Last Enemy* (originally titled *Falling through Space*). Hillary,
an English pilot terribly disfigured and maimed by burns in the
Battle of Britain, had been unable to fly again. Sent on a mission
to the United States in 1941, he was introduced to Saint-Exupéry
by Galantière. Saint-Exupéry presented him to his editors and even
wanted to write a preface for his book. Hillary was much influenced
by Saint-Exupéry, for he also had the urgent need to participate
before he could bear witness. His one book is written to justify "my
right to fellowship with my dead and to the friendship of those
. . . still living who would go on fighting" for the ideals for which
their comrades had died.[34] It contains some passages similar to Saint-
Exupéry's writing: "It is only in the air that the pilot can grasp
that . . . flash of knowledge . . . that matures him beyond his
years, only in the air that he knows suddenly he is a man in a world
of men."[35] Like Saint-Exupéry, Hillary later returned valiantly to
active flying and he died in action in January 1943.

Articles in the American Press

In May 1942, the *Senior Scholastic* magazine published Saint-Exupéry's "Message to Young Americans," translated by Lewis Galantière. Until recently the original French text was presumed lost, but the 1978 volume of *Icare* published one which Consuelo de Saint-Exupéry had rediscovered. In this short article, Saint-Exupéry succinctly offers his philosophy of life to the young Americans who must prepare for war, after Pearl Harbor. If man is to fight for liberty, he must first know himself, as he contributes to the community of which he is a part. Saint-Exupéry gives the essential "device" in creating the greater entity which will in turn enrich the individual, and that is sacrifice, the free gift of self. Finally, Saint-Exupéry recalls his years with the Line in North Africa and South America, realizing that what enriched him there were the hard times, those moments of struggle shared with his comrades.

During 1942 Saint-Exupéry moved several times to other homes outside New York City. With Consuelo, he rented a villa in Westport, Connecticut, then another in Eton Neck, Northport, New York. It was here that Saint-Exupéry apparently was finally persuaded by Consuelo to take some English lessons; and his teacher, Adèle Bréaux, has written an account of her brief association with her famous pupil.[36] However, he continued to protest that he would learn only the most basic, practical English, as any real study of another language might spoil his command of his own.

Although Saint-Exupéry was fully occupied with his writing, he remained on call for the War Department because of his military and aeronautical knowledge. That summer of 1942 he evolved a dramatic scheme to rescue Général Giraud, who had just escaped from prison camp, and let him lead French troops in a landing in North Africa. When Saint-Exupéry persuaded Galantière to present this plan to some influential friends in Washington, their violent reaction was only proof that Saint-Exupéry had come too close to guessing secret plans for the African landing. Yet soon one of the top officers in American military aviation came to see Saint-Exupéry and, shortly thereafter, the military authorities had assembled detailed information on landing fields and flying conditions in North Africa.

In November 1942 the first allied landing took place in North Africa; and in France, the authority of the Vichy government in the "free zone" had expired. Saint-Exupéry was moved to write his "Open Letter to Frenchmen" which was published in the *New York Times Magazine.* As France seemed to disappear totally in the darkness, like a silent ship at night, the spiritual flame of the country is kept alight by those within the country, who "nourish it with their very substance, as with candle-wax."[37] Those outside France in her suffering can serve her, but not represent her, for "there is no common measure between the role of a soldier and that of a hostage."[38] So Saint-Exupéry calls on all Frenchmen to be reconciled in their differences so that they might serve their country together. As he had proclaimed in *Pilote de guerre,* France must be saved both in her spirit and in her body: "Of what value is the spiritual heritage if there are no more heirs. What purpose does the heir serve, if the Spirit is dead?"[39] Where Frenchmen had been divided over the role of the Vichy government, now that the Vichy puppets had fallen, there was no more reason to argue. Saint-Exupéry exhorts Frenchmen to abandon any partisan spirit and to unite. There is no more room for rivalry, for "the only places to be taken are those of soldiers and, perhaps, quiet beds in some little cemetery in North Africa."[40] Saint-Exupéry denies any importance to the question of party or leader, declaring, "The true chief is France, who is condemned to silence."[41] For once, Saint-Exupéry names de Gaulle as he expresses his willingness to follow any military leader in the freeing of his country. "We know about General de Gaulle as we do about General Giraud, what they think about authority: they serve. They are the first of the servants. That is sufficient for us."[42]

The partisan quarrels of many French exiles in New York had given a false image of France, and Saint-Exupéry calls all those who have remained silent to prove the true state of mind of the French by sending a telegram to Cordell Hull: "We beg the honor of serving in any form that may be. We desire the military mobilization of all the French in the United States. We accept in advance any organization deemed desirable. But, hating any spirit of division among Frenchmen, we simply wish it to be outside politics."[43] And Saint-Exupéry recalls how in the Group, after battle, he would drink with comrades of many political persuasions, "and we touched glasses with deep affection."[44]

Despite some misunderstandings caused by the translation, the effect of this "Call to Frenchmen" was considerable in America, where many editorials commented on it. Delange quotes one such editorial by Stanley Walker: "When historians will start to recount the story of the resurrection of France and of the French Spirit, the words of Saint-Exupéry must have a high and honorable place."[45] In his study of Saint-Exupéry, Maxwell Smith expresses the opinion that: "this lofty and noble utterance served as a rallying call for many Frenchmen and helped to forge the union of all factions into what was later to become a revived French army of liberation."[46]

Lettre à un otage

In his "Call to Frenchmen," Saint-Exupéry had quietly stated that the only dream which he cherished was to rediscover the comrades of the Group II/33. Early in 1943 he would finally realize that wish, but first he would publish two more works which have taken an essential place in his writings: *Letter to a Hostage* and *The Little Prince.*

The slim booklet, *Lettre à un otage,* "one of the most exquisite of Saint-Exupéry's writings, both for purity of style and warmth of personal emotion,"[47] was first published in New York in 1943. The next year it appeared in the magazine *L'Arche* in Algiers where, according to Smith, the Information Service of the Provisional Government made multiple copies to be widely circulated. Finally, in December 1944, following the Liberation and after Saint-Exupéry's death, it was published by Gallimard in Paris, where it seemed to bring Saint-Exupéry's final message to his newly liberated countrymen.

The hostage to whom this long letter is addressed is essentially Léon Werth, an older, cherished friend in occupied France, who symbolizes for Saint-Exupéry all those held captive by the invading Nazis because, as a Jew, he is in special danger. In a larger way, it is also addressed to all the people of France, held hostage by the Nazis. In fact, the *Lettre à un otage* was originally intended to be a preface to a work on the Occupation by Léon Werth. The long, meditative epistle, divided into six sections, is rich with echoes of Saint-Exupéry's earlier writings on the war, the *Lettre aux Français* and *Pilote de guerre,* and the reader recognizes now familiar themes and images, refined and polished in a tauter text.

The opening section describes the falsely bright and cheerful Lisbon in which Saint-Exupéry found himself on his way to America, after the fall of France. There he sees all the rich refugees who so distress him, with their "remnants of identity." Strangely, Saint-Exupéry, who had so admired the old slave, Bark, refusing to "abdicate his identity"[48] amongst the desert Arabs, now seems almost repelled by these sad, safe refugees who try to retain some individual significance. Perhaps he feels too strongly the danger of becoming one of them himself, unless he can hold on to the rich treasure of memories and associations which make up his identity. Saint-Exupéry discovers that it is the certainty of return which keeps the traveler from becoming an emigrant. Saint-Exupéry illustrates this concept in a beautiful image of Breton sailors who were preparing their return to their fiancées from the moment they set sail to Cape Horn; the rich emigrants on board ship are like those Breton sailors bereft of their fiancées; "Then there begins the real journey, which is out of oneself" (20). This is the journey which Saint-Exupéry dreads making, for how can one reconstruct or replace "the heavy skein of memories within oneself?" Going alone into exile, he wants to feel the demands of long-cultivated friendship.

In the second section, Saint-Exupéry tries to discover those poles of his being which can help him survive exile without abdicating: "The essential is that there should remain somewhere that on which one has lived. And habits. And family celebration. And the house filled with memories. The essential is to live for the return" (25). Yet he feels threatened by the very fragility of those distant poles. If he loses them he will be in the true desert, after all his years in the Sahara.

Here Saint-Exupéry glimpses the mystery of the desert, and he begins a long, poetic evocation of that beloved desert. This passage, which at first appears unrelated, in fact illustrates Saint-Exupéry's concept of the invisible poles which magnetize and vitalize the otherwise empty space between them. Even the silences are different in the desert, signifying peace, plot, or mystery, and an invisible oasis can polarize the desert. Almost unreal poles magnetize from afar: the childhood home which Saint-Exupéry had recalled in the desert, and now a friend of whom one knows nothing except that he exists. "Thus you feel yourself stretched and vitalized by the magnetic fields which pull you or repell you, solicit or resist you. You are well-founded, well-determined, well-installed in the center of the cardinal directions" (29). In the desert, whether of sand or of exile, man is moved by invisible forces, for he is governed by the spirit. Saint-Exupéry declares, "I am worth, in the desert, what my divinities are worth" (29–30). These memories, friendships, and loyalties are his magnetic poles, and they all draw him to the essence of his country, giving him his own essence: "if I lived in a planet that was still alive, it was thanks to a few friends lost behind me in the night of France and who were beginning to be essential to me. France . . . was not for me an abstract goddess or an historian's concept, but indeed, a flesh on which I depended, a network of bonds which governed me, a combination of poles which founded the bent of my heart" (30). The awareness of these friends becomes a bright symbol of his country, as a lighthouse symbolizes a whole continent. As France seems to disappear into the darkness, like a ship at night, Saint-Exupéry is anxious for the fate of all these friends, on whom his own essence depends. He thinks especially of Léon Werth for, as long as he is alive somewhere, Saint-Exupéry can retain his own being: "Then only, walking afar in the empire of his friendship, which has no frontiers, I may feel that I am not an immigrant but a traveller" (32).

These are the magnetic poles of friendship, but what created them? The simple events which build such affections and, through them, the love of country, are the quiet miracles of life. In the third section, probably the best-known passage of the book, Saint-Exupéry remembers the uneventful, peaceful lunch by the river, which he had once shared with Léon Werth, and which now seems to him one of the "invisible celebrations" of life, nurturing an essential friendship. They had become aware of this special sense of celebration growing within them, as they drank with boatmen whom they invited from the river: "We tasted a kind of perfect state where, all desires being granted, we had nothing more to confide in each other" (38). In a humorous, self-indulgent exaggeration, Saint-Exupéry feels that all creation had somehow tended to that one perfect moment of fellowship, of almost religious communion.

Gradually, Saint-Exupéry and his old friend Werth, with their new friends the boatmen, feel a bond of understanding grow between them, so strong that they would have fought to save its substance. For want of better words, Saint-Exupéry defines that substance by the smile which they all exchange and share. Foreshadowing the secret which the Fox gives to the Little Prince, Saint-Exupéry writes: "The essential, most often, has no weight. Here the essential was, in appearance, only a smile" (41). Léon Werth considered this text sacred to their friendship and would not attempt to summarize it for fear of lessening it. He said simply that it is "the account of a miracle, a humble miracle. But it is all the miracle of friendship, of the quality of a smile and of a perfect hour."[49]

The intangible quality of a smile, which had for Saint-Exupéry defined the essence of that privileged moment of companionship, inspires the whole fourth section, which is "the story of another smile" (41). Caught by a group of militants while reporting on the Spanish Civil War, Saint-Exupéry could find no means of explaining his position as a journalist, as they did not understand his South-American Spanish, and he expected to be shot. As Saint-Exupéry asked by gestures for a cigarette, he gave a little smile: his guard responded with a smile, and "It was like the sunrise. . . . This miracle did not solve the drama, it quite simply effaced it, as light does to shadow" (52). Delivered by this smile, Saint-Exupéry suddenly felt his kinship with these men who, moments before, had seemed another species.

Then, most beautifully, Saint-Exupéry realizes how the human smile had always marked every significant event: "I entered their smile as, in other days (I entered) into our rescuers' (smile) in the Sahara. . . . The smile of rescuers, if I was stranded, the smile of the stranded, if I was the rescuer, I remember these also as a home-land where I felt so very happy" (55). It illumines every human exchange: "We come together in a smile beyond languages, castes and parties" and, however different our customs, we feel our fellowship.

In the fifth section, Saint-Exupéry moves to the proclamation of the essential quality of our civilization, which was being threatened by the Nazi power. A totalitarian tyranny might satisfy material needs, but never the spiritual needs, for those raised believing in the respect for man. In a long, passionate passage, which is the climax of the *Letter,* Saint-Exupéry proclaims the creed of the respect for Man, which is the touchstone of our civilization, as he had proclaimed it in *Pilote de guerre.* He condemns the totalitarian Nazi who wants everything to resemble him and who "refuses creative contradictions, ruins all hope of ascension, and founds for a thousand years, instead of man, the robot of an ant-heap" (60). To this soul-killing idea he contrasts our civilization which believes in the con-tinual ascension of man, and which recognizes the kinship of all men. "It is founded on the future, not on the past. . . . We are to each other as pilgrims who, along various paths, strive toward the same meeting-place" (60–61). It was that respect for Man, the condition of our ascension, which was in peril in the war.

To defend our civilization, to ensure our continued ascension, Saint-Exupéry calls for all to unite, forgetting all political squabbles. "We have tasted, in the hours of miracle, a certain quality of human relationship: there is the truth for us" (62). The vocation which commands us is "to found respect for Man" (62). Even if we do not agree with a man's reasoning, we must respect him on the level of the Spirit "if he is striving toward the same star" (63).

Confidently, Saint-Exupéry asserts that if the respect for Man is well rooted in men's hearts, there is no need to worry about political systems, for men will finally establish whatever system consecrates that respect. Idealistically, he believes that a civilization is founded first in its substance, rather than in its form. Returning again to a favorite image, he declares that this substance is like a blind desire for warmth, so that Man will feel his way along the path which leads to the fire.

In the final section, Saint-Exupéry returns in thought to his friend, Léon Werth, the companion who respects in him "the pilgrim of that fire." Their friendship is strong because they respect each other's differences: "You consider in me simply Man. You honor in me the ambassador of particular beliefs, customs and loves. If I differ from you, far from lessening you, I enrich you" (68).

Hoping always to return to the battle, Saint-Exupéry promises Werth, "If I fight again, I will fight a little for you. I need you in order to believe better in the coming of that smile" (69). In a passage rich in imagery and reminiscent of *Pilote de guerre* and of *Lettre aux Français,* he proclaims his passionate belonging to his country: "We are all of France as being of a tree, and I will serve your truth as you would have served mine. . . . We must free the provision of grain frozen by the snow of the German presence . . . we must make you free in the land where you have the fundamental right to thrust your roots" (70).

It is not only Werth who is hostage, but forty million Frenchmen. It is they who keep the flame burning, nourishing it by their very substance. To them, he declares his loyalty: "We cannot found France, we can only serve her." In his anguish at the suffering of his countrymen, Saint-Exupéry cries out, "There is no common measure between the profession of a soldier and the profession of a hostage. You are saints" (71).

Chapter Eight
Allegory and Apotheosis: *Le Petit Prince*

Just at the time that the *Lettre à un otage* was being published, Saint-Exupéry was coming closer to realizing his cherished desire to return to battle. In January 1943 Général Béthouard arrived in New York from North Africa, on a mission from Général Giraud to obtain weapons. Saint-Exupéry immediately went to see Béthouard and, in March, finally received sailing orders. On 1 April he was officially mobilized into the Béthouard Mission, and he sailed a few days later for North Africa.

Almost simultaneously with his sailing, came the publication of *Le Petit Prince* on 6 April. This book, so often mistaken for "only" a children's book, is in fact a delicate crystallization of Saint-Exupéry's philosophy of life, in allegorical form. The success of this book has been so great that Saint-Exupéry is often thought of simply as "the author of the *Little Prince*," and the book itself has become a beginning French reader in America. It is, indeed, sad that such sensitive, exquisitely wrought writing should be subjected to the impatient deciphering of beginning students, as a butterfly being dissected to see what makes it fly. As Maxwell Smith says: "To analyze in detail so lovely and fragile a tale would be like removing the petals of a rose to discover its charm."[1]

It is perhaps surprising to find this gentle allegory written at a time when Saint-Exupéry was so agonizingly concerned for his country, yet there are many signs of the gradual growth of the figure of the Little Prince in the author's thoughts. On a copy of *Pilote de guerre*, Saint-Exupéry sketched a child standing on a cloud, watching the burning of Arras. To the suggestion that the child be made to reveal his thoughts, Saint-Exupéry replied, "No, not his thoughts. They are too melancholy."[2] Fleury also mentions the frequent sketching of *un petit bonhomme* leaning from a cloud;[3] and, on a letter to Léon Werth, reproduced in *Icare,* there is again "a little fellow" on a cloud, quietly watching a country road, while a Messerschmitt plane approaches menacingly.[4] Reynal, the editor, claims that the book originated in a drawing of a little winged figure, made as a joke on the margin of Lamotte's sketch for the illustrations in *Flight to Arras:* Reynal kept urging Saint-Exupéry to write a book on the figure, finally suggesting a children's book for Christmas 1942. Yet, as Pélissier points out, the book rapidly progresses from its childlike beginning to become a philosophical fable.[5] Just as the drawings of the Little Prince can be traced back over several years, it will be seen that many of the ideas expressed so poignantly in *Le Petit Prince* have their source in earlier writings.

Le Petit Prince

Le Petit Prince begins with the well-known pair of drawings which the narrator, Saint-Exupéry himself, discouraged in his childhood artistic attempts, now uses whenever he meets an apparently lucid adult to see if he really has understanding. Drawing number one is of a boa constrictor which has swallowed an elephant whole; most grown-ups see a hat shape, for they cannot see beyond the exterior. For them, he produces his drawing number two, the open snake, so that they may see the elephant inside. Now that they have failed the test, Saint-Exupéry comes down to their level and talks to them of politics, bridge, and neckties, instead of virgin forests and stars. So the theme is proclaimed that "grown-ups" have lost the gift of perception and only those who keep the child alive within them can continue to see through the exterior to the essence which lies within. As the *Time* review of the book recognized, this "fairy-tale for grown-ups . . . challenges man the adult and deplores the loss of the child in man."[6] Saint-Exupéry laments that "Grown-ups never understand anything alone, and it is tiring for children always, always to give them explanations" (10), a comment which recurs as a leitmotif, with variations, at the end of many chapters.

After living for many years alone in the world of grown-ups, Saint-Exupéry is stranded one day in the desert, trying to repair his plane, when suddenly the Little Prince miraculously appears and demands "Please, draw me a sheep." Accepting the mystery, Saint-Exupéry starts to draw but first he sketches his drawing number one, and the Little Prince immediately protests that he does not want an elephant in a boa constrictor. At last, here is someone who does understand; and so Saint-Exupéry starts to draw a sheep for him. The Little Prince rejects each attempt until, at last, Saint-Exupéry simply draws a box in which the sheep might be. Then the Little Prince is content for he sees the sheep inside the box and even sees that it is asleep. So begins the gentle friendship between the Little Prince and the narrator, Saint-Exupéry. Little by little, the pilot learns about his new friend's life, but always by indirect allusion, for the Little Prince never tells about himself and never answers questions, although he is always asking them. Soon Saint-Exupéry discovers that his little visitor fell from the sky and that the planet from which he came was very small.

As Saint-Exupéry puzzles over the Little Prince's appearance, he concludes that he must have come from one of the small asteroids. To satisfy the grown-ups, Saint-Exupéry gives the number of the asteroid, B 612, but he would rather have begun his story like a fairy-tale: "Once upon a time there was a little prince who lived in a planet hardly any bigger than he was and who needed a friend" (20).

One day Saint-Exupéry discovers the story of the baobab trees on the Little Prince's planet. Their powerful seeds take root and, unless one carefully weeds them out each day, soon giant trees will take over the planet. Besides the daily discipline of weeding baobab shoots, there was also the responsibility of sweeping out the planet's three volcanoes to avoid chimney fires. It would be easy to analyze this episode as a morality tale but, following Maxwell Smith's advice, we will not tear the rose apart.

On the fourth day, Saint-Exupéry realizes the Little Prince's melancholy, revealed by an ingenuous reference to the sunsets which the Prince could see so often on his tiny planet. The Little Prince confides that when he is sad he likes to watch a sunset; and one day he had watched forty-three sunsets. Nostalgically, Saint-Exupéry wishes that, like the Little Prince, he could just move his chair to see the sun setting in France, but "sadly, France is much too far away" (27).

Suddenly, on the fifth day, Saint-Exupéry discovers the secret of the Little Prince's melancholy; it is the beautiful, temperamental Rose, which grew unexpectedly on his planet and so tormented him with her whims that he finally decided to leave. When the Little Prince first mentions his Rose, however, Saint-Exupéry is so concerned with the plane which he still cannot repair, and with his dwindling water supply, that he casually dismisses the Little Prince's questions about flowers, thorns, and sheep, with the almost unpardonable remark, "I am concerned with serious things" (28). Immediately, the Little Prince accuses him of speaking like a grownup and compares him to the red-faced man he had met, who loved nobody and cared only for numbers. He, declares the Little Prince, was not a man but a mushroom! Then the Little Prince launches into a passionate, beautiful proclamation of what is truly important in life: "And if I know a flower unique in the world, which exists nowhere except on my planet and which a little sheep can annihilate in one stroke . . . without realizing what he is doing, isn't that important?" (29). Suddenly he bursts into tears, and Saint-Exupéry, recalled to a realization of what is truly important, forgets his tools, his plane, thirst, and death. "There was on one star, on one planet, my planet the Earth, a little prince to console" (30). And he takes him in his arms to console him.

Soon Saint-Exupéry comes to know about the beautiful, coquettish Rose who had tormented the Little Prince by her moody vanity. Only when, driven to despair by her tantrums, the Little Prince had decided to leave his planet, did the Rose finally admit that she loved him; and as the Little Prince now recognizes he was foolish not to have understood: "I ought to have judged her on acts and not on words. She perfumed me and illumined me. . . . I ought to have guessed her affection behind her poor wiles. . . . But I was too young to know how to love" (33).

Many critics maintain that the Rose symbolizes Consuelo, and this theory was encouraged by Consuelo herself. However, it must be remembered that Saint-Exupéry had also deeply loved his fiancée, Louise de Vilmorin, when he was indeed "too young" to understand. Carlo François points out an interesting parallelism between the description of the Rose and that of Geneviève in the semiautobiographical *Courrier sud,* written before Saint-Exupéry met Consuelo.[7] It is also conceivable that Saint-Exupéry had loved other women, of whom we know nothing, so that the Rose could represent a composite portrait. She is best understood, perhaps, in the old, literary tradition of the *Roman de la rose,* as an allegorical image of the loved one. As the Little Prince grows in wisdom, he learns to love simply for what the Rose is in her essence, and she becomes unique for him because of his love for her.

The Little Prince sets out on his travels, aided by a flight of migratory birds, and he visits a number of other planets before he reaches the Earth of men. Each planet is inhabited by a unique, solitary figure, who comes to represent some aspect of men, foible or quality. There is first the King, who eagerly adopts the Little Prince as a subject whom he can command. He believes that he rules over the whole universe, obeyed by the very stars, but his authority is reasonable, based only on what can be expected. When the Little Prince, named minister of justice by the King, protests that there is nobody on the planet to judge, the monarch replies: "You will judge yourself. . . . It is the most difficult. . . . If you succeed in judging yourself, you must be a true sage" (41).

On the second planet the Little Prince finds the Vain Man, who sees in his visitor only an admirer. The Little Prince soon tires of applauding him and travels on, declaring, "Grown-ups are decidedly very strange" (44). On the third planet he meets the pathetic Drunk-ard, caught in his vicious circle of drinking to forget that he is ashamed of drinking. The Little Prince is even more puzzled.

Arriving on the fourth planet, the Little Prince meets a more formidable species, the Businessman (the English term is used in the French text). This man can do nothing but count his riches, uncertain even of what he thinks he possesses. To the Little Prince's insistent question, he replies that he is counting those "little gold things in the sky which make the lazy folk dream" (47), for he believes that he owns the stars, simply by writing down their numbers. Like the King, he believes that the stars are his; like the Drunkard, he is caught in a vicious circle, for he explains that the purpose of being rich in stars is simply to buy more stars. At every interruption by the Little Prince, he repeats, "I am serious, I have no time to waste." Here, indeed, is the red-faced man, the "mush-room" whom the Little Prince had accused Saint-Exupéry of resem-bling. The Little Prince finds the Businessman rather foolish in his belief that he can possess anything by recording the number on a paper. He remembers his own precious possessions, the flower which he waters and the volcanoes which he sweeps, realizing "It is useful to my volcanoes, it is useful to my flower, that I should possess them" (49).

Traveling on to the fifth planet, the Little Prince finds the enig-matic, poetic figure of the Lamplighter who, as his planet turns faster and faster, must continuously light and extinguish his lamps.

For the Little Prince, this seemingly senseless work has a meaning and is useful because it is beautiful: "When he lights his lamp, it is as though he brought to life another star, or a flower" (49–50). This man, who would seem ridiculous to the King or to the Businessman, is lovable to the Little Prince because he is faithful to his task. He alone does not seem ridiculous, for he is concerned with something other than himself. The Lamplighter is perhaps related to the church sacristan mentioned in *Pilote de guerre:* "the love of his God, in the sacristan, becomes the love of lighting the candles . . . he is satisfied to make the candelabras flower."[8] The Lamplighter is, in fact, for the Little Prince, the only one of his new acquaintances of whom he could have made his friend.

On the sixth planet, the Little Prince meets the Geographer, who spends his time writing about what others have discovered, while he stays at his desk. Here is truly the antithesis of Saint-Exupéry's conviction that only by participating can he have the right to speak; and, in his journal, Saint-Exupéry had commented on the Geographer who "separates thought from action."[9] Here, however, the Little Prince meets some new ideas: he has his first inkling of mortality, when the Geographer refuses to record flowers because they are "ephemeral"; and when the Geographer defines that term as meaning "threatened with future disappearance," the Little Prince knows his first feeling of regret and thinks of his flower. Especially, it is the Geographer who recommends that he visit the Earth, which has a good reputation.

The Earth is, therefore, for the Little Prince, the seventh planet, a number of perhaps biblical significance. Perhaps biblically again, he is greeted by the Serpent, who speaks in enigmas: "I am more powerful than the finger of a king. . . . I can carry you away further than a ship" (60). He promises to help if some day the Little Prince yearns to return to his planet. Like Saint-Exupéry the Little Prince is looking for mankind. He inquires of a flower, who considers men too rootless, then climbs a mountain peak, where only the echo answers him.

Suddenly in his quest he comes to a garden filled with roses and he is deeply disappointed, for his Rose had always said that she was unique. Reflecting sorrowfully, "I believed myself rich in a unique flower and I possess only an ordinary rose" (66), the Little Prince lies down in the grass and weeps.

Now the little Fox appears, who will console the Little Prince and teach him his secrets, as the little desert fox had comforted Saint-Exupéry when he was stranded in the desert, and had taught him wisdom. The Little Prince is looking for friends, but the Fox says that, before he can become his friend, he must be "tamed." (Here, we encounter a problem of translation, for the one English word "to tame" translates two very different French ones: *domestiquer* in the sense of training an animal to behave suitably, and *apprivoiser* in the sense of creating bonds of affection between man and animal. The French text here is *apprivoiser*.) When the Fox explains that *apprivoiser* means that, "If you tame me, we shall need each other. I shall be for you unique in the world" (68), the Little Prince begins to understand that his Rose has "tamed" him. The Little Prince is at first too impatient to tame the Fox, for he is in a hurry to discover more friends, but the wise Fox explains that "one only knows those things which one tames" (69). Then the Fox teaches the Little Prince the slow, gentle patience of making friends, not by words, for "language is the source of misunderstanding" (69), but just by coming closer every day. Every day, too, he must come at the same time, so that one hour may become unique; and so the Fox teaches the importance of ritual.

When, at last, the Little Prince must leave to continue his quest, the Fox sends him first to visit the garden of roses again. There the Little Prince suddenly understands, and he exclaims: "You are nothing yet. Nobody has tamed you and you have tamed nobody. . . . You are beautiful but you are empty. One cannot die for you. . . . My Rose alone is more important than all of you, for it is she whom I have watered. . . . Since she is my Rose" (72). Then he returns to the Fox, who gives him his three-fold secret, "One sees well only with the heart. The essential is invisible to the eyes. . . . It is the time which you have spent for your rose which makes your rose so important. . . . You become responsible for always for whatever you have tamed" (72–73).

Enriched with this vital secret, the Little Prince leaves the Fox to continue his journey. He meets a railway switch-man, sending trains to left and right, and wonders what the busy travelers are seeking. "Nothing at all," says the switch-man, pointing out that only the children look out of the windows. The Little Prince agrees, saying: "Only children know what they are seeking" (75). Then the Little Prince meets a merchant of antithirst pills designed to save the time usually spent on drinking, and the puzzled Little Prince reflects that, if he had that time to spend he would walk quietly toward a fountain.

It is now the eighth day of Saint-Exupéry's breakdown in the desert, and he has drunk the last drop of water. Still the Little Prince cannot understand his anxiety, for "it is good to have had a friend, even if one is going to die" (77). Then he suggests, simply, though rather unreasonably, that they start looking for a well. Gradually, as they walk on the sand beneath the stars, the Little Prince imparts the Fox's secret to Saint-Exupéry, distilling it in quiet phrases: "Water can also be good for the heart. . . . The stars are beautiful because of a flower which one does not see . . . what makes the desert beautiful is that it hides a well somewhere" (77–78). Suddenly, Saint-Exupéry understands the mysterious radiance of the sand, he remembers his childhood home, enchanted by the legend of a treasure hidden in its heart, and he discovers the secret: "Whether it concerns a house, stars or the desert, what makes their beauty is invisible" (78). When the Little Prince falls asleep and Saint-Exupéry carries him, he realizes that he sees only the shell, for the important is invisible. "What moves me so much about this little sleeping prince is his faithfulness to a flower, it is the image of a rose which radiates within him like the flame of a lamp" (78).

Miraculously they do find a well in the desert, a simple village well, and Saint-Exupéry draws up the bucket on the groaning pulley. When the Little Prince says "I am thirsty for that water," Saint-Exupéry understands the quality of the water: "It was born of the walk beneath the stars, of the song of the pulley, of the effort of my arms. It was good for the heart, like a gift" (81). Gently meditating on the blindness of men, the Little Prince teaches Saint-Exupéry that what they keep seeking could be found in a single rose or in a drop of water.

Suddenly the Little Prince starts to talk of his planet, anxiously asking Saint-Exupéry to draw a muzzle on the sheep to protect his Rose, and Saint-Exupéry realizes that the Little Prince is intending to return home. Quietly the Little Prince dismisses him to work on his plane, while he seeks the help of the Serpent. First, however, he gives the lonely Saint-Exupéry a special gift: just as all the stars flower for the Little Prince because of his Rose, so will all the stars ring with laughter for Saint-Exupéry, because of the Little Prince's laughter. "Since I will laugh in one of them, it will be for you as though all the stars were laughing. . . . It will be as though I had given you, instead of stars, a mass of little sleigh-bells which can laugh" (87–88).

Bravely then, the Little Prince speaks of his coming return to his star, his death by the Serpent. To lessen Saint-Exupéry's grief, he tells him not to mourn over his body: "I will look as though I am dead, but it will not be true. . . . I cannot carry that body away. It is too heavy. . . . Old, empty shells are not sad" (89). Just like Saint-Exupéry's young brother, François, the Little Prince affirms that his body is not his essential self. The Little Prince walks toward the Serpent, there is a flash of yellow, and he falls like a tree. The reader is reminded of Bernis's death in *Courrier sud,* when "a lost child filled the desert,"[10] and of Fabien's death in the desert when "two children seem to sleep."[11] Here, though, is the enigma of the book which is never explained, for, at day-break, Saint-Exupéry does not find the Little Prince's body.

Six years later, as Saint-Exupéry tells his story, he wonders over this enigma. A little consoled by time, he can enjoy listening to the stars at night; but, because he forgot to add a fastening to the muzzle he drew for the sheep, he always wonders whether the Rose is safe. This unanswerable mystery can change the stars' laughter to tears. "But no grown-up will ever understand that it is of such importance" (93).

Saint-Exupéry had difficulty persuading his publishers to accept the death of the Little Prince, but he argued that children accept all natural things. He insists, perhaps, on the idea of the continued life of the spirit, by his plea to his readers to let him know if by chance they meet the Little Prince in the desert. Perhaps, too, the mysterious disappearance of the body is a suggestion, even subconscious, of resurrection. After all, Saint-Exupéry, without being a practicing Catholic, frequently claimed the enriching influence of his religious upbringing which teaches that belief.

The Little Prince was probably Saint-Exupéry's favorite book of all his writings, with the possible exception of *Citadelle.* Benouville, who knew Saint-Exupéry in Algiers, writes that Saint-Exupéry seemed to consider the book his autobiography and that he gave it to his friends as he might offer his photo.[12] Albérès says that the Little Prince is Saint-Exupéry's alter ego. "This resolute, courageous and hopelessly sentimental little fellow, standing on his miniscule planet, is indeed his double who lived in the astral world while Saint-

Exupéry's body lived among men."[13] The Little Prince, says Albérès, is the symbol of life, the discoverer of all the essential values of life; he is, indeed, the child whom Saint-Exupéry never had.[14] But this comes too close to the analysis which "tears the rose apart." Borgal more simply recognizes that *Le Petit Prince* is "a long fable in which the principal themes of Saint-Exupéry's thoughts are transfigured into the most delicate poetry. . . . This book is the purest masterpiece of exupérian art."[15] The immediate reaction to *The Little Prince* was hesitant, perhaps confused, for, as the critic, Binsse, realized, it did not fit into the category in which the public had placed the author.[16] Yet, as Smith foresaw in 1956, the book would perhaps become one of the immortals with La Fontaine's *Fables,* Swift's *Gulliver's Travels,* Carroll's *Alice,* and Maeterlinck's *Blue Bird.*[17]

Return to the Group

While *The Little Prince* was appearing in the United States, Saint-Exupéry was sailing on a troop ship to North Africa, and was finding in the military convoy "all the joy of a crusade."[18] He landed in Algiers on 4 May 1943, and was greeted by his old friend, Dr. Pélissier. He had come to the war front as "the first French civilian to rally to the call in North Africa,"[19] and now he had to wait for a military assignment. Meanwhile, his first action was to go to see his old Group II/33, now stationed at Laghouat. After visiting his old friends and celebrating with them, Saint-Exupéry flew back to Algiers to try to obtain an assignment to join them. This would be difficult, as part of the Group had been sent to join the American Third Photo Group of the Seventh Army, under Colonel Roosevelt, who had equipped the squadron with the new Lockheed Lightnings; and Saint-Exupéry, at forty-three, was well past the age limit to fly these latest, fastest planes.

In his attempts to obtain the coveted assignment to the Group II/33, Saint-Exupéry appealed, through an old friend, Général Chambe, to Général Giraud, then head of the French forces in North Africa. Although there are conflicting accounts in different sources, it is possible that Général Giraud himself may have appealed directly to Eisenhower to waive the age limit. While waiting for action on his appeal, Saint-Exupéry went on a goodwill mission to Morocco, at Giraud's request.

Finally, on June 4th, newly named Major Saint-Exupéry obtained the authorization to join the Group now stationed at Oujda and to

begin his training to fly the Lightnings. He submitted quite mod-
estly to this training, although he found much less delight in flying
these large planes, loaded with instruments, than in the old, simple
craft of the pioneer days of aviation. To his American friend, Curtice
Hitchcock, he wrote almost jovially of barracks life on the American
base, where the Group was stationed, expressing his admiration for
the young flyers and declaring, "I have quite fallen in love with
your country."[20] Yet writing to Dr. Pélissier, in Algiers, he admits
his moments of depression and of physical fatigue. Still, however,
he proclaims his determination to fight for his country: "I have
obstinately done what I believed I had to do."[21] As Delange writes,
Saint-Exupéry had "come to sign with his presence the message
which, a few months earlier, he had sent to Frenchmen everywhere."[22]

The specially equipped squadron was moved to the Maison-Blanche
base at Algiers, but Saint-Exupéry longed to see his whole Group
reunited. He made an appeal to Counselor Robert Murphy, Roosevelt's special envoy, to reestablish the whole Group as an active
fighting force, in association with the American Roosevelt Group.
Soon the French flyers were sent to the La Marsa base at Tunis, to
start on active duty.

On 21 July 1943, Saint-Exupéry flew his first reconnaissance
mission over occupied France, and he was deeply moved to see his
country once more, observing the land which seemed to lie so
peacefully beneath him. Pélissier recalls his account of this experience: "You cannot imagine how moving it is, when one has not
seen one's country for three years, to reach the land of France, and
to say to oneself, 'I am flying over my country. I am defying the
occupying force. I am seeing what I am forbidden to see.' "[23] He
was so eager for his next flight that he schemed like a schoolboy to
have his turn advanced.

This joy was short-lived, however, for on 31 July, returning from
another mission, Saint-Exupéry over-shot his landing and damaged
his plane. As a result, the American command withdrew its authorization for Saint-Exupéry to fly the Lightnings and, on August
1st, he was effectively grounded. After his long, determined struggle
to reenter the fray, it was heartbreaking to be excluded after only
two flights. Saint-Exupéry was sent back to Algiers, where he settled
into Dr. Pélissier's home. There, for almost a year, he would continue to fight to be allowed to fly again; and these were probably
the most unhappy months of his life.

"Lettre au Général X"

Shortly before his desperate disappointment, Saint-Exupéry had written a letter which he never posted and which was found later amongst his papers; it is generally presumed to have been written to Général Chambe. It was eventually published by *Le Figaro* in April 1948, and now forms part of the collection *Un Sens à la vie,* as the "Lettre au Général X."[24] It is so sad and despondent a letter that, as Smith suggests, we could be tempted to attribute it to the disappointment of being grounded, although it is dated before this event.[25] In this letter, Saint-Exupéry expresses a deep pessimism about the materialism of his epoch, in which it seems that "any lyricism sounds with a ridiculous ring, and men refuse to be awakened to any spiritual life whatever" (225). Saint-Exupéry diagnoses the sickness of the times as the refusal of any of the "great refreshing myths," and he then makes what is surely the most pessimistic statement of all his writings, otherwise so positive: "I hate my era with all my strength. Man is dying of thirst in it" (225). It is this thirst that Saint-Exupéry yearned to assuage by his writing, always wanting to write "a book which would give something to drink."[26] He then writes a passionate solution for the ills of his time: "there is only one problem in the world. To give back to men a spiritual significance, spiritual concerns. To make something resembling a Gregorian chant shower upon them. . . . One can no longer live without poetry, color or love . . . (the only problem is) to rediscover that there is a life of the spirit higher still than the life of the intelligence (and it is) the only one which can satisfy man. . . . One must absolutely speak to mankind" (226–27). With striking accuracy, Saint-Exupéry foresees the period of disillusionment and disintegration which will come after the war, when all the essential problems will arise to divide mankind. "For want of a strong, spiritual current, innumerable sects will grow, like mushrooms, and will be divided, one from another" (227). He feels a lack of commitment in the modern world. "The bonds of love which tie today's man to beings or to things are so lax, so lacking in density, that man no longer feels absence as he used to do" (228). Now Saint-Exupéry condemns all forms of totalitarianism: "I hate this era when man becomes, under a universal totalitarianism, like quiet, polite and calm cattle. . . . What I hate in marxism is the totalitarianism to which it leads. . . . What I hate in nazism, is the totalitarianism which it claims by its very essence" (229). Here is the answer to those critics who variably try to classify Saint-Exupéry as a communist or a fascist.

Modern man, laments Saint-Exupéry, has been deprived of all his creative power and can no longer create a folkdance or folksong. Instead, he is fed with ready-made culture. To this he compares the passionate, burning love which inspired the novel, *La Princesse de Clèves* just three hundred years ago.

Saint-Exupéry returns to the urgent problem which will arise as soon as the war has removed the German threat, the problem of the significance of man. Since no solution has been prepared, he feels that he is moving toward "the darkest times of the world" (230). If he survives the war, what will be left of all that he loves? "As well as of people, I am speaking of customs, irreplaceable intonations, of a certain spiritual light, of lunch in a Provençal farm under the olive trees, but also of Händel. I don't give a damn for the things which will survive. What has value is a certain arrangement of things. . . ." (230). If he returns alive from the "necessary but thankless job" of the war, his only concern will be, "What can one, what must one say to men?" (231). It is the task which Saint-Exupéry sets himself.

Grounded in Algiers

This was Saint-Exupéry's mood even before his grounding in Algiers, pessimistic about the materialism of his time, yet yearning to give to his fellow men the spiritual riches to water their souls and reawaken their creativity. The long months of enforced inactivity, when he longed to participate in the fight to free his country, were agonizing to him. He found some relief in continuing to work on his notes for *Citadelle*, yet he could not really write, for he was not participating, which was for him the essential condition to validate any writing. He worked on mathematical and scientific problems, foreseeing concepts of jet reaction and atomic power, to the amazement of scientific friends like Professor von Karman. He spent a month in Casablanca, invited by his friend, Dr. Henri Comte; and in Algiers he saw many friends, including André Gide. Yet nothing could relieve his distress which began to affect his physical health. Deprived of the privilege of responsibility, of sharing action with others, he grew more and more somber in mood.

"How can one think on the subject of France if one does not take share of the risk. . . . To love is to participate, to share."[27] Chevrier relates passages of *Citadelle* to this period: "Lord, bind me again to the tree from which I come. I have no meaning if I am alone. Let others lean on me. Let me lean on others. Let the hierarchies contain me. I am here, undone and temporary. I need to be."[28]

When his friends realized that Saint-Exupéry could not rest content in placid security, when he longed to participate in the essential battle for his country, they tried to find relatively safe missions for him. Three possible assignments which may have been suggested were as assistant air attaché to London or to China, or as chargé d'affaires to the United States. However, the unfortunate but growing antagonism of the Gaullist authorities toward Saint-Exupéry prevented him from getting the necessary approval; instead he was to remain as a reserve officer. As we have seen, Saint-Exupéry had refused to join any partisan group in New York, where the de Gaulle and Giraud factions were bickering, far from their leaders. To Chevrier, Saint-Exupéry described this conflict as one between the ideas and the individuals: "A group of 'individuals' . . . fights for conquered France which has saved her substance. And that is good. She must be present in the fight. . . . The general of the volunteers of such a foreign legion would have had me in the fight. But the tragedy is that these individuals think that they *are* France, instead of being *of* France."[29] That, as Saint-Exupéry wrote so often, he could never accept. De Gaulle was no doubt hurt by the refusal of this other great patriot to join him. In a speech in Algiers in which he named some of the outstanding figures of the French intellect, de Gaulle deliberately omitted Saint-Exupéry. Many biographers, notably Cate, like to insist upon the tragic misunderstanding between these two great Frenchmen, exaggerating it into a feud. Chassin, who was in Algiers at the time, explains it more simply:

The two men had never met and it is no doubt a pity. It had been represented to de Gaulle that by refusing to join the Free French Forces in the United States, Saint-Exupéry had acted as a bad Frenchman. In fact, Antoine, who believed above all in freedom and truth, judged rather severely a group of the Gaullists whom he had seen in America.

Carefully nurtured by certain people, the misunderstanding grew worse. The general's entourage did not forgive Saint-Exupéry for the independence of spirit which he had shown.[30]

Smith also realizes the tragedy of this misunderstanding "between the two men who symbolized in different ways French resistance and patriotism"[31] and he believes that it might have been resolved if they could have known each other. This belief that the rift between these two generous patriots could have been healed by simply meeting is supported by André Gide's account of the one time when Saint-Exupéry heard de Gaulle in person, at a meeting of the Consultative Assembly. Struck by his calm presence and persuasive arguments, Saint-Exupéry told a friend, "He is evidently stronger, wiser and greater than I expected to see him."[32] It is rewarding to find in de Gaulle's war memoirs a similarly generous readiness to change a wrong opinion. Discussing the importance of the French air forces in North Africa and Italy, de Gaulle refers to the heroic deaths of several airmen: "The records of Clostermann, a Maridor, a Marin la Meslée, the deliberate sacrifice of Saint-Exupéry, as well as still other valorous actions, were like sparks flying out of the over-whelming machinery. . . ."[33]

Yet this recognition by the man whom he should have known came too late. For awhile even Saint-Exupéry's *Pilote de guerre,* while being published in clandestine editions in occupied France, ironically was forbidden in Algeria. Saint-Exupéry suffered much from this antagonism fostered against him. In a cry from the heart, he wrote to a close friend: "I can no longer bear this calumny, nor the insults nor this prodigious idleness. I don't know how to live outside love. I have never spoken, nor acted nor written except by love. I love my country more, all on my own, than all of them together."[34]

Saint-Exupéry's friends continued trying to help him find the participation he so craved. Général Bethouard offered a headquarters post with him, but Saint-Exupéry could accept no desk job. Finally, in April 1944, a partial solution was found to this agonizing impasse, when Général Chassin asked Saint-Exupéry to accompany him as a staff officer to his new posting in Sardinia, as commander of a squadron of Marauder bombers, at Villacidro. Saint-Exupéry accepted this offer, with the understanding that he would be flying at least part of the time. Still, however, he continued his campaign to be allowed to return to his reconnaissance group.

From Villacidro, Saint-Exupéry finally contrived to make a direct appeal to General Eakers, the chief of allied air forces in the Mediterranean area. There are varying versions of how he managed this personal appeal, either through Général Chassin or through two

Americans who took up his cause and intervened with General Eakers on his behalf. One was Colonel Rockwell, to whom Saint-Exupéry explained his need to participate in the fighting so that he could write another *pilote de guerre*, an Allied one extolling the camaraderie between American and French flyers.[35] The other American was the reporter, John Phillips, to whom Saint-Exupéry promised an article for *Life* magazine, if only he would help him return to active duty with the Group. Phillips devoted a chapter of his book, *Odd World*, to Saint-Exupéry, and this chapter was later published in French translation by the Air Force Museum, together with the promised text by Saint-Exupéry (which had never appeared in *Life* because of the front-page events of the landings in Provence).[36] Whatever the exact details may be, the important fact remains that Saint-Exupéry did meet General Eakers who granted him the exceptional permission to fly five more reconnaissance missions on Lightnings with his Group, now stationed at Alghero in Sardinia.

Return to Action

From that moment Saint-Exupéry was revitalized, restored to his ebullient, youthful self. Jean Leleu recalls seeing him at that time, "overflowing with joy at the idea of his coming reunion."[37] He rejoined his beloved Group on 16 May and was welcomed joyfully by Gavoille and all his comrades: "There he was, simple and jovial, radiant at feeling himself in friendly surroundings."[38] His happiness in rediscovering his purpose, in being allowed once more to participate, is perhaps best reflected in the article which he wrote for Phillips. "I have found again all those of whom I said that, beneath the heel of the invader, they were not the defeated, but seeds buried in the silence of the earth. After the long winter of the armistice, the seed has germinated. My squadron of other days has flourished like a tree. Once again, I have the joy of participating in the deep-sea dives which high-altitude missions represent."[39] Movingly, this unpublished text closes on the description of the long-sought missions over France, still occupied by the Nazis: "And then there is the poignant meditation of the hours of flight over France, at once so close and so far! One is separated from her as though by centuries. All tender feelings, all memories, all reasons for living are there, laid out 35 thousand feet beneath your eyes, well lighted by the sun and yet more inaccessible than the Pharoah's treasures beneath a museum window."[40]

The opening of this hitherto unpublished text is also very interesting, for it suggests the new *pilote de guerre* that Saint-Exupéry would have liked to write, associating French and American flyers. Like a troubadour, he sings the high purpose of the modern crusader, the American soldier setting out on a troopship to save mankind. Whatever dissension may later occur between his country and the land of his exile, Saint-Exupéry wants to acknowledge the generous spirit of those soldiers: "To the quality of your profound substance, I will always bear witness. . . . The 50 thousand soldiers of my convoy set off to war to save, not the citizens of the United States, but Man himself, respect for Man, the liberty of Man, the greatness of Man."[41] Moved by this expression of the "solidarity of men," Saint-Exupéry feels that the world is drawing together in a physical closeness, but that this new body is still in search of a soul. It is this soul that the young soldiers are striving to find: "Your young men are dying in a war which, for the first time in the history of the world, is for them, despite all its horrors, a confused experience of love. Do not betray them. Let it be they who dictate their peace, when the day comes! Let that peace resemble them! This war is noble, let their faith in the Spirit ennoble the peace, also."[42]

These last months of his life were, perhaps, as Smith suggests, the happiest for Saint-Exupéry. He was with his beloved Group, surrounded by the comrades-in-arms whom he loved and respected; he was participating in the great effort to free his country; and every time he flew a reconnaissance mission, he could see his country lying in the sunshine beneath him. When not actively flying, Saint-Exupéry enjoyed the simple life which he shared with his fellow pilots, in a little house on the coast of Sardinia. One day, too, he had joined Gavoille's family in Tunis to become godfather to their new baby. Sometimes he could fly to Algiers to see his friends, Dr. Pélissier or the writer André Gide. Yet there was always in his heart the persistent anxiety for his family in occupied France. In a letter smuggled into France by a Resistance worker, he laments the long, sad winter of France's trial. In the last letter to his mother, which reached her a year after his death, he writes, "When will it be possible to say to those one loves that one loves them?"[43]

Because of his constant preoccupation with France, with his family and friends, held hostage by the Occupation, Saint-Exupéry continuously wanted to fly more missions, especially over the regions of Agay and Annecy so familiar to him. He would beg the operations officer, Jean Leleu, for more than the other pilots, saying: "For me, since I have been delayed, it is vital, . . . I need it, with a physical and moral need."[44] Soon he passed the stipulated five flights granted by General Eakers, and still he wanted to fly more, although these missions were often difficult. On one mission he was attacked by two fighter planes, but threw them off by his speed. On another the oxygen supply leaked, but he brought the plane down to an altitude where he could breathe, even if he was vulnerable to anti-aircraft fire. On yet another mission, on his 44th birthday, his left engine broke down, and he had to limp home on one engine, threading his way through the Alpine valleys and flying dangerously low over Genoa. That time he put down at the Bastia airport for repairs, and his comrades, waiting to welcome him with a birthday feast, lived through hours of anxiety until they received news of his safety.

A letter which Saint-Exupéry wrote to Pierre Dalloz at this time reveals much of his quiet mood of fulfillment in this determined, daily offering of his life for his beliefs: "I am making war as profoundly as possible, I am certainly the dean (oldest) of fighter-pilots in the world. . . . I have experienced everything since my return to the squadron. This return is a miracle. . . . It is my only satisfaction. And also to wander . . . for hours at a stretch, over France, taking photos. That is strange."[45]

Once again Saint-Exupéry's friends grew increasingly concerned at his determination to continue risking his life. Général Chassin appealed to him to stop when he had carried out eight missions, pleading, "You now have (earned) the right to speak. In consequence, you no longer have the right to risk your life." But Saint-Exupéry only smiled and replied, "It is impossible, I will go on to the end, now. It is not very far off, I think. I will stay with my comrades—until the end."[46] Léon Werth had once tried to dissuade Saint-Exupéry from active duty in 1940, talking of a higher duty than risking his life in battle, and Saint-Exupéry had simply replied, "Towards my comrades, it would be lacking in courtesy."[47]

In July 1944 the Group was moved to Corsica, to the base of Borgo, as preparation intensified for the final thrust to liberate France. Everybody knew that the landing in the south of France must soon take place, and Saint-Exupéry was vibrant with joyous anticipation, "more enthusiastic, younger, more radiant than ever."[48] Desperately trying to save him from almost certain death in action if he continued flying missions, some of Saint-Exupéry's officer friends in the Group devised a plot to ground him once more. They would brief him on all the latest plans for the Allied landing in southern France, for nobody with that knowledge was allowed to fly, lest he fall into enemy hands and, under torture, divulge it. They finally arranged with the American authorities for a formal briefing of Saint-Exupéry on August 1st.

Last Mission

Saint-Exupéry, unaware of these drastic measures being prepared to ground him, had asked to fly the reconnaissance flight scheduled for July 31st over the regions of Annecy which he loved so well. Knowing that Saint-Exupéry would soon be deprived of the privilege of flying, Commandant Leleu reluctantly gave in to his insistence and assigned the flight to him. Early that morning Leleu and Gavoille helped Saint-Exupéry don the cumbersome flight gear and clamber into the tight-fitting cockpit, where he used jokingly to say that he fitted like a pipe in its case. Then, in bright sunshine, Saint-Exupéry took off to fly his tenth reconnaissance mission. Leleu and Gavoille watched his plane disappear over the coastal mountains towards France. From that flight Saint-Exupéry never returned; no radio message was received from him, and no sign was ever found of his plane. "He disappeared without trace, like a god of ancient legends in a mysterious assumption."[49]

On the Borgo base all Saint-Exupéry's comrades, pilots and mechanics, gathered to wait through the vigil of the last hours when hope could persist, of which Saint-Exupéry had written so vividly in *Vol de nuit*. Now it was Captain Courtin who described the anguish of their waiting, as they wondered how to make the impersonal higher authorities realize who Saint-Exupéry was to them: "We must make the Wing understand who Saint-Exupéry is. But who could explain to General W . . . that Saint-Exupéry may have appeared to be one of us and that, indeed, he asked for nothing more, but that he was also a rare being, an exceptional and precious being, a Prince, a debonair, absent-minded Prince, stranded amongst us. And who has suddenly disappeared." Instinctively calling on Saint-Exupéry's essential quality of responsibility, which had made him struggle to survive in the desert, Courtin continues: "Men, all men—the earth, the whole earth—everyone must know that Saint-

Exupéry is in peril, everything must move and be moved and throw out to the pilot in distress a cry so tremendous that, however wounded, however broken, however annihilated he may be, he cannot fail to hear it and respond to it."[50]

If Saint-Exupéry were still alive, he would respond to that call, and all his friends clung to this hope, as they had when he had had engine failure just a month earlier, on his birthday. Pélissier wanted to believe the young lieutenant who tried to reassure him that they would surely find Saint-Exupéry in some *maquis* Resistance group in France. Gavoille's report in the Group's daily logbook reflects both his grief and this unreasoning hope:

A very sad event has come to dull the joy which we were all feeling at the approach of a victory. Commandant Saint-Exupéry has not returned. . . .

We lose in him not only our dearest comrade but the one who was for us all a great example of faith. If he came to share our risks despite his age, it was not to add any vain glory to an already magnificently fulfilled career, but because he felt the need of it, for himself. . . .

Of course, we all have the great hope of seeing him again soon. . . . He may have landed in Switzerland or be hidden in the "maquis" of Savoy. . . .[51]

This hope to which Saint-Exupéry's friends clung was not fulfilled. Saint-Exupéry had disappeared and, like the Little Prince, had not even left the shell of his body to mark his going. In their distress his friends continued to call out to him, but "The total gift of his smile comes to wound them in the heart and they discover the extent of their love."[52]

The mystery of Saint-Exupéry's death has never been fully clarified. For several years there was no indication at all of what might have happened to him, despite repeated searches and investigations. Pélissier explains that there are basically three possibilities: a breakdown in the oxygen supply, a mechanical accident, or enemy attack in some region which cannot be determined. Saint-Exupéry had often explained to his friends that he had given up watching for the approach of enemy fighters, as there was so little he could do if he did spot them. Gavoille, in a letter to Pélissier, expressed the degree of renunciation which Saint-Exupéry had reached in these continued flights: "Because he was very big, he could not make any movement within the narrow cockpit. His numerous fractures and wounds caused him severe pain at high altitude. He had, I think, resigned himself to giving up any watching of the sky which would have forced him to make exhausting movements."[53] Pélissier, his friend, was deeply moved by the nobility of such abnegation, which made of each flight a full offering of self.

Four years after Saint-Exupéry died, Gaston Gallimard, his French editor, received a letter from a German theology student, Herman Korth, who had been an officer in the German Luftwaffe in southern France in 1944. Korth, an admirer of Saint-Exupéry's works, had just read of the author's disappearance in a German article and, struck by the dates, had consulted his diary of that year. On the page for the night of 31 July he found the abbreviated notes: "An(ruf) Trib(un) K(ant) abschuss 1 aufkl(ärer) brennend üb(er) See. Aukfl(ärung) Ajacc(io) unver(ändert) (Call from Tribun Kant a reconnaissance shot down burning over the sea. Reconnaissance Ajaccio unchanged.)[54] These notes recorded a call from the pilot Kant, which Korth had been awaiting late that night. After checking with Allied flight journals for that period, it was found that Saint-Exupéry was the only pilot to have failed to return that day, in that area. Newspapers immediately published this explanation of Saint-Exupéry's death as an established fact. Delange's book appeared that year, and accepted the conclusion suggested by Korth's letter. Soon this certainty was shaken by the discovery that an American pilot, Meredith, had been shot down in the same area, on 30 July, and might be the subject of Korth's report. Pélissier gives an extensive discussion of this possibility, as do other biographers. Some of the confusion concerning this report arises from careless translation of the German, and some from exaggerated reporting. Yet Migéo's careful study of the various reports and translations, and his personal interview of Korth, seem to establish beyond reasonable doubt that the report did, in fact, refer to Saint-Exupéry's plane.[55] Perhaps the best conclusion is in Pastor Korth's own words: "The sea was the destiny of this man, delightful as an aviator and a poet, who was venerated with a very deep love also among German aviators."[56]

Because Saint-Exupéry's death has never been fully explained and because of the sadness of some of his last writings, some commentators have tantalized their readers with suggestions of suicide. Such suggestions reveal little understanding of the man whose whole philosophy of life was founded on the concept of responsibility. Saint-Exupéry carried in his heart the responsibility for all those who believed in his living: his comrades, his family, his countrymen, even his readers. He would not have betrayed that sense of responsibility which had already brought him back from death so many times. One must not confuse his acceptance of death, his readiness to die each day, or even a sometimes weary indifference to death, with any purpose of death. It is true that Saint-Exupéry frequently expressed his distress at the world which would emerge from the cauldron of the war years for, as Roy says, "he loves all that of which we are more and more deprived, the substance of soul which enriches the acts of men, even into their death."[57] Yet he was ready to play his part in restoring that substance to the war-gutted world. As he had written to Général X, "What can one, what must one say to men?",[58] so to Pélissier he wrote, "I wish, that this sinister war might finish before I have quite melted away like a candle in the burning of the oxygen. I have another task to do later."[59]

In *Terre des hommes*, Saint-Exupéry had contrasted the acceptance of death through fulfilled responsibility with the pettiness of suicide: "Before this meager destiny, I remembered a true man's death. That of a gardener who said to me 'You know . . . sometimes I sweated when I dug the earth. . . . Well now, I would like to dig, to dig the earth. To dig would seem so beautiful to me! . . . And then, who is going to prune my trees?' . . . He left land lying fallow. He left a planet lying fallow. He was bound in love to all the soils and the trees of the earth. He was the generous one, the prodigal one, the great lord."[60] Saint-Exupéry too, in his acceptance of death, must have wondered who would tend all those lives for which he felt responsible; and he would never deliberately have cast off that responsibility or willingly have left the earth of men lying fallow. Saint-Exupéry, who wrote to Dalloz, "I was made to be a gardener,"[61] did die indeed like the old gardener whom he admired, having all his life fulfilled his responsibility and ready, if he could live still, to till the earth again.

On 3 November 1944 the provisional government issued a citation of Saint-Exupéry, to the order of the army, for the two dangerous reconnaissance missions carried out on 23 and 29 June: "Major, reconnaissance pilot, always giving proof of the finest qualities of daring and skill. During the months of June and July 1944, carried out over France, on an unarmed, single-seater plane, a very fine series of greater photo reconnaissance missions over a very great distance. . . ."[62] This citation order was signed by Général de Gaulle.

On 31 July 1945, a year after Saint-Exupéry's death, two years after the grounding which he had fought so passionately, a memorial service was held in Colmar, attended by family, friends, and comrades-in-arms. On 12 March 1950 a citation to the order of the air forces "summarized the life of Saint-Exupéry and all the reasons which we have to love and admire him."[63]

Major Antoine de Saint-Exupéry (reconnaissance Group II/33)
Pioneer of airlines, has, by his unfailing tenacity and his thoughtful daring made French wings shine with a new brilliance.
Ardent war-pilot, proved in 1940 as in 1943, his passion to serve and his faith in the destiny of his country.
Knew how to express his taste for action and the generosity of his ideal in a literary work which counts among the most important of our times and which celebrates the spiritual mission of France.
He met a glorious death on July 31st 1944 returning from a distant reconnaissance mission over his country, occupied by the enemy.
This citation carries with it the award of Croix de Guerre 1939–45, with palm.[64]

Chapter Nine

The Wisdom of the Sands: *Citadelle*

"Citadelle, je te construirai
dans le coeur de l'homme"

When Saint-Exupéry died he left as his final legacy to his friends, those who knew him and those who read him, the voluminous manuscript on which he had been working since before the war, and which had followed him into exile and back again to the war front. This was his "poem," his "posthumous work" of which he said to Dalloz, "Beside this writing, all my other books are only exercises."[1] Yet what his intention was for this manuscript is uncertain. Cate, taking Saint-Exupéry's oft-repeated reference to a "posthumous" work in its usual sense, asserts that he certainly intended it to be his "magnum opus."[2] Yet Saint-Exupéry's cousin, André de Fonscolombe, states that he never felt that Saint-Exupéry wanted to make of this work any philosophical summation.[3] Reynal, Saint-Exupéry's publisher, in personal notes sent to Maxwell Smith, insists that it was an entirely personal notebook, kept to elaborate his own thinking, with no intention of publication at all:

Citadelle was a curious composition in that it was something which Saint-Exupéry wrote purely for himself. . . . He referred to it jokingly as his "oeuvre posthume" not because he had any premonition of dying before it could be completed and not because he was saying anything in it that could not be published while he was alive, but purely because he regarded it as part of his life, something that grew as he grew and changed as he changed, to which he never saw any real end. It presented his own personal philosophy and his own personal view of things.[4]

When Saint-Exupéry's papers were sent first to Dr. Pélissier and then to the literary executor whom Saint-Exupéry had designated in a scribbled note on the back of a flight order, there were over one thousand manuscript pages of *Citadelle*. Dr. Pélissier, in whose home Saint-Exupéry had lived during the agonizing months of inactivity before his final return to duty, recalls how Saint-Exupéry continued to work on his manuscript during that period. He had arrived in Algiers in 1943 with five binders of typed manuscript and a notebook to which he continuously added changes or elaborations of previously worked themes. Pélissier explains that as Saint-Exupéry's handwriting grew progressively smaller and more illegible during this time of stress, this all-important final notebook was almost impossible to decipher, so that the friends editing the manuscript gave up the attempt to "decode" these final notes. Furthermore, for lack of any reference indications, it was impossible to insert them into the typewritten script. Pélissier, who watched Saint-Exupéry during his last months of writing, asserts that, in the published text, "one can read only an incomplete manuscript, printed still in its matrix. . . . It is therefore impossible to say what the structure of the finished work would have been."[5]

The concept of the "matrix" is one which Saint-Exupéry often used, and in all his other books he had laboriously and meticulously reworked the texts to remove the "matrix" of the raw material, as a sculptor removes the stone, to reveal the envisioned shape within. Léon Werth also asserts that the published text of the whole manuscript is only a "matrix," probably the outside one of many, for Saint-Exupéry had said that he wanted to work another ten years on the manuscript. For Werth *Citadelle* is an "organist's improvisation" not a composition.[6]

There has been much controversy over the publishing of this monumental manuscript which, in its unrefined, unpolished state, within its layers of "matrix," is about as long as all of Saint-Exupéry's other works together; and Werth quotes one critic as saying that this publication was a "betrayal."[7] In later editions, however, much of the work of deciphering the notes and reconciling the various sections of the manuscript had been carried out by the editors Pierre Chevrier, Simone Lamblin, and Léon Wencélius. Recent editions, although still resembling a "monumental labyrinth," or a "not yet constructed ruin,"[8] are organized with some sequence of theme. The English version, *Wisdom of the Sands,* represents even more editing, for the American publisher, Reynal, decided to have the volume edited much as Saint-Exupéry might have done, so that the translation is only about two-thirds the length of the French version.

Most of the "redundancies and obscurities" have been removed, leaving the "rich cadencies and poetic imagery of the original," in Smith's opinion.[9]

The Citadel and the Berber Prince

Citadelle grew over some eight years from the original first sketch, a short article which the *Table ronde* eventually published in 1948, under the title "Seigneur berbère."[10] Saint-Exupéry had entrusted the manuscript of this article to Dr. Pélissier and later, when he was working on his notes in New York in 1942, he sent an urgent cable to his friend, begging him not to give the manuscript to a publisher who had requested it, because he was transforming the article into a book. This article, read without the present context of *Citadelle* or without any knowledge of Saint-Exupéry's other work, would be extremely enigmatic, presenting a surprising harshness of philosophy otherwise not found in Saint-Exupéry's writing, except for some aspects of Rivière's character in *Vol de nuit*. Starting with the quiet statement "I was a Berber chief and I was going home" (1091), the chieftain meditates upon his empire and his power, upon his slaves and the wives of his harem, and on his sleeping people, whom he has always sought to bind together into an entity. All of this seems far removed from the Saint-Exupéry whom we know in his other books until we recognize, in this strange, exotic setting, some familiar themes in transposed form. He speaks of the art of "taming": "To tame is to call, to hold close, to draw to oneself the one who is fleeing through the one whom we possess" (1098). The chieftain too, knows responsibility, feeling it for those with whom his life is bound up. In a strong echoing of the story of the old sergeant on the Spanish front, who found an unknown self emerging, the chieftain speaks of the "archangel" within each man who is released at the moment of death. All human companionship is with this mute "archangel," which resides within each person. In a striking image of the bonds of human companionship, the chief says of the "archangel" that "he is scattered amongst us all and in no one will he be assembled. . . . I will talk to you of the archangel who has been crossed with the human species" (1096). There is, too, in this first *Citadelle*, the endless search of Saint-Exupéry for God, who is present even by his very silence. Throughout his long life, the old chieftain has taught his people prayer, "so that the word of God might nourish, as with oil, these lamps lighted for life" (1100).

The monumental *Citadelle* which grew from the germ idea retains the same setting of a fortress city, a citadel, in the desert, ruled with benevolent despotism by the Berber chieftain. Here, however, it is a young chieftain, ruling his people after the assassination of his father. All his long meditations are upon what he learned either from that wise father or from his own experience; and the themes are all those which can be seen growing through Saint-Exupéry's books, developed, abstracted, and transposed through multiple variations. Léon Wencélius, a friend of Saint-Exupéry's and later one of the editors of *Citadelle,* counts some hundred themes and recalls Saint-Exupéry's saying of his manuscript: "It is a torrent which drags too many pebbles"[11]; it is these "pebbles" which Saint-Exupéry would have plucked out of the torrent of ideas. The work is a great granary where all the rich seeds of Saint-Exupéry's thought are found, ready to spring forth in new forms in his other works. Yet it is also a grandiose finale to a great symphony, where all the themes reverberate in triumphant, glorious recapitulation. (André de Fonscolombe, however, would compare it to a symphony begun by one musician and finished by another!)[12] The style of the book is that epic, almost biblical prose which became so dominant at the end of *Pilote de guerre,* a final development of the latent poetic quality found even in Saint-Exupéry's earlier works. For Saint-Exupéry, style was a cherished value, not to be lightly exploited, and he decried writers who, for personal advantage, "break the vase of common treasure."[13]

Interpretations and Criticism

Maxwell Smith points out that there are two interpretations for the French title, *Citadelle:* it can be the "empire of traditions, rituals and patriotic fervor which shall bind all its citizens together in a common cause greater than themselves," or it can be "the city of the spirit to be founded in each individual heart" for it is the virtues of the citizen which make the empire.[14] A radically different interpretation is given by Cate, who asserts that the "Citadelle" created by the chief's father obviously represents the Middle Ages.[15] Yet Saint-Exupéry's own statement, "Citadelle, I shall build you in the heart of man" (27), clearly situates that citadel in the future and within the spirit.

There is even more controversy over the actual philosophy of the book. Because of the harsh rule imposed by the chieftain, some critics have considered *Citadelle* to be fascist inclined, proposing totalitarianism, a strange accusation to make against the author who writes that all men are "ambassadors of God," or the "dwelling of God" (52–53). It is true that the old father's concept of justice depends on the choice between being "just towards the archangel or just towards the man" (52–53), which suggests an inquisitor's benevolence. Yet Werth suggests that sometimes the fictitious character of the Berber prince takes over from Saint-Exupéry, in some of the harsher statements. It must be remembered, too, that Saint-Exupéry had spent several years in the desert civilization and had come to have some insight into the Arab mores, without adopting them. Several critics, notably Carlo François, maintain that Saint-Exupéry was strongly influenced by Nietzsche and his philosophy of the superman, with whom they identify the chieftain, as earlier Rivière had been identified. Yet others, such as Devaux, Borgal, and Werth himself, consider *Citadelle* to be a Christian parable and identify the chieftain with God: "God and the Chieftain are only one, and the acts of the Chieftain are the thoughts of God."[16] This interpretation, however, fails in those passages where the chieftain is seeking God. A related interpretation asserts the influence of Pascal, maintaining that the figure of the Geomètre in *Citadelle* represents this philosopher, whom Saint-Exupéry so admired, carrying his *Pensées* always with him. "I who have known the only true geometer, my friend, who could instruct me by night and day. . . . I who have known in him expanse and I who used to go to him as one seeks the sea-wind, or solitude . . ." (656–66). Ravoux insists in his presentation of *Citadelle* that the Geometer represents Pascal: "Like him, the geometer has in vain sought the proofs of the existence of God and he has never let himself be guided by reason alone."[17] Indeed, the Geometer laments, "I should have liked to discover in the universe the trace of a divine mantel . . ." (243). In an echo of Pascal's phrase, "The heart has reasons which reason does not know," Saint-Exupéry writes, "there is no reasoning to reason upon the love of the domain" (347).

This seemingly irreconcilable relationship between the philosophies of Nietzsche and Pascal is one of the enigmas of the book for which many critics, notably Jean Cau, have criticized Saint-Exupéry. Cau, claiming to have discovered the "trickery" in Saint-Exupéry's philosophy, protests that one cannot proclaim a lordly Nietzschean ethic and, at the same time seek "mystic, fraternal, virile communion with men."[18] Cate refutes this argument as being typical of the exclusiveness of pure logic, which Saint-Exupéry rejected. Instead of considering this apparent contradiction as a weakness, Cate writes of the book: "if it had one central aim . . . it was probably to marry the warring philosophies of Nietzsche and Pascal. It was nothing less than to fuse Christian compassion and Nietzschean hard-heartedness, the cult of Reason and the Gospel of faith. . . ."[19] Saint-Exupéry, indeed, had frequently written of the danger of intelligence which believes that language can fully grasp a concept, explaining that "in a language which formulates but does not grasp, two truths can oppose each other" (113).

An even more fascinating interpretation of the book is that developed by Carlo François. In the same study which elaborates the influence of Nietzsche, François asserts that the art critic, Elie Faure, whom Saint-Exupéry had met at the Ecole des beaux arts,[20] exerted a strong influence on Saint-Exupéry's philosophy, style, and language. In fact, François believes that the father of the Chieftain represents Elie Faure, who had taught Saint-Exupéry so much.[21] This is probably an exaggerated assumption, given François's own admission that neither Léon Werth, a mutual friend of both men, nor Saint-Exupéry's family believes that Saint-Exupéry actually met Faure. François, however, builds an elaborate case for Faure's influence, especially with regard to the strong vocabulary of key words which permeate Saint-Exupéry's writing, such as the "matrix," the "key-stone" and the "poem," in the sense of creation. Whatever the origin of this intense personal vocabulary of Saint-Exupéry's, it is essential for the reader to have grasped it, to have grown into it, through reading all Saint-Exupéry's other books, before attempting to read *Citadelle,* in order to understand that last book thoroughly.

Themes and Images

Although *Citadelle* is not an autobiography, an awareness of Saint-Exupéry's life can also help in understanding otherwise enigmatic passages in this deeply personal book. When the chieftain says "he who emigrates with his heart, the people will deny him and he himself will deny his people," it is Saint-Exupéry refusing to forget France, in his exile. When he describes the camp where the refugees, lacking for no physical good, nevertheless become vicious to each other, he is remembering the squabbles of the political refugees in New York. When he talks of the ceremony of the well, he is recalling the life-giving desert water of his Sahara adventures, as he did in *Le Petit Prince*. Surely, too, the chieftain meditating on the ramparts, as he watches over the sleeping people for whom he is responsible, is related to Saint-Exupéry the war pilot, walking in his village at night, after his mission.

Some of the images frequently suggested in Saint-Exupéry's earlier books here find their fullest poetic development. The image of the tree, for instance, is a constantly recurring motif in *Citadelle*, a symbol of the collaboration of the many varied roles of roots, trunk, and branches to raise the whole from earth to sky: "it is the pathway of exchange, between the stars and us" (62). The tree does not live for itself but is: "the source of winged seeds and it is transformed and grows more beautiful from generation to generation . . . it is only a way and a path" (509). The image of the cathedral, consummate expression of the loose stones which find their meaning within it, recurs strongly too: "if each stone is in its place and serves the temple, then alone count the silence which is born from them and the prayer which is formed there" (85). Although "stupid language" may say that cathedrals are useless, men everywhere seek these "granaries for the soul and the heart" (98). The symbol of the ship which has grown through Saint-Exupéry's writing, often associated with the house which carries the generations, now is interwoven with that of the cathedral, for cathedrals are "half-buried ships which alone lead somewhere" (99). Those who visit the ancient cathedrals "dream of being aboard them," for during the crossing aboard these ships of stone, they could make for themselves "souls which are rich and generous" (99). The image of the ship interweaves, too, with that of the tree, for once the yearning of the sea has been established in men, then the ship will grow from an assembly of nails and planks, "just as the cedar drains the sap and salts of the rock to establish them in the sun" (334).

As the images intertwine to make a new language, so do the many themes of Saint-Exupéry's rich philosophy. In one striking, allegorical passage, these themes are well revealed. In *Pilote de guerre*, Saint-Exupéry had spoken of comrades of his Group who volunteered for service in snow-covered Scandinavia as though they accepted to die "for a certain taste of the Christmas celebrations" adding, "if we had been the Christmas of the world, the world would have saved itself through us."[22] Now, in *Citadelle,* he returns to this mood of Christmas which he often used for that mysterious exhilaration, writing of the one who wanted to die because he had heard the "legend of a Northern country where, on a certain night of the year, one walks on crackling snow toward lighted wooden houses" (345); and the light comes from a tree. It is a night when every face is radiant because everyone is awaiting a miracle, and that miracle will be the elusive, priceless thought which will shine a moment in the children's eyes, created by the ceremonial of Christmas: "For you have built it all year by waiting and by stories and by promises and especially by your knowing airs and your secret allusions and the immensity of your love. And now you will detach from the tree some humble object of painted wood and will offer it to the child according to the tradition of your ceremonial. And that is the moment" (346). As the sleepy child thanks you with a kiss, he gives you "something which is a fountain for the heart and for which you thirst" (346). If the color of that moment were: "the only recompense for your year, and the sweat of your work . . . and your nights of meditation, and the affronts and sufferings endured, it would pay you richly and you would be filled with wonder. For you would gain in that exchange" (347).

Quest for God

The themes again knit closely in another strongly autobiographical passage. Saint-Exupéry is surely recalling the village of Orconte of *Pilote de guerre* when he writes, speaking through the chieftain: "Your village becomes one as it sleeps, with . . . its little cargo of wishes, coveting, angers and pity. . . . And now I can say to you: . . . 'the fountain of your village' and so awaken your heart and little by little teach you that walk towards God which alone can satisfy you for, from sign to sign you will reach him. He who is read through the woven strands. . . . He binds together for you the raw materials in order to draw their significance . . ." (476). Suddenly, from the quiet meditation in the village, we have moved to the meditation on God, the ceaseless quest of Saint-Exupéry, the agnostic, who yet treasured his Christian culture.

As a young student in Switzerland, Saint-Exupéry had lost the practicing Catholic faith in which he had been brought up; yet he had always retained a yearning for that faith and he cherished the western culture which is founded on Christian belief. In *Courrier sud*, the lonely young pilot, Bernis, who wandered into Notre-Dame cathedral in nostalgic search of a meaning to the passing moments but was discouraged by the stylized sermon, echoes Saint-Exupéry's ambivalent agnosticism. In *Pilote de guerre*, Saint-Exupéry confesses his long alienation from his traditional faith: "if I have kept the image of the civilization which I claim as mine, I have lost the rules which bore it."[23] Yet he treasures that civilization which "contemplated God through men" and which, "inheriting from God, has made men equal in Man."[24] There are, indeed, several references to God in *Pilote de guerre*, although there had not been in *Vol de nuit* and in *Terre des hommes*. Through those ten years between *Courrier sud* and *Pilote de guerre*, however, Saint-Exupéry had kept his *Carnets* (or personal journal), a precursor to the later *Citadelle* notes. In these *Carnets*, we find his preoccupation with the concept of God, from whom he and others were "weaned too early," so that they now struggle through life as "lonely little fellows."[25] He finally admits the difficulty of having authority derive from anything but God, for one "sows seed from above."[26] In the "Lettre au Général X," Saint-Exupéry had expressed his yearning for a religion, saying "If I had (religious) faith, I could no longer bear anything but Solesmes (the monastery)."[27] Now, in *Citadelle*, there stands revealed Saint-Exupéry's long quest for God. The chieftain's references to God are so many that it would be difficult to select the most significant. The search for perfection is itself a quest for God:

—Perfection is not a goal which one attains. It is exchange into God. (88)
—You will teach the taste for perfection, for every work is a walk towards God. (118)
—The voice of God is inexpressible need, search and thirst. (176)
—You want to be. You will be only in God. He will garner you in his granary when you are slowly become (fulfilled). (127)

God is to be found in beauty, too: "The one who recognizes the smile of the statue or the beauty of the landscape, or the silence of the temple, finds God" (255).

As the chieftain meditates upon God, he comes to understand His silence. After climbing the mountain to ask of God the reason for this "exchange," and finding only a silent rock, he understands the essence of prayer:

> For the first time, I divined that the greatness of prayer resides firstly in that it is not answered and that there enters into this exchange none of the ugliness of barter. And that the apprenticeship of prayer is the apprenticeship of silence. And that love begins only where there is no gift to expect. Love is firstly the exercise of prayer, and prayer the exercise of silence.
>
> And I came back to my people, for the first time enclosing them in the silence of my love. . . . And by me, they and I, we were nothing else but prayer which was founded in the silence of God. (234–35)

Just as silence is of God, so does doubt prove Him: "Doubt is the ransom of God, for His lack is in you and hurts you" (299). God cannot be seen but only perceived for "if He resembles me to show Himself to me, He is not God. . . . I can only recognize Him by His resonance on me . . . in the way a blind man reaches towards the fire" (390). God gives the meaning to those "empires" of unity which men must build around themselves, and He descends into the house as "the duty of lighting candles" (470). Most richly, He is "the celebration and crowning of the ceremonial of your sorrows" (538).

Man's quest toward God intensifies and grows, as a tree, in the space left between the inattainability of God and the concept of Him, and the chieftain says, "I go toward Thee as a tree which develops according to the lines of force of its seed" (598). Finally, in the ultimate recognition of God, through the chieftain, Saint-Exupéry says: "Thou art the essential knot of diverse acts" (617).

If Saint-Exupéry had not died in action, how much further would he have traveled in his quest for God? Léon Werth, writing about *Citadelle,* asks this question, which can never be answered: "The god of Saint-Exupéry is at the center of the multiple 'matrices' which death did not allow him to tear away. Only he could have told us if his god was a god or if his god was God."[28]

From Cap Juby, the outpost in the desert which he had come to love so well, Saint-Exupéry used to write that he was "leading the life of a monk." There, in austere solitude, he had read and meditated, beginning that ascension of soul which is so marked from that time. His friend Renée de Saussine, to whom he wrote his *Lettres à l'amie inventée,* comments thoughtfully on this "monk's life" that it is "as if he were meditating upon the perturbing passage of Scripture": "I will draw you, says God, I will lead you into the desert, and there I will speak to your heart, and you will answer as in the day of your youth. Then shall I affiance you to me in justice and judgement, in strength and in tenderness."[29] Whether Saint-Exupéry ever rediscovered a full belief in God, we can never know, but surely his quest began then, in the desert. That is why his *Citadelle* is set in the desert and why he speaks through the Berber prince. Now, says Renée de Saussine, "a whole universe of the heart, that of brotherhood and solicitude" took shape, and there was "this lonely crusade" which lay before him.

It is this "lonely crusade" which became Saint-Exupéry's purpose in life and which he proclaims with all the resonance of his intensely personal vocabulary in the intimacy of his private meditation in *Citadelle*.

Chapter Ten
Conclusion

In this study, there have been frequent references to Saint-Exupéry's personal vocabulary of key words. It is beyond the scope of this study to analyze and explain the very many rich symbol words which Saint-Exupéry created, but an awareness of them can greatly enhance the understanding of all of his work. They are an example of the "essential which is invisible," for within each apparently simple word, there vibrates a whole new idea. Just as the stars ring with the Little Prince's laughter for Saint-Exupéry, so do these words ring with rich music for those readers who have been "tamed" by Saint-Exupéry's spirit. These bell words form a new instrument on which Saint-Exupéry can create a music all his own: exchange, to tame, the tree, the cathedral, the archangel, ritual, dwelling, becoming, fête. . . . If we respond to his personal vocabulary, we are answering his concept: "To move me, you must knit me in the bonds of your language, and that is why style is a divine operation" (*Citadelle*, 260).

In *Citadelle*, Saint-Exupéry uses these vibrant key words in such close juxtaposition as to form virtually a new language, an intensely personal form of expression which, in cold translation, often loses most of its meaning. An example is this declaration of the chieftain's: "I love man delivered by his religion and vivified by the gods whom I found in him: house, domain, empire, kingdom of God, so that he may exchange himself always for that which is more vast than himself" (113).

In this passage, "to deliver" is to free from the "matrix"; "religion" is those values in which man believes; while the "gods" are those entities for which a man will live or die, and which give meaning to his life. "Fonder," as in the English "to found" (not "to find") is here to set up and establish; and the "gods" which the chieftain has "founded" are themselves key words. The "house" is the love and cherishing of the home, which carries generations of a family like a ship; the "domain" is the symbolic earth which man has tilled and worked until he is bound to it in love; the "empire" is that community of man to which all men contribute as the stones do to a cathedral; the "kingdom of God" is men's relationship to each other and to a world around them through God, who, though often silent, is manifest through them. Eventually, by free gift of himself in participation, man will "exchange" himself for that in which he most believes, the cause to which he engages himself. Even in explaining this passage, we have used other "exupérian" vocabulary, such as the "ship" and the "cathedral," which Saint-Exupéry had enriched with special meaning.

If we are truly "knit in the bonds" of Saint-Exupéry's language, then we can perhaps grasp and express his philosophy, the passionate crusade of his life, in his own language, as he expresses it in *Citadelle*.

Saint-Exupéry, in the intensity of his love for Man, wants to teach him the *fervor* that he has lost, and that gives meaning to life. Man must be moved again by the yearnings *founded* within his heart and the *bonds* of responsibility and friendship that *knit* him together into a *knot of relationships*. These yearnings are *slopes* of tendency and weight along which he will move toward his own *being* and *becoming*. "This slope . . . is more powerful than reason and alone governs" (335). Man, grown lax in the modern world, must be *founded* anew: "If I found Man, I deliver the *archangel* within him . . . and if I make of you an archangel, I set free winged words and *steps* as sure as those of a dancer" (292). Man is founded when he feels *responsibility* for all that he has *tamed*, people or things; he is founded when his *empire* is strong around him with all the *gods* which give it meaning. "You have been governed only by the gods which are *temple, domain, empire, slope* toward the sea . . ." (335). Man is founded, too, through accepted constraints which liberate him, as discipline frees the artist: "So that you shall be free with the liberty of the singer who improvises on his instrument, must I not first train your fingers and teach you the singer's art?" (411).

To restore a *meaning to life,* Man must rediscover the invisible *essential* within the things around him. "It is the *weight* of things which one must change. And this act is a *poem* or the *modeling* of a sculptor, or a *canticle*" (228). Indeed, objects in themselves offer no hope unless "they echo one against the other, which is the only music for the heart" (278). But objects can only have such meaning within the *domain* that one has built of one's life by *giving* and *sacrifice* and the *time* which one has spent for it. To *be,* Man needs to be *of* some domain or *dwelling,* and must know and feel his *patrimony.* If he is not given the keys of his patrimony, he will wander joylessly in his homeland, which will seem empty to him. Each generation must teach the next to *read the face* of the *domain* from the diverse face of things. "I have taken stars, fountains, regrets. . . . I have modeled them according to my spirit, and they have served as a pedestal to a *divinity* which is contained in none of them" (72–73).

Just as things have an invisible meaning within a unity, just as the *cathedral* is the expression of loose stones, so can moments have meaning within a pattern of time that is marked by *rituals:* "Rituals are in time, what the dwelling is in space. . . . I walk from *celebration* to celebration" (29). Those who lack a sense of time, enriched by ritual and by celebration, want to pick flowers before they are *become* and so find nothing; or they choose a flower already opened elsewhere, but meaningless because it is not "the fulfillment of the *ceremonial* of the rose-bush" (493). The anticipation of celebration is what "perfumes the ordinary days" (513) and each celebration must be prepared by its ceremonial, which creates its meaning, for the *fête* is created of "the instant in which you pass from one state to another, when the observance of ceremonial has prepared a birth for you" (569).

"Life only has meaning if one *exchanges* it" (41). In working toward something that will last longer than themselves, a *ship* or a *temple,* men "exchange themselves in joy for something more precious" (43) and so build their own eternity. Yet this can only happen with complete dedication to the object of exchange, as a flower becomes uniquely beautiful only when all other flowers are refused (44). Especially must one's *craft,* one's work, have this element of *exchange,* for then "the sound of your hammers will be a *canticle* . . . and your launching of a ship will be a miraculous gesture, for you will have flowered the waters" (236). The old artisan who has given his life to weaving a brocade, "becomes more and more luminous and bright . . . in the object of his *exchange*" and his work becomes "a subtle elixir" (44); and more and more imperishable, he goes to his death, "with his hands full of stars."

Man thus *founded* by his *responsibility* and his creative constraints is established within his *domain,* whose *face* is made clear by all the *divinities* that give it life. Rich in a *craft* that obliges him to "espouse the world" (222), *exchanging* himself for his domain and his poem, Man can now find a *meaning to life,* which is "duration in the very object of your exchange" (461). This is the "palace . . . where all the steps (have) a meaning" (33). "There you are in the peace of the tree, and [in] the meaning of life which is to raise you from level to level in the glory of God" (501).

Now man is *knit* into life and has become a *"knot* of relationships" (468), the essential knotting of all the strands that create the rich tapestry of life. This is the *"divine knot* which knits things together" (278), giving them meaning, and if it is unknotted, everything loses its magnetic bonding. It is the "divine knot which binds things to the God who is the meaning of your life" (312). This *knotting* of everything into a *meaning of life* is the source of the essential nourishment that Man seeks, and he will die to save that invisible knot. Now, indeed, has he rediscovered *fervor,* for "fervor is simply the fruit of the divine knot which binds things" (255). Now, in this invisible knotting, life is enriched by the *invisible essential,* and so "the sea has the meaning of the black pearl once found there, the year [has] the meaning of the unique fête, and life the meaning of fulfillment in death" (523).

So did Saint-Exupéry fulfill his lonely crusade and restore fervor to Man. He died like the old peasant of whom he wrote, "the death of the aged parent become earth, after having exchanged himself completely, is nothing else than a marvel" (45), for Saint-Exupéry, too, had exchanged himself completely into his love for fellow man and his country, and into his writings, in which he builds his eternity. In his full belief that he was not enclosed in his body which "cracks like an old shell" (164), his chivalric spirit stands there to guide Man to fervent life. As "the essential of a candle is not the wax which leaves traces, but the flame" (20), the essential of Saint-Exupéry is his radiant spirit, which shines still. "I will awaken you to fervor."

Notes and References

Chapter One

1. *Pilote de guerre* (Paris: Gallimard, 1942), p. 101.
2. Pierre Chevrier, *Antoine de Saint-Exupéry*, NRF (Paris: Gallimard, 1949), pp. 20–21.
3. Maxwell Smith, *Knight of the Air* (New York: Pageant Press, 1956), p. 15.
4. *Terre des hommes* (Paris: Gallimard, 1939), p. 81.
5. Adèle Bréaux, *Saint-Exupéry in America, 1942–1943: A Memoir* (Rutherford, N.J.: Fairleigh Dickinson University Press, 1971), p. 156.
6. *Icare, Revue de l'aviation française*, Saint-Exupéry: Première Epoque, no. 69 (Summer-Fall 1974), p. 60.
7. Chevrier, *Saint-Exupéry*, p. 11 (note).
8. Smith, *Knight of the Air*, p. 6.
9. Curtis Cate, *Antoine de Saint-Exupéry: His Life and Times* (New York: Putnam, 1970), p. 21.
10. Chevrier, *Saint-Exupéry*, p. 11.
11. *Lettres à sa mère*, NRF (Paris: Gallimard, 1955), p. 40.
12. Ibid., p. 160.
13. *Terre des hommes*, p. 140.
14. Simone de Saint-Exupéry, "Jeux d'Enfants," *Confluences, Revue des lettres et des arts*, VIIIᵉ année, nos. 12–14 (1947), p. 46.
15. Ibid., p. 45.
16. Simone de Saint-Exupéry, *Icare*, no. 69, p. 65.
17. Simone de Saint-Exupéry, "Jeux d'Enfants," pp. 47–51.
18. *Pilote de guerre*, p. 155.
19. Chevrier, *Saint-Exupéry*, p. 19.
20. Yvonne de Lestrange, *Icare*, no. 69, p. 95.
21. Simone de Saint-Exupéry, "Antoine, mon frère," in *Saint-Exupéry*, Collection Génies et Réalités (Paris: Hachette, 1963), p. 59.
22. Jean Escot, *Icare*, no. 69, p. 114.
23. Jacques Néri, *Icare*, Saint-Exupéry: Deuxième Epoque, no. 71 (Winter 1974–75), p. 51.
24. Cate, *Saint-Exupéry*, p. 36.
25. *Confluences*, p. 45.
26. *Pilote de guerre*, pp. 150–52.
27. *Terre des hommes*, p. 82.
28. *Courrier sud* (Paris: Gallimard, 1929), p. 100.
29. *Pilote de guerre*, p. 112.

30. *Courrier sud,* p. 146.
31. Charles Salles, *Icare,* no. 69, p. 83.
32. *Lettres à sa mère,* p. 153.
33. Ibid., p. 93.
34. Chevrier, *Saint-Exupéry,* p. 22.
35. Cate, *Saint-Exupéry,* p. 29.
36. Chevrier, *Saint-Exupéry,* p. 25.
37. *Icare,* no. 69, p. 81.
38. Chevrier, *Saint-Exupéry,* p. 27.
39. *Courrier sud,* pp. 23–26.
40. *Icare,* no. 69, p. 84.
41. *Pilote de guerre,* p. 153.
42. Simone de Saint-Exupéry, "Antoine, mon frère," p. 58.
43. Cate, *Saint-Exupéry,* p. 163.
44. *Pilote de guerre,* pp. 171–72.
45. Chevrier, *Saint-Exupéry,* p. 29

Chapter Two

1. Henri de Segogne, *Icare,* no. 69, p. 91.
2. Ibid., p. 92.
3. Général Chassin, "Voyage de l'universel," *Confluences,* p. 77.
4. *Lettres à sa mère,* pp. 51, 54.
5. Simone de Saint-Exupéry, "Antoine, mon frère," p. 61.
6. *Icare,* no. 69, p. 92.
7. Bernard Lamotte, *Icare,* no. 69, p. 96.
8. Carlo François, *L'Esthétique d'Antoine de Saint-Exupéry* (Neuchâtel and Paris: Delachaux et Niestle, 1957).
9. *Icare,* no. 69, pp. 96–97.
10. *Lettres à sa mère,* p. 56.
11. Ibid., p. 68.
12. Robert Aéby, *Icare,* no. 69, pp. 100–101.
13. Marcel Migéo, *Saint-Exupéry* (Paris: Flammarion, 1958), pp. 37–40.
14. *Lettres à sa mère,* p. 79.
15. Ibid., p. 81.
16. Migéo, *Saint-Exupéry,* pp. 30, 43.
17. André de Vilmorin, *Poètes d'aujourd'hui,* no. 91 (Paris: Seghers, 1962), p. 35.
18. Ibid., p. 36.

Chapter Three

1. *Icare,* no. 69, p. 83.
2. Chevrier, *Saint-Exupéry,* p. 38.

3. Migéo, *Saint-Exupéry*, p. 47.

4. De Vilmorin, *Poètes*, p. 36.

5. Louise de Vilmorin, "Ma Fièvre me raconte de belles histoires d'Amour," *Marie-Claire*, no. 13 (October 1955), p. 109.

6. Marcelle Auclair, *Icare*, no. 69, p. 127.

7. Louise de Vilmorin, "Fiançailles pour rire," *Poèmes*, NRF (Paris: Gallimard, 1970), pp. 21–22.

8. De Vilmorin, *Poètes*, p. 37.

9. *Lettres à sa mère* (Paris: Gallimard, 1955), p. 94.

10. Ibid., p. 94.

11. Ibid., p. 97.

12. Ibid., p. 103.

13. Ibid., p. 104.

14. Ibid., p. 114.

15. *Lettres de jeunesse* (Paris: Gallimard, 1953), p. 28.

16. *Lettres à sa mère*, p. 109.

17. Ibid., p. 108.

18. *Lettres de jeunesse*, p. 14.

19. Ibid., p. 44.

20. Ibid., p. 45.

21. Ibid.

22. *Lettres à sa mère*, p. 116.

23. Ibid., p. 116.

24. Ibid.

25. *Icare*, no. 69, p. 47.

26. Chevrier, *Saint-Exupéry*, p. 45.

27. Cate, *Saint-Exupéry*, p. 151.

28. *Lettres à sa mère*, p. 100.

29. *Un Sens à la vie*, NRF (Paris: Gallimard, 1956), p. 15.

30. Ibid., p. 15.

31. Ibid., pp. 17–29.

32. Luc Estang, *Saint-Exupéry par lui-même*, "Ecrivains de toujours" series (Paris: Seuil, 1956), p. 7.

33. *Icare*, no. 69, p. 182.

34. *Lettres de jeunesse*, p. 58.

Chapter Four

1. Migéo, *Saint-Exupéry*, p. 55.

2. Smith, *Knight of the Air*, p. 28.

3. Migéo, pp. 56–57.

4. Chevrier, *Saint-Exupéry*, p. 51.

5. "Saint-Exupéry: Ecrivain et Pilote," *Icare*, no. 30 (Summer 1964), p. 6.

6. *Lettres de jeunesse,* p. 61.
7. *Terre des hommes,* p. 13.
8. Ibid., p. 15.
9. Ibid., p. 16.
10. Ibid., p. 17.
11. Ibid., p. 18.
12. Chevrier, *Saint-Exupéry,* p. 51.
13. *Lettres de jeunesse,* pp. 70–71.
14. Ibid., p. 75.
15. Ibid., p. 76.
16. Ibid., p. 83.
17. *Terre des hommes,* p. 19.
18. Ibid., pp. 34–35.
19. Ibid., p. 7.
20. *Lettres à sa mère,* pp. 124, 131.
21. Ibid., p. 125.
22. Ibid., p. 131.
23. Ibid., p. 133.
24. Ibid., p. 134.
25. *Icare,* no. 69, p. 138.
26. Ibid., p. 140.
27. *Lettres à sa mère,,* p. 139.
28. *Icare,* no. 69, p. 142.
29. Smith, *Knight of the Air,* p. 50.
30. *Lettres à sa mère,* p. 140.
31. Migéo, *Saint-Exupéry,* p. 85.
32. *Terre des hommes,* pp. 44–45.
33. Chevrier, *Saint-Exupéry,* p. 62.
34. *Icare,* no. 69, pp. 173–76.
35. Ibid., p. 173.
36. *Citadelle* (Paris: Gallimard, 1948), pp. 272, 312.
37. Chevrier, *Saint-Exupéry,* p. 60.
38. Ibid., p. 176.
39. *Lettres à sa mère,* p. 145.
40. Ibid., p. 146.
41. Migéo, *Saint-Exupéry,* p. 89.
42. Chevrier, *Saint-Exupéry,* p. 50.
43. *Lettres à sa mère,* p. 140.
44. Ibid., p. 141.
45. *Terre des hommes,* p. 109.
46. Ibid., pp. 109–10.
47. Ibid., p. 111.
48. Ibid., p. 112.

49. Ibid., p. 110.
50. Ibid., p. 114.
51. Ibid., p. 105.
52. Ibid., pp. 116–17.
53. Ibid., pp. 120–21.
54. Ibid., p. 108.
55. *Le Petit Prince* (Paris: Gallimard, 1946), p. 72.
56. *Terre des hommes*, p. 98.
57. J. Huguet, *Saint-Exupéry ou l'enseignement du désert* (Paris: Vieux Colombier, 1956), pp. 29–30.
58. Ibid., p. 21.
59. Chevrier, *Saint-Exupéry*, p. 67.
60. Cate, *Saint-Exupéry*, p. 149.
61. Ibid., p. 151.
62. *Lettres à sa mère*, p. 130.
63. Ibid., pp. 143–44.
64. Ibid., p. 125.
65. Chevrier, *Saint-Exupéry*, p. 71.
66. Cate, *Saint-Exupéry*, p. 159.
67. "Books I Remember," *Harper's Bazaar*, April 1941, p. 82.
68. Hans Christian Andersen, *The Little Mermaid* (Copenhagen: Host, 1959), p. 38.
69. André Beucler, preface to *Courrier sud*, pp. 8–9.
70. Ibid.
71. Edmond Jaloux, *Les Nouvelles littéraires*, 6 July 1929.
72. *Lettres à sa mère*, p. 152.
73. Ibid., p. 151.

Chapter Five

1. *Icare*, no. 69, p. 190.
2. *Lettres à sa mère*, p. 156.
3. *Lettres de jeunesse*, p. 104.
4. Ibid., pp. 104–5.
5. Ibid., p. 103.
6. *Terre des hommes*, p. 71.
7. Ibid., p. 72.
8. Jean-Gérard Fleury, *La Ligne* (Paris: Gallimard, 1949), p. 211.
9. *Terre des hommes*, p. 26.
10. Ibid., p. 38.
11. Ibid., p. 86.
12. *Terre des hommes*, p. 94.
13. Ibid., p. 47.
14. Ibid., p. 48.

15. Ibid.
16. Ibid., p. 53.
17. Ibid., pp. 58–59.
18. Ibid., p. 57.
19. Ibid., p. 58.
20. Ibid., p. 55.
21. Ibid., p. 57.
22. *Icare,* no. 30, pp. 29–31.
23. *Icare,* no. 71, p. 50.
24. Bréaux, *Saint-Exupéry,* p. 33.
25. *Lettres à sa mère,* p. 120.
26. Consuelo de Saint-Exupéry, *Kingdom of the Rocks* (Paris: Brentano, 1945), p. 231; (reprint ed., New York: Random House, 1946), p. 293.
27. *Icare,* no. 30, p. 76.
28. Bréaux, *Saint-Exupéry in America,* p. 103.
29. *Lettres à sa mère,* p. 167.
30. André Gide, *Journal* (Paris: Gallimard, Pleiade), p. 1040–41.
31. *Lettres à sa mère,* pp. 161–62.
32. Daniel Anet, *Antoine de Saint-Exupéry: poète, romancier, moraliste* (Paris: Corréa, 1946), p. 83.
33. Cate, *Saint-Exupéry,* p. 230.
34. Smith, *Knight of the Air,* p. 84.
35. *Vol de nuit* (Paris: Gallimard, 1931), p. 11.
36. Smith, *Knight of the Air,* pp. 90-91.
37. Richard Rumbold and Margaret Stewart, *The Winged Life* (New York: McKay, n.d.), p. 110.
38. Didier Daurat, *Dans le Vent des hélices* (Paris: Seuil, 1956), p. 234.
39. Clément Borgal, *Saint-Exupéry, mystique sans foi* (Paris: Centurion, 1965), p. 59.
40. Cate, *Saint-Exupéry,* p. 230.
41. *Icare,* no. 69, pp. 211–12.
42. Léon Werth, "Tel que je l'ai connu," in René Delange, *La Vie de Saint Exupéry* (Paris: Seuil, 1948), p. 183.
43. "Books I Remember," p. 82.
44. Cate, *Saint-Exupéry,* p. 226.
45. *Icare,* no. 69, p. 153.

Chapter Six

1. Jules Roy, *Passion de Saint-Exupéry* (Paris: Gallimard, 1951), p. 17.
2. Cate, *Saint-Exupéry,* p. 240.

3. Delange, *La Vie de Saint-Exupéry*, p. 60.
4. *Terre des hommes*, p. 141.
5. Smith, *Knight of the Air*, pp. 101–4.
6. Cate, *Saint-Exupéry*, p. 251.
7. *Icare*, no. 71, pp. 71–73.
8. Chevrier, *Saint-Exupéry*, p. 109.
9. *Terre des hommes*, p. 170.
10. *Icare*, no. 71, p. 91.
11. Cate, *Saint-Exupéry*, p. 284.
12. Chevrier, *Saint-Exupéry*, p. 124.
13. *Icare*, no. 75, pp. 116–20.
14. Daurat, *Dans le Vent des hélices*, p. 208.
15. *Un Sens à la vie*, p. 45.
16. Ibid., pp. 45–46.
17. Ibid., pp. 46–47.
18. Ibid., p. 47.
19. Ibid., p. 48.
20. Ibid., p. 57.
21. Delange, *La Vie de Saint-Exupéry*, pp. 66–67.
22. *Terre des hommes*, p. 152.
23. Smith, *Knight of the Air*, p. 106.
24. *Terre des hommes*, pp. 143–208. (Page numbers in next paragraphs refer to this chapter.)
25. *Un Sens à la vie*, p. 121.
26. Ibid., p. 123.
27. Ibid., p. 140.
28. Ibid.
29. *Terre des hommes*, p. 211.
30. Ibid., p. 218.
31. *Icare*, Saint-Exupéry: Troisieme Epoque, no. 75 (Winter 1975–76), pp. 79–81.
32. *Un Sens à la vie*, pp. 161–62.
33. *Icare*, no. 75, p. 66.
34. Smith, *Knight of the Air*, p. 123.
35. See chapters 4 and 5 in this volume.
36. See chapter 5 in this volume.
37. See chapter 6 in this volume.
38. See chapter 6 in this volume.
39. Anne Morrow Lindbergh, *War Within and Without* (New York: Harcourt Brace, 1980), p. 33.

Chapter Seven

    1. Chevrier, *Saint-Exupéry*, pp. 215–16.
    2. Georges Pélissier, *Les Cinq Visages de Saint-Exupéry* (Paris: Flammarion, 1951), p. 35.
    3. *Icare*, Saint-Exupéry: Quatrième Epoque, no. 78 (Autumn 1976), p. 39.
    4. *Pilote de guerre*, p. 51.
    5. *Icare*, no. 78.
    6. Ibid., p. 62.
    7. *Pilote de guerre*, pp. 80–81.
    8. Ibid., p. 186.
    9. Ibid., p. 188.
    10. *Icare*, no. 78, p. 85.
    11. Delange, *La Vie de Saint-Exupéry*, p. 91.
    12. Pélissier, *Cinq Visages*, po. 37.
    13. *Icare*, Saint-Exupéry: Cinquième Epoque, no. 84, p. 47.
    14. Cate, *Saint-Exupéry*, p. 425.
    15. Smith, *Knight of the Air*, pp. 162–63.
    16. *Icare*, no. 78, p. 121.
    17. *Lettre à un otage*, NRF (Paris: Gallimard, 1945), p. 14.
    18. Chevrier, *Saint-Exupéry*, p. 230.
    19. *Lettre à un otage*, p. 17.
    20. Smith, *Knight of the Air*, p. 140.
    21. *Icare*, no. 84, p. 47.
    22. Consuelo de Saint-Exupéry, *Kingdom of Rocks*, p. 142.
    23. See chapters 4 and 5 in this volume.
    24. *Icare*, no. 84, p. 32.
    25. See chapter 7 in this volume.
    26. See chapter 1 in this volume.
    27. See chapter 6 in this volume.
    28. Smith, *Knight of the Air*, pp. 160–61.
    29. *Time*, 23 February 1942, pp. 88, 90–91.
    30. Lewis Galantière, "Antoine de Saint-Exupéry," *Atlantic Monthly*, April 1947, pp. 133–41.
    31. Smith, *Knight of the Air*, pp. 160–61.
    32. *Icare*, no. 84, p. 133.
    33. Ibid., p. 139.
    34. Richard Hillary, *The Last Enemy* (London: Pan Books, 1956), p. 184.
    35. Ibid., p. 47.
    36. Bréaux, *Saint-Exupéry in America*.
    37. *Un Sens à la vie*, p. 209.
    38. Ibid., p. 210.

39. Ibid., p. 211.
40. Ibid., p. 214.
41. Ibid., p. 215.
42. Ibid., p. 216.
43. Ibid.
44. Ibid., p. 217.
45. Delange, *La Vie de Saint-Exupéry*, p. 102.
46. Smith, *Knight of the Air*, p. 177.
47. Ibid., p. 178.
48. *Terre des hommes*, p. 129.
49. Delange, *La Vie de Saint-Exupéry*, p. 169.

Chapter Eight

1. Smith, *Knight of the Air*, p. 199.
2. Rumbold and Stewart, *The Winged Life*, p. 186.
3. *Icare*, no. 84, p. 35.
4. *Icare*, no. 78, p. 84.
5. Smith, *Knight of the Air*, p. 191.
6. Pélissier, *Cinq Visages*, pp. 69-70.
7. François, p. 182.
8. *Pilote de guerre*, p. 43.
9. *Carnets* (Paris: Gallimard, 1953), p. 145.
10. *Courrier sud*, pp. 178-81.
11. *Vol de nuit*, p. 148.
12. Benouville, "Saint-Exupéry fraternel," *Confluences*, p. 150.
13. R. M. Albérès, *Saint-Exupéry* (Paris: Editions Albin Michel, 1961), p. 160.
14. Ibid., p. 164.
15. Borgal, *Saint-Exupéry*, p. 143.
16. Cate, *Saint-Exupéry*, p. 464.
17. Smith, *Knight of the Air*, p. 200.
18. Ibid., p. 201.
19. Pélissier, *Cinq Visages*, pp. 42-43.
20. Cate, *Saint-Exupéry*, p. 495.
21. Pélissier, *Cinq Visages*, p. 40.
22. Delange, *La Vie de Saint-Exupéry*, p. 103.
23. Pélissier, *Cinq Visages*, p. 45.
24. *Un Sens à la vie* (the following page quotations refer to this collection).
25. Smith, *Knight of the Air*, p. 205.
26. *Lettres à sa mère*, p. 168.
27. Inédit, *Saint-Exupéry* (Paris: Editions du Musée Air France, 1973), p. 6.

28. Chevrier, *Saint-Exupéry*, p. 267.
29. Ibid., p. 259.
30. Chassin, "Voyage de l'Universel," *Confluences*, pp. 81–82.
31. Smith, *Knight of the Air*, p. 207.
32. Ibid., p. 208.
33. Charles de Gaulle, *War Memoirs: Unity 1942–44* (New York: Simon & Schuster, 1959), pp. 312–13.
34. Chevrier, *Saint-Exupéry*, p. 261.
35. Cate, *Saint-Exupéry*, p. 525.
36. Inédit, *Saint-Exupéry*.
37. Jean Leleu, "Saint-Exupéry fraternel," *Confluences*, pp. 172–73.
38. Smith, *Knight of the Air*, p. 210.
39. Inédit, *Saint-Exupéry*, p. 5.
40. Ibid., p. 6.
41. Ibid., pp. 1–2.
42. Ibid., p. 4.
43. *Lettres à sa mère*, p. 171.
44. Jean Leleu, "Pilote au 2/33," *Confluences*, p. 177.
45. Pierre Dalloz, "Dernières Rencontres," *Confluences*, p. 166.
46. Ibid., p. 88.
47. Delange, *La Vie de Saint-Exupéry*, p. 184.
48. Leleu, "Saint-Exupéry fraternel," p. 186.
49. Ibid., p. 187.
50. Delange, *La Vie de Saint-Exupéry*, pp. 123–24.
51. Pélissier, *Cinq Visages*, pp. 53–54.
52. Chevrier, *Saint-Exupéry*, p. 280.
53. Pélissier, *Cinq Visages*, p. 57.
54. Migéo, *Saint-Exupéry*, p. 274.
55. Ibid., pp. 270–78.
56. Ibid., p. 271.
57. Roy, *Passion de Saint-Exupéry*, p. 98.
58. See above.
59. Pélissier, *Cinq Visages*, p. 47.
60. *Terre des hommes*, pp. 59–60.
61. Dalloz, "Dernières Rencontres," p. 166.
62. *Icare*, Saint-Exupéry: Sixième Epoque (Spring 1981), no. 96, p. 185.
63. P. Kessel, *La Vie de Saint-Exupéry* (Paris: Gallimard, 1954), p. 112.
64. *Icare*, no. 96, p. 185.

Chapter Nine

1. Dalloz, "Dernières Rencontres," p. 164.
2. Cate, *Saint-Exupéry*, p. 557.
3. *Icare,* no. 71, p. 33.
4. Smith, *Knight of the Air,* p. 227.
5. Pélissier, *Cinq Visages,* p. 72.
6. Delange, *La Vie de Saint-Exupéry,* p. 135.
7. Ibid., p. 135.
8. Cate, *Saint-Exupéry*, p. 556.
9. Smith, *Knight of the Air,* p. 229.
10. "Seigneur berbère," *La Table ronde,* no. 7 (July 1948), pp. 1091–1101. (The following quotations refer to this article.)
11. Cate, *Saint-Exupéry*, p. 557.
12. *Icare,* no. 71, p. 32.
13. *Citadelle* (Paris: Gallimard, 1948), p. 116.
14. Smith, *Knight of the Air,* p. 230.
15. Cate, *Saint-Exupéry*, p. 562.
16. Delange, *La Vie de Saint-Exupéry,* p. 160.
17. Jean-Phillippe Ravoux, *Saint-Exupéry: Citadelle* (Paris: Bordas, 1969), p. 73.
18. *Icare,* no. 30, p. 91.
19. Cate, *Saint-Exupéry*, p. 560.
20. See chapter 2 in this volume.
21. François, *L'Esthetique d'Antoine de Saint-Exupéry,* p. 52.
22. *Pilote de guerre,* pp. 212–13.
23. Ibid., p. 217.
24. Ibid., pp. 224–25.
25. *Carnets,* p. 35.
26. Ibid., p. 42.
27. *Un Sens à la vie,* p. 226.
28. Delange, *La Vie de Saint-Exupéry,* p. 146.
29. *Lettres à l'amie inventée* (Paris: Plon, 1953), p. 75. (Original edition of *Lettres de jeunesse.*)

Selected Bibliography

PRIMARY SOURCES

1. Books

Courrier sud. Paris: Gallimard, 1929. *Southern Mail.* Translated by Stuart Gilbert. New York: Smith & Hass, 1933.

Vol de nuit. Paris: Gallimard, 1931. *Night Flight.* Translated by Stuart Gilbert. New York: Century Co., 1932.

Terre des hommes. Paris: Gallimard, 1939. *Wind, Sand, and Stars.* Translated by Lewis Galantière. New York: Reynal & Hitchcock, 1939.

Pilote de guerre. Paris: Gallimard, 1942. *Flight to Arras.* Translated by Lewis Galantière. New York: Reynal & Hitchcock, 1942.

Airman's Odyssey. New York: Reynal & Hitchcock, 1942. Contains *Wind, Sand, and Stars, Night Flight,* and *Flight to Arras.*

Lettre à un otage. Paris: Gallimard, 1945. *Letter to a Hostage.* Translated by John Rodker. In *French Short Stories.* New York: New Directions, 1948.

Le Petit Prince. Paris: Gallimard, 1946. *The Little Prince.* Translated by Katherine Woods. New York: Reynal & Hitchcock, 1943.

Citadelle. Paris: Gallimard, 1948. *The Wisdom of the Sands.* Translated by Stuart Gilbert. New York: Harcourt Brace, 1949.

Lettres de jeunesse. Paris: Gallimard, 1953. Preface by Renée de Saussine.

Lettres à l'amie inventée. Paris: Plon, 1953. Presented by Renée de Saussine, with illustrations by the author. Same letters as the *Lettres de jeunesse.*

Carnets. Paris: Gallimard, 1953. Introduced by Michel Quesnel and Pierre Chevrier.

Lettres à sa mère. Paris: Gallimard, 1955. Introduction by Madame de Saint-Exupéry, his mother.

Un Sens à la vie. Paris: Gallimard, 1956. *A Sense of Life.* Translated by Adrienne Foulke. New York: Funk & Wagnalls, 1965. A collection of articles and prefaces by Saint-Exupéry, and also his first published short story, "L'Aviateur," and important letters.

Oeuvres. Bibliothèque de la Pléiade, NRF Paris: Gallimard, 1959.

2. Articles

"L'Aviateur." *Le Navire d'argent,* edited by Jean Prévost, April 1926. Also in *Un Sens à la vie.*

"Une Lettre de M. de Saint-Exupéry." *Annales politiques et littéraires,* December 1931.

170

Preface to *Destin de Le Brix,* by José le Boucher. Nouvelle Librairie française, 1932. Also in *Icare,* no. 71.

Preface to *Grandeur et servitude de l'aviation,* by Maurice Bourdet. Paris: Corrêa, 1933. Also in *Un Sens à la vie.*

"Souvenirs de Mauritanie." *Air France Revue,* no. 2 (1935). Also in *Icare,* no. 71.

Articles on Moscow. *Paris-Soir,* May 3, 14, 16, 19, 20, and 22, 1935. Also in *Un Sens à la vie.*

Articles on Spanish Civil War. *L'Intransigeant,* August 12, 13, 14, 15, and 19, 1936; and *Paris-Soir,* June 27, 28, and 3 July, 1937. Also in *Un Sens à la vie.*

"La Paix ou la guerre." *Paris-Soir,* October 2, 3, and 4, 1938. Also in *Un Sens à la vie.*

"Le Pilote et les puissance naturelles." *Marianne,* 16 August, 1939. Chapter omitted from *Terre des hommes* but found as "The Elements" in the English version. Also in *Un Sens à la vie.*

"Aventures et escales." *Paris-Soir,* 15 November 1938. Also in *Icare,* no. 75.

Preface to *Le Vent se lève,* by Anne Morrow Lindbergh. Paris: Corrêa, 1939. Also in *Un Sens à la vie.*

Preface to *Pilotes d'essai,* by Jean-Marie Conty. Paris: Spès, 1939. Also in *Un Sens à la vie.*

"Books I Remember." *Harper's Bazaar,* April 1941.

"Letter to Young Americans." *Senior Scholastic,* May 25, 1942. Translated by Lewis Galantière. Original now discovered and published in *Icare,* no. 84.

"An Open Letter to Frenchmen Everywhere." *New York Times Magazine,* 29 November 1942. French original in *Pour la victoire,* 19 December 1942. Also in *Icare,* no. 84 and *Un Sens à la vie.*

"Voulez-vous, Français, vous réconcilier?" *Le Canada,* Montreal, 30 November 1942.

"Lettre inédite au Général X." *Le Figaro littéraire,* 10 April 1948. Also in *Un Sens à la vie.*

"Seigneur berbère." *La Table ronde,* no. 7 (July 1948).

SECONDARY SOURCES

1. Books

Anet, Daniel. *Antoine de Saint-Exupéry.* Paris: Corrêa, 1946. A study of Saint-Exupéry's major works, analyzing the aspects of the poet, the novelist, and the moralist.

Albérès, R.-M. *Saint-Exupéry.* Paris: Albin Michel, 1961. A reworking of his original biography to study the poetry and vision of Saint-Exupéry through his use of images.

Borgal, Clément. *Saint-Exupéry, mystique sans foi.* Paris: Centurion, 1965. Studies the mystical or spiritual aspects of the works to establish a "religion" for Saint-Exupéry. Tends to overanalyze each work in an attempt to prove his thesis.

Bréaux, Adèle. *Saint-Exupéry in America, 1942–43.* Rutherford, N.J.: Fairleigh Dickinson University Press, 1971. A memoir by his English teacher during the war. A natural glimpse of Saint-Exupéry and Consuelo in their summers in New England.

Cate, Curtis. *Antoine de Saint-Exupéry: His Life and Times.* New York: Putnam, 1970. A voluminous work in conversational style, giving a wealth of detail and anecdote, but is often exaggerated or insufficiently documented. Tends to caricature Saint-Exupéry as spoiled eccentric and shows excessive prejudice against de Gaulle.

Chevrier, Pierre. *Antoine de Saint-Exupéry.* Paris: Gallimard, 1949. Sensitive biography and study by a personal friend of Saint-Exupéry. Contains extracts of letters not published elsewhere. One of the essential sources.

Confluences. Revue des lettres et des arts 7 (1947). Edited by René Tavernier. An early anthology of articles about Saint-Exupéry, many written by those who knew him personally. Includes articles and a preface by Saint-Exupéry, later included in *Un Sens à la vie.* Contains a chronology.

Crane, Helen Elizabeth. *L'Humanisme dans l'oeuvre de Saint-Exupéry.* Evanston, Ill.: Principia Press, 1957. Another study of the elements of formal, Christian religion within the humanism of Saint-Exupéry's philosophy of life. Contains a very detailed bibliography.

Daurat, Didier. *Dans le Vent des hélices.* Paris: Seuil, 1956. The history of La Ligne written by Saint-Exupéry's revered director. Many references to Saint-Exupéry and to incidents in his works. Contains official reports by Saint-Exupéry and Guillaumet. Also a discussion by Daurat of his relationship to the character of Rivière in *Vol de nuit.*

Delange, René. *La Vie de Saint-Exupéry,* followed by "Tel que je l'ai connu," by Léon Werth. Paris: Seuil, 1948. An excellent source containing the personal reminiscences of those who knew Saint-Exupéry personally. The meditation by Léon Werth is a very personal tribute to their friendship. The appendix includes an aviation report by Saint-Exupéry as well as articles later published in *Un Sens à la vie.*

Devaux, André. *Saint-Exupéry.* Les Ecrivains devant Dieu. Paris: De Brouwer, 1965. A small volume devoted to Saint-Exupéry's lifelong quest for God, studying his concept of God as it appears in his different works.

Estang, Luc. *Saint-Exupéry par lui-meme.* Ecrivains de toujours. Paris: Seuil, 1956. Comprises a biography of Saint-Exupéry and a study of his philosophy, all illustrated by direct quotations from his works. An excellent integration of the works into the life of Saint-Exupéry. Contains interesting photos and a chronology.

Fleury, Jean-Gérard. *La Ligne.* Paris: Gallimard, 1944. An interesting history of the Latécoère Line by one of Saint-Exupéry's fellow pilots. Many references to Saint-Exupéry or to anecdotes contained in his books.

François, Carlo. *L'Esthétique d'Antoine de Saint-Exupéry.* Neuchatel, Switzerland: Delachaux & Niestlé, 1957. A study of the aesthetic aspects of Saint-Exupéry's work: the influences and the poetic art, with illustrations and judgment. A difficult work for the average reader but interesting for its thesis that the art critic Elie Faure was a major influence.

Huguet, Jean. *Saint-Exupéry ou l'enseignement du désert.* Paris: La Colombe, 1956. Studies the influence of his years in the desert on Saint-Exupéry's spirit and writing, especially in response to silence in which there is the presence of God. Specific reference to *Citadelle.*

Icare. Revue de l'aviation française (originally, "Revue des pilotes de Ligne"), Orly. No. 30 was devoted to Saint-Exupéry in 1964. A later series on Saint-Exupéry began in 1974 with vol. 1, no. 69. Vol. 6 appeared in 1981 and the final volume is planned for 1984. These are excellent sources, with articles by those who knew Saint-Exupéry, each volume relating to a period of his life. They include facsimile copies of letters, newspaper articles, and documents, and many photos and maps. Several hitherto unpublished texts.

Kessel, Joseph. *Vent de sable.* Paris: Hachette, 1929. History of pioneer aviation at the time of La Ligne, with many references to Saint-Exupéry's work at Cap Juby.

Kessel, P. *La Vie de Saint-Exupéry.* Paris: Gallimard, 1954. An interesting, even moving, photographic biography of Saint-Exupéry. Simple, informative text links the photos chronologically. An excellent introduction to the life of Saint-Exupéry.

Mermoz, Jean. *Mes Vols.* Paris: Flammarion, 1937. The famous pilot's personal account of his flights. Contains four articles by Saint-Exupéry written for different newspapers at the time of Mermoz's death.

Migéo, Marcel. *Saint-Exupéry.* Paris: Flammarion, 1958. An interesting, reliable source written by a fellow pilot who knew Saint-Exupéry during his military service. Contains a detailed discussion of the theories on Saint-Exupéry's disappearance.

Ouellet, Réal. *Les Relations humaines dans l'oeuvre de Saint-Exupéry.* Paris: Minard, 1971. An advanced thesis analyzing some of the major principles of Saint-Exupéry's philosophy of life. Contains a very detailed bibliography.

Pagé, Pierre. *Saint-Exupéry et le monde de l'enfance.* Ottawa: Fidés, 1963. Studies the recurring themes of childhood throughout most of the works of Saint-Exupéry, but especially in *Courrier sud* and *Le Petit Prince.* Concludes that *The Little Prince* is a poem containing the essentials of the author's spiritual experience.

Pélissier, Georges. *Les Cinq Visages de Saint-Exupéry.* Paris: Gallimard, 1951. One of the essential sources, written by a personal friend. Pélissier faithfully presents the five facets of his friend's personality: the pilot, the writer, the man, the inventor, and (surprisingly) the magician. Contains detailed chronology, lists of war missions, bibliography, and list of patents.

Ravoux, Jean-Phillipe. *Saint-Exupéry: Citadelle.* Paris: Classiques contemporains Bordas, 1969. Introduction to the posthumous work with brief biography and study of Saint-Exupéry. Extracts of the work are linked by summaries of passages omitted. Useful condensation, although choice of extracts can be questioned at times.

Roy, Jules. *Passion de Saint-Exupéry.* Paris: Gallimard, 1951. A meditation by a fellow pilot from North Africa on the impulse that drove Saint-Exupéry to offer his life for his country. Includes comparison to the British pilot, Richard Hillary.

Rumbold, Richard, and **Stewart, Margaret.** *The Winged Life.* New York: McKay, n.d. A sincere, well-written biography of two British aviators. Saint-Exupéry's books are placed in the context of his life, but with no literary analysis. Interesting parallel drawn to the British author-pilot, Richard Hillary.

Saint-Exupéry. Collection: Génies et Réalités. Paris: Hachette, 1963. An anthology of articles by some of the best-known biographers and critics of Saint-Exupéry, as well as by his sister, Simone, and his director, Daurat. Contains many interesting photographs and a good chronology.

Smith, Maxwell A. *Knight of the Air.* New York: Pageant Press, 1956; rev. ed., London: Cassell & Co., 1959. A sensitive biography and study based on interviews with those who knew Saint-Exupéry personally. An essential source, of which Saint-Exupéry's mother wrote that it showed the understanding of a friend with the same quality of soul.

2. Articles (including representative early reviews)

Borgal, Clément. "La religion de Saint-Exupéry." *La Table ronde,* nos. 198–99, pp. 55–63. Article related to Borgal's long work on Saint-Exupéry as a "mystic without faith."

Crémieux, Benjamin. Review of *Vol de nuit. Nouvelle Revue française,* October 1931, pp. 609–13.

Daurat, Didier. "Saint-Exupéry, tel que je l'ai connu." *Figaro littéraire,* 16 February 1952, p. 1.

———. "Saint-Exupéry, pionnier de La Ligne." *Figaro littéraire,* 31 July 1954.

Devaux, André. "Saint-Exupéry et Dieu." *Revue de Paris,* October 1975, pp. 65–73. Article related to Devaux's study of Saint-Exupéry's long quest for God.

Fleury, Jean-Gérard. "Saint-Exupéry, l'aviateur du désert." *Candide,* 9 January 1936.

———. "Aux quatre vents de l'esprit: Antoine de Saint-Exupéry." *Pour la victoire,* 4 August 1945. Articles by Saint-Exupéry's fellow pilot in La Ligne before and after his comrade's death.

Galantière, Lewis. "Antoine de Saint-Exupéry." *Atlantic Monthly,* April 1947, pp. 133–41. Reminiscences by the translator of *Wind, Sand, and Stars* and *Pilote de guerre.*

Gide, Andrè. "Saint-Exupéry." *France-Amérique.* 25 March 1945, p. 2.

———. "Saint-Exupéry." *Le Figaro,* 17 February 1945. Appreciations by the novelist who was also a friend of Saint-Exupéry in France and in North Africa during the war.

Jaloux, Edmond. Review of *Vol de nuit. Nouvelles littéraires,* 7 September 1931, p. 3.

———. Review of *Terre des hommes. Nouvelles littéraires,* 8 April 1939, p. 4.

Kessel, Joseph. "Portrait: Saint-Exupéry." *Gringoire,* 10 January 1936, p. 3. Study of Saint-Exupéry by the historian of pioneer aviation in *Vent de sable.*

Lindbergh, Anne Morrow. "Adventurous Writing." *Saturday Review of Literature,* 14 October 1939, pp. 8–9. Review of *Terre des hommes* by the wife of Charles Lindbergh, and the author of *Listen, the Wind* for which Saint-Exupéry had written a preface.

Maurois, André. Review of *Pilote de guerre. Yale Review,* Summer 1942, p. 819.

Peyre, Henri. "French Novel at mid-century." *New Republic,* 7 September 1953, pp. 16–17. Places Saint-Exupéry within the context of contemporary writings.

Prévost, Jean. Review of *Courrier sud. Nouvelle Revue française,* September 1929, pp. 417–18. Written by Saint-Exupéry's first editor.

Reynal, Thérèse. Review of *Le Petit Prince. La France libre,* 15 August 1944, pp. 302–3.

Smith, Maxwell A. Review of *Lettre à un otage. French Review,* December 1949, pp. 110–18.

————. Review of *Citadelle*. *French Review*, October 1951, pp. 16–22.

Wencélius, Léon. Review of *Citadelle*. *Modern Language Notes*, May 1951, pp. 289–95.

Index

DATE DUE

GAYLORD			PRINTED IN U.S.A.